OUR DAILY BREAD®

DEVOTIONAL JOURNAL

DISCOVERY HOUSE
PUBLISHERS

Discovery House Publishers is affiliated with RBC Ministries, Grand Rapids, Michigan.

Discovery House books are distributed to the trade exclusively by Barbour Publishing, Inc., Uhrichsville, Ohio.

Requests for permission to quote from this book should be directed to: Permissions Department, Discovery House Publishers, P.O. Box 3566, Grand Rapids, MI 49501, or contact us by e-mail at permissionsdept@dhp.org

ISBN: 978-1-57293-389-7

Printed in the United States of America

11 12 13 14 15 / BP / 10 9 8 7 6 5 4 3 2 1

QUIET TIME WITH GOD

He makes me to lie down in green pastures;
He leads me beside the still waters.
—Psalm 23:2

The word *connected* captures our contemporary experience of life. Many people rarely go anywhere without a cell phone, iPod, laptop, or pager. We have become accessible twenty-four hours a day. Some psychologists see this craving to stay connected as an addiction. Yet a growing number of people are deliberately limiting their use of technology. Being a "tech-no" is their way of preserving times of quiet, while limiting the flow of information into their lives.

Many followers of Christ find that a daily time of Bible reading and prayer is essential in their walk of faith. This "quiet time" is a disconnection from external distractions in order to connect with God. The "green pastures" and "still waters" of Psalm 23:2 are more than an idyllic country scene. They speak of our communion with God whereby He restores our souls and leads us in His paths (v. 3).

All of us can make time to meet with God, but do we? In Robert Foster's booklet "7 Minutes with God" he suggests a way to begin: Start with a brief prayer for guidance, then read the Bible for a few minutes, and close with a short time of prayer that includes adoration, confession, thanksgiving, and supplication for others. It's vital to take time today to connect with the Lord, who is our life. (David C. McCasland)

Keeping a daily appointment with God is a vital part of the Christian life. The more time we spend with God—reading His Word, conversing with Him in prayer, meditating on thoughts from His Word—the better we get to know Him and the more our lives begin to reflect His image and His truth.

We hope that this devotional journal will help you keep those daily appointments and give you spiritual guidance along your way.

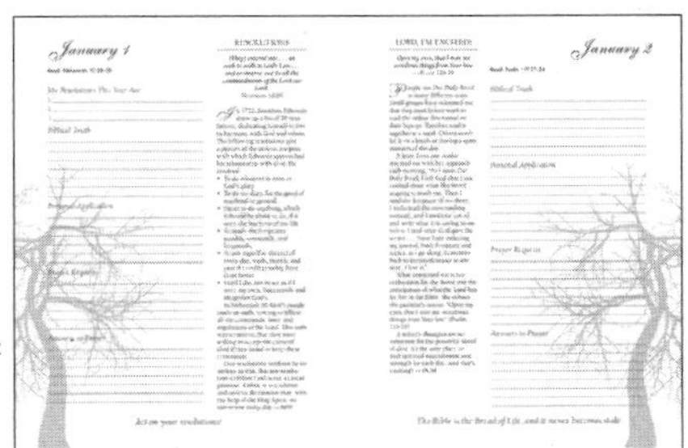

How to Use This Devotional Journal

Here are some suggestions for getting the most out of your reading and your daily time with God:

Select a time and place. If possible, set aside a time and place each day for reading the Scripture passages and the daily *ODB* devotional and thinking about what you've read. Your time will be more meaningful if you can concentrate and establish a regular practice.

Read the Bible passage. Begin by reading the suggested verses from the Bible at the top of the column. Note the key verse, which is printed above the devotional article and relates to the theme of the day.

Read the article thoughtfully. As you read, seek to learn more about God, your relationship with Him, and how He wants you to live each day. The closing "thought for the day" at the bottom of the page is intended to help you remember a key idea from the article.

Use the journaling section to help you remember. Use the journaling section for each day to record truths you see in the Bible passage and insights you gain from the article. There is a place to record: (1) Biblical Truth—highlights and insights that you see in the daily Bible passage and in the devotional article; (2) Personal Application; (3) Prayer Requests; and (4) Answers to Prayer.

Take time to pray. After you have read the Scripture passages and the article, talk with the Lord about what you've discovered in His Word and what your response will be to Him. Use the journaling sections provided to note your prayer requests and answers to prayer.

May you find encouragement, hope, challenge, and comfort throughout the year as you draw closer to God and grow in your love for Him.

READ THROUGH THE BIBLE IN A YEAR

JANUARY

- ❑ 1 Gen. 1–3; Mt. 1
- ❑ 2 Gen. 4–6; Mt. 2
- ❑ 3 Gen. 7–9; Mt. 3
- ❑ 4 Gen. 10–12; Mt. 4
- ❑ 5 Gen. 13–15; Mt. 5:1-26
- ❑ 6 Gen. 16–17; Mt. 5:27-48
- ❑ 7 Gen. 18–19; Mt. 6:1-18
- ❑ 8 Gen. 20–22; Mt. 6:19-34
- ❑ 9 Gen. 23–24; Mt. 7
- ❑ 10 Gen. 25–26; Mt. 8:1-17
- ❑ 11 Gen. 27–28; Mt. 8:18-34
- ❑ 12 Gen. 29–30; Mt. 9:1-17
- ❑ 13 Gen. 31–32; Mt. 9:18-38
- ❑ 14 Gen. 33–35; Mt. 10:1-20
- ❑ 15 Gen. 36–38; Mt. 10:21-42
- ❑ 16 Gen. 39–40; Mt. 11
- ❑ 17 Gen. 41–42; Mt. 12:1-23
- ❑ 18 Gen. 43–45; Mt. 12:24-50
- ❑ 19 Gen. 46–48; Mt. 13:1-30
- ❑ 20 Gen. 49–50; Mt. 13:31-58
- ❑ 21 Ex. 1–3; Mt. 14:1-21
- ❑ 22 Ex. 4–6; Mt. 14:22-36
- ❑ 23 Ex. 7–8; Mt. 15:1-20
- ❑ 24 Ex. 9–11; Mt. 15:21-39
- ❑ 25 Ex. 12–13; Mt. 16
- ❑ 26 Ex. 14–15; Mt. 17
- ❑ 27 Ex. 16–18; Mt. 18:1-20
- ❑ 28 Ex. 19–20; Mt. 18:21-35
- ❑ 29 Ex. 21–22; Mt. 19
- ❑ 30 Ex. 23–24; Mt. 20:1-16
- ❑ 31 Ex. 25–26; Mt. 20:17-34

FEBRUARY

- ❑ 1 Ex. 27–28; Mt. 21:1-22
- ❑ 2 Ex. 29–30; Mt. 21:23-46
- ❑ 3 Ex. 31–33; Mt. 22:1-22
- ❑ 4 Ex. 34–35; Mt. 22:23-46
- ❑ 5 Ex. 36–38; Mt. 23:1-22
- ❑ 6 Ex. 39–40; Mt. 23:23-39
- ❑ 7 Lev. 1–3; Mt. 24:1-28
- ❑ 8 Lev. 4–5; Mt. 24:29-51
- ❑ 9 Lev. 6–7; Mt. 25:1-30
- ❑ 10 Lev. 8–10; Mt. 25:31-46
- ❑ 11 Lev. 11–12; Mt. 26:1-25
- ❑ 12 Lev. 13; Mt. 26:26-50
- ❑ 13 Lev. 14; Mt. 26:51-75
- ❑ 14 Lev. 15–16; Mt. 27:1-26
- ❑ 15 Lev. 17–18; Mt. 27:27-50
- ❑ 16 Lev. 19–20; Mt. 27:51-66
- ❑ 17 Lev. 21–22; Mt. 28
- ❑ 18 Lev. 23–24; Mk. 1:1-22
- ❑ 19 Lev. 25; Mk. 1:23-45
- ❑ 20 Lev. 26–27; Mk. 2
- ❑ 21 Num. 1–3; Mk. 3
- ❑ 22 Num. 4–6; Mk. 4:1-20
- ❑ 23 Num. 7–8; Mk. 4:21-41
- ❑ 24 Num. 9–11; Mk. 5:1-20
- ❑ 25 Num. 12–14; Mk. 5:21-43
- ❑ 26 Num. 15–16; Mk. 6:1-29
- ❑ 27 Num. 17–19; Mk. 6:30-56
- ❑ 28 Num. 20–22; Mk. 7:1-13

(if a leap year—no reading on 29)

MARCH

- ❑ 1 Num. 23–25; Mk. 7:14-37
- ❑ 2 Num. 26–27; Mk. 8:1-21
- ❑ 3 Num. 28–30; Mk. 8:22-38
- ❑ 4 Num. 31–33; Mk. 9:1-29
- ❑ 5 Num. 34–36; Mk. 9:30-50
- ❑ 6 Dt. 1–2; Mk. 10:1-31
- ❑ 7 Dt. 3–4; Mk. 10:32-52
- ❑ 8 Dt. 5–7; Mk. 11:1-18
- ❑ 9 Dt. 8–10; Mk. 11:19-33
- ❑ 10 Dt. 11–13; Mk. 12:1-27
- ❑ 11 Dt. 14–16; Mk. 12:28-44
- ❑ 12 Dt. 17–19; Mk. 13:1-20
- ❑ 13 Dt. 20–22; Mk. 13:21-37
- ❑ 14 Dt. 23–25; Mk. 14:1-26
- ❑ 15 Dt. 26–27; Mk. 14:27-53
- ❑ 16 Dt. 28–29; Mk. 14:54-72
- ❑ 17 Dt. 30–31; Mk. 15:1-25
- ❑ 18 Dt. 32–34; Mk. 15:26-47
- ❑ 19 Josh. 1–3; Mk. 16
- ❑ 20 Josh. 4–6; Lk. 1:1-20
- ❑ 21 Josh. 7–9; Lk. 1:21-38
- ❑ 22 Josh. 10–12; Lk. 1:39-56
- ❑ 23 Josh. 13–15; Lk. 1:57-80
- ❑ 24 Josh. 16–18; Lk. 2:1-24
- ❑ 25 Josh. 19–21; Lk. 2:25-52
- ❑ 26 Josh. 22–24; Lk. 3
- ❑ 27 Jud. 1–3; Lk. 4:1-30
- ❑ 28 Jud. 4–6; Lk. 4:31-44
- ❑ 29 Jud. 7–8; Lk. 5:1-16
- ❑ 30 Jud. 9–10; Lk. 5:17-39
- ❑ 31 Jud. 11–12; Lk. 6:1-26

APRIL

❑ 1 Jud. 13–15; Lk. 6:27-49
❑ 2 Jud. 16–18; Lk. 7:1-30
❑ 3 Jud. 19–21; Lk. 7:31-50
❑ 4 Ruth 1–4; Lk. 8:1-25
❑ 5 1 Sam. 1–3; Lk. 8:26-56
❑ 6 1 Sam. 4–6; Lk. 9:1-17
❑ 7 1 Sam. 7–9; Lk. 9:18-36
❑ 8 1 Sam. 10–12; Lk. 9:37-62
❑ 9 1 Sam. 13–14; Lk. 10:1-24
❑ 10 1 Sam. 15–16; Lk. 10:25-42
❑ 11 1 Sam. 17–18; Lk. 11:1-28
❑ 12 1 Sam. 19–21; Lk. 11:29-54
❑ 13 1 Sam. 22–24; Lk. 12:1-31
❑ 14 1 Sam. 25–26; Lk. 12:32–59
❑ 15 1 Sam. 27–29; Lk. 13:1-22
❑ 16 1 Sam. 30–31; Lk. 13:23-35
❑ 17 2 Sam. 1–2; Lk. 14:1-24
❑ 18 2 Sam. 3–5; Lk. 14:25-35
❑ 19 2 Sam. 6–8; Lk. 15:1-10
❑ 20 2 Sam. 9–11; Lk. 15:11-32
❑ 21 2 Sam. 12–13; Lk. 16
❑ 22 2 Sam. 14–15; Lk. 17:1-19
❑ 23 2 Sam. 16–18; Lk. 17:20-37
❑ 24 2 Sam. 19–20; Lk. 18:1-23
❑ 25 2 Sam. 21–22; Lk. 18:24-43
❑ 26 2 Sam. 23–24; Lk. 19:1-27
❑ 27 1 Ki. 1–2; Lk. 19:28-48
❑ 28 1 Ki. 3–5; Lk. 20:1-26
❑ 29 1 Ki. 6–7; Lk. 20:27-47
❑ 30 1 Ki. 8–9; Lk. 21:1-19

MAY

❑ 1 1 Ki. 10–11; Lk. 21:20-38
❑ 2 1 Ki. 12–13; Lk. 22:1-20
❑ 3 1 Ki. 14–15; Lk. 22:21-46
❑ 4 1 Ki. 16–18; Lk. 22:47-71
❑ 5 1 Ki. 19–20; Lk. 23:1-25
❑ 6 1 Ki. 21–22; Lk. 23:26-56
❑ 7 2 Ki. 1–3; Lk. 24:1-35
❑ 8 2 Ki. 4–6; Lk. 24:36-53
❑ 9 2 Ki. 7–9; Jn. 1:1-28
❑ 10 2 Ki. 10–12; Jn. 1:29-51
❑ 11 2 Ki. 13–14; Jn. 2
❑ 12 2 Ki. 15–16; Jn. 3:1-18
❑ 13 2 Ki. 17–18; Jn. 3:19-36
❑ 14 2 Ki. 19–21; Jn. 4:1-30
❑ 15 2 Ki. 22–23; Jn. 4:31-54
❑ 16 2 Ki. 24–25; Jn. 5:1-24
❑ 17 1 Chr. 1–3; Jn. 5:25-47
❑ 18 1 Chr. 4–6; Jn. 6:1-21
❑ 19 1 Chr. 7–9; Jn. 6:22-44
❑ 20 1 Chr. 10–12; Jn. 6:45-71
❑ 21 1 Chr. 13–15; Jn. 7:1-27
❑ 22 1 Chr. 16–18; Jn. 7:28-53
❑ 23 1 Chr. 19–21; Jn. 8:1-27
❑ 24 1 Chr. 22–24; Jn. 8:28-59
❑ 25 1 Chr. 25–27; Jn. 9:1-23
❑ 26 1 Chr. 28–29; Jn. 9:24-41
❑ 27 2 Chr. 1–3; Jn. 10:1-23
❑ 28 2 Chr. 4–6; Jn. 10:24-42
❑ 29 2 Chr. 7–9; Jn. 11:1-29
❑ 30 2 Chr. 10–12; Jn. 11:30-57
❑ 31 2 Chr. 13–14; Jn. 12:1-26

JUNE

❑ 1 2 Chr. 15–16; Jn. 12:27-50
❑ 2 2 Chr. 17–18; Jn. 13:1-20
❑ 3 2 Chr. 19–20; Jn. 13:21-38
❑ 4 2 Chr. 21–22; Jn. 14
❑ 5 2 Chr. 23–24; Jn. 15
❑ 6 2 Chr. 25–27; Jn. 16
❑ 7 2 Chr. 28–29; Jn. 17
❑ 8 2 Chr. 30–31; Jn. 18:1-18
❑ 9 2 Chr. 32–33; Jn. 18:19-40
❑ 10 2 Chr. 34–36; Jn. 19:1-22
❑ 11 Ezra 1–2; Jn. 19:23-42
❑ 12 Ezra 3–5; Jn. 20
❑ 13 Ezra 6–8; Jn. 21
❑ 14 Ezra 9–10; Acts 1
❑ 15 Neh. 1–3; Acts 2:1-21
❑ 16 Neh. 4–6; Acts 2:22-47
❑ 17 Neh. 7–9; Acts 3
❑ 18 Neh. 10–11; Acts 4:1-22
❑ 19 Neh. 12–13; Acts 4:23-37
❑ 20 Est. 1–2; Acts 5:1-21
❑ 21 Est. 3–5; Acts 5:22-42
❑ 22 Est. 6–8; Acts 6
❑ 23 Est. 9–10; Acts 7:1-21
❑ 24 Job 1–2; Acts 7:22-43
❑ 25 Job 3–4; Acts 7:44-60
❑ 26 Job 5–7; Acts 8:1-25
❑ 27 Job 8–10; Acts 8:26-40
❑ 28 Job 11–13; Acts 9:1-21
❑ 29 Job 14–16; Acts 9:22-43
❑ 30 Job 17–19; Acts 10:1-23

JULY

❑ 1 Job 20–21; Acts 10:24-48
❑ 2 Job 22–24; Acts 11

- ❑ 3 Job 25–27; Acts 12
- ❑ 4 Job 28–29; Acts 13:1-25
- ❑ 5 Job 30–31; Acts 13:26-52
- ❑ 6 Job 32–33; Acts 14
- ❑ 7 Job 34–35; Acts 15:1-21
- ❑ 8 Job 36–37; Acts 15:22-41
- ❑ 9 Job 38–40; Acts 16:1-21
- ❑ 10 Job 41–42; Acts 16:22-40
- ❑ 11 Ps. 1–3; Acts 17:1-15
- ❑ 12 Ps. 4–6; Acts 17:16-34
- ❑ 13 Ps. 7–9; Acts 18
- ❑ 14 Ps. 10–12; Acts 19:1-20
- ❑ 15 Ps. 13–15; Acts 19:21-41
- ❑ 16 Ps. 16–17; Acts 20:1-16
- ❑ 17 Ps. 18–19; Acts 20:17-38
- ❑ 18 Ps. 20–22; Acts 21:1-17
- ❑ 19 Ps. 23–25; Acts 21:18-40
- ❑ 20 Ps. 26–28; Acts 22
- ❑ 21 Ps. 29–30; Acts 23:1-15
- ❑ 22 Ps. 31–32; Acts 23:16-35
- ❑ 23 Ps. 33–34; Acts 24
- ❑ 24 Ps. 35–36; Acts 25
- ❑ 25 Ps. 37–39; Acts 26
- ❑ 26 Ps. 40–42; Acts 27:1-26
- ❑ 27 Ps. 43–45; Acts 27:27-44
- ❑ 28 Ps. 46–48; Acts 28
- ❑ 29 Ps. 49–50; Rom. 1
- ❑ 30 Ps. 51–53; Rom. 2
- ❑ 31 Ps. 54–56; Rom. 3

AUGUST

- ❑ 1 Ps. 57–59; Rom. 4
- ❑ 2 Ps. 60–62; Rom. 5
- ❑ 3 Ps. 63–65; Rom. 6
- ❑ 4 Ps. 66–67; Rom. 7
- ❑ 5 Ps. 68–69; Rom. 8:1-21
- ❑ 6 Ps. 70–71; Rom. 8:22-39
- ❑ 7 Ps. 72–73; Rom. 9:1-15
- ❑ 8 Ps. 74–76; Rom. 9:16-33
- ❑ 9 Ps. 77–78; Rom. 10
- ❑ 10 Ps. 79–80; Rom. 11:1-18
- ❑ 11 Ps. 81–83; Rom. 11:19-36
- ❑ 12 Ps. 84–86; Rom. 12
- ❑ 13 Ps. 87–88; Rom. 13
- ❑ 14 Ps. 89–90; Rom. 14
- ❑ 15 Ps. 91–93; Rom. 15:1-13
- ❑ 16 Ps. 94–96; Rom. 15:14-33
- ❑ 17 Ps. 97–99; Rom. 16
- ❑ 18 Ps. 100–102; 1 Cor. 1
- ❑ 19 Ps. 103–104; 1 Cor. 2
- ❑ 20 Ps. 105–106; 1 Cor. 3
- ❑ 21 Ps. 107–109; 1 Cor. 4
- ❑ 22 Ps. 110–112; 1 Cor. 5
- ❑ 23 Ps. 113–115; 1 Cor. 6
- ❑ 24 Ps. 116–118; 1 Cor. 7:1-19
- ❑ 25 Ps. 119:1-88; 1 Cor. 7:20-40
- ❑ 26 Ps. 119:89-176; 1 Cor. 8
- ❑ 27 Ps. 120–122; 1 Cor. 9
- ❑ 28 Ps. 123–125; 1 Cor. 10:1-18
- ❑ 29 Ps. 126–128; 1 Cor. 10:19-33
- ❑ 30 Ps. 129–131; 1 Cor. 11:1-16
- ❑ 31 Ps. 132–134; 1 Cor. 11:17-34

SEPTEMBER

- ❑ 1 Ps. 135–136; 1 Cor. 12
- ❑ 2 Ps. 137–139; 1 Cor. 13
- ❑ 3 Ps. 140–142; 1 Cor. 14:1-20
- ❑ 4 Ps. 143–145; 1 Cor. 14:21-40
- ❑ 5 Ps. 146–147; 1 Cor. 15:1-28
- ❑ 6 Ps. 148–150; 1 Cor. 15:29-58
- ❑ 7 Prov. 1–2; 1 Cor. 16
- ❑ 8 Prov. 3–5; 2 Cor. 1
- ❑ 9 Prov. 6–7; 2 Cor. 2
- ❑ 10 Prov. 8–9; 2 Cor. 3
- ❑ 11 Prov. 10–12; 2 Cor. 4
- ❑ 12 Prov. 13–15; 2 Cor. 5
- ❑ 13 Prov. 16–18; 2 Cor. 6
- ❑ 14 Prov. 19–21; 2 Cor. 7
- ❑ 15 Prov. 22–24; 2 Cor. 8
- ❑ 16 Prov. 25–26; 2 Cor. 9
- ❑ 17 Prov. 27–29; 2 Cor. 10
- ❑ 18 Prov. 30–31; 2 Cor. 11:1-15
- ❑ 19 Eccl. 1–3; 2 Cor. 11:16-33
- ❑ 20 Eccl. 4–6; 2 Cor. 12
- ❑ 21 Eccl. 7–9; 2 Cor. 13
- ❑ 22 Eccl. 10–12; Gal. 1
- ❑ 23 Song 1–3; Gal. 2
- ❑ 24 Song 4–5; Gal. 3
- ❑ 25 Song 6–8; Gal. 4
- ❑ 26 Isa. 1–2; Gal. 5
- ❑ 27 Isa. 3–4; Gal. 6
- ❑ 28 Isa. 5–6; Eph. 1
- ❑ 29 Isa. 7–8; Eph. 2
- ❑ 30 Isa. 9–10; Eph. 3

OCTOBER

- ❑ 1 Isa. 11–13; Eph. 4
- ❑ 2 Isa. 14–16; Eph. 5:1-16
- ❑ 3 Isa. 17–19; Eph. 5:17-33
- ❑ 4 Isa. 20–22; Eph. 6
- ❑ 5 Isa. 23–25; Phil. 1

- ❑ 6 Isa. 26–27; Phil. 2
- ❑ 7 Isa. 28–29; Phil. 3
- ❑ 8 Isa. 30–31; Phil 4
- ❑ 9 Isa. 32–33; Col. 1
- ❑ 10 Isa. 34–36; Col. 2
- ❑ 11 Isa. 37–38; Col. 3
- ❑ 12 Isa. 39–40; Col. 4
- ❑ 13 Isa. 41–42; 1 Th. 1
- ❑ 14 Isa. 43–44; 1 Th. 2
- ❑ 15 Isa. 45–46; 1 Th. 3
- ❑ 16 Isa. 47–49; 1 Th. 4
- ❑ 17 Isa. 50–52; 1 Th. 5
- ❑ 18 Isa. 53–55; 2 Th. 1
- ❑ 19 Isa. 56–58; 2 Th. 2
- ❑ 20 Isa. 59–61; 2 Th. 3
- ❑ 21 Isa. 62–64; 1 Tim. 1
- ❑ 22 Isa. 65–66; 1 Tim. 2
- ❑ 23 Jer. 1–2; 1 Tim. 3
- ❑ 24 Jer. 3–5; 1 Tim. 4
- ❑ 25 Jer. 6–8; 1 Tim. 5
- ❑ 26 Jer. 9–11; 1 Tim. 6
- ❑ 27 Jer. 12–14; 2 Tim. 1
- ❑ 28 Jer. 15–17; 2 Tim. 2
- ❑ 29 Jer. 18–19; 2 Tim. 3
- ❑ 30 Jer. 20–21; 2 Tim. 4
- ❑ 31 Jer. 22–23; Ti. 1

NOVEMBER

- ❑ 1 Jer. 24–26; Ti. 2
- ❑ 2 Jer. 27–29; Ti. 3
- ❑ 3 Jer. 30–31; Philemon
- ❑ 4 Jer. 32–33; Heb. 1
- ❑ 5 Jer. 34–36; Heb. 2
- ❑ 6 Jer. 37–39; Heb. 3
- ❑ 7 Jer. 40–42; Heb. 4
- ❑ 8 Jer. 43–45; Heb. 5
- ❑ 9 Jer. 46–47; Heb. 6
- ❑ 10 Jer. 48–49; Heb. 7
- ❑ 11 Jer. 50; Heb. 8
- ❑ 12 Jer. 51–52; Heb. 9
- ❑ 13 Lam. 1–2; Heb. 10:1-18
- ❑ 14 Lam. 3–5; Heb. 10:19-39
- ❑ 15 Ezek. 1–2; Heb. 11:1-19
- ❑ 16 Ezek. 3–4; Heb. 11:20-40
- ❑ 17 Ezek. 5–7; Heb. 12
- ❑ 18 Ezek. 8–10; Heb. 13
- ❑ 19 Ezek. 11–13; Jas. 1
- ❑ 20 Ezek. 14–15; Jas. 2
- ❑ 21 Ezek. 16–17; Jas. 3
- ❑ 22 Ezek. 18–19; Jas. 4
- ❑ 23 Ezek. 20–21; Jas. 5
- ❑ 24 Ezek. 22–23; 1 Pet. 1
- ❑ 25 Ezek. 24–26; 1 Pet. 2
- ❑ 26 Ezek. 27–29; 1 Pet. 3
- ❑ 27 Ezek. 30–32; 1 Pet. 4
- ❑ 28 Ezek. 33–34; 1 Pet. 5
- ❑ 29 Ezek. 35–36; 2 Pet. 1
- ❑ 30 Ezek. 37–39; 2 Pet. 2

DECEMBER

- ❑ 1 Ezek. 40–41; 2 Pet. 3
- ❑ 2 Ezek. 42–44; 1 Jn. 1
- ❑ 3 Ezek. 45–46; 1 Jn. 2
- ❑ 4 Ezek. 47–48; 1 Jn. 3
- ❑ 5 Dan. 1–2; 1 Jn. 4
- ❑ 6 Dan. 3–4; 1 Jn. 5
- ❑ 7 Dan. 5–7; 2 John
- ❑ 8 Dan. 8–10; 3 John
- ❑ 9 Dan. 11–12; Jude
- ❑ 10 Hos. 1–4; Rev. 1
- ❑ 11 Hos. 5–8; Rev. 2
- ❑ 12 Hos. 9–11; Rev. 3
- ❑ 13 Hos. 12–14; Rev. 4
- ❑ 14 Joel 1–3; Rev. 5
- ❑ 15 Amos 1–3; Rev. 6
- ❑ 16 Amos 4–6; Rev. 7
- ❑ 17 Amos 7–9; Rev. 8
- ❑ 18 Obadiah; Rev. 9
- ❑ 19 Jonah 1–4; Rev. 10
- ❑ 20 Mic. 1–3; Rev. 11
- ❑ 21 Mic. 4–5; Rev. 12
- ❑ 22 Mic. 6–7; Rev. 13
- ❑ 23 Nahum 1–3; Rev. 14
- ❑ 24 Habakkuk 1–3; Rev. 15
- ❑ 25 Zephaniah 1–3; Rev. 16
- ❑ 26 Haggai 1–2; Rev. 17
- ❑ 27 Zech. 1–4; Rev. 18
- ❑ 28 Zech. 5–8; Rev. 19
- ❑ 29 Zech. 9–12; Rev. 20
- ❑ 30 Zech. 13–14; Rev. 21
- ❑ 31 Malachi 1–4; Rev. 22

January

January 1

Read: Nehemiah 10:28–31

My Resolutions This Year Are:

1. ______
2. ______
3. ______

Biblical Truth

Personal Application

Prayer Requests

Answers to Prayer

RESOLUTIONS

[They] entered into . . . an oath to walk in God's Law . . . and to observe and do all the commandments of the Lord our Lord.
—Nehemiah 10:29

In 1722, Jonathan Edwards drew up a list of 70 resolutions, dedicating himself to live in harmony with God and others. The following resolutions give a picture of the serious purpose with which Edwards approached his relationship with God. He resolved:

- To do whatever is most to God's glory.
- To do my duty, for the good of mankind in general.
- Never to do anything, which I should be afraid to do, if it were the last hour of my life.
- To study the Scriptures steadily, constantly, and frequently.
- To ask myself at the end of every day, week, month, and year if I could possibly have done better.
- Until I die, not to act as if I were my own, but entirely and altogether God's.

In Nehemiah 10, God's people made an oath, vowing to follow all the commands, laws, and regulations of the Lord. This oath was so serious that they were willing to accept the curse of God if they failed to keep these commands.

Our resolutions need not be so serious as that. But any resolution to follow God is not a casual promise. Rather, it is a solemn and serious declaration that, with the help of the Holy Spirit, we can renew every day. —MW

Act on your resolutions!

LORD, I'M EXCITED!

Open my eyes, that I may see wondrous things from Your law.
—Psalm 119:18

January 2

Read: Psalm 119:17–24

People use *Our Daily Bread* in many different ways. Small groups have informed me that they meet before work to read the online devotional on their laptops. Families read it together at a meal. Others reach for it on a break or during a quiet moment of the day.

A letter from one reader inspired me with her approach each morning: "As I open *Our Daily Bread,* I tell God that I am excited about what His Word is going to teach me. Then I read the Scripture (if it's short, I include all the surrounding context), and I meditate [on it] and write what it is saying to me before I read what God gave the writer . . . Since I am indexing my journal, both Scripture and topics, as I go along, I can refer back to pertinent topics at any time. I love it."

What impressed me is her enthusiasm for the Word and the anticipation of what the Lord has for her in the Bible. She echoes the psalmist's prayer, "Open my eyes, that I may see wondrous things from Your law" (Psalm 119:18).

A writer's thoughts are no substitute for the powerful Word of God. It's the only place to find spiritual nourishment and strength for each day. And that's exciting! —DCM

Biblical Truth

Personal Application

Prayer Requests

Answers to Prayer

The Bible is the Bread of Life, and it never becomes stale.

January 3

Read: Psalm 119:25–32

Biblical Truth

Personal Application

Prayer Requests

Answers to Prayer

START TODAY!

I cling to Your testimonies; O Lord, do not put me to shame! I will run the course of Your commandments.
—Psalm 119:31–32

Many people make resolutions on New Year's Day, promising themselves (and sometimes God) that the next year of life will be different. We determine that habits are going to be changed and new patterns of behavior developed.

Resolutions like these are highly commendable and can often serve as a stimulus to spiritual growth. But not always. Sometimes our resolutions are carried out only for a little while and all too soon are forgotten.

Samuel Johnson, a deeply committed Christian who lived in the 18th century, frequently wrote resolutions in his journals. Here is a typical entry: "I have corrected no external habits, nor kept any of the resolutions made in the beginning of the year, yet I hope still to be reformed, and not to lose my whole life in idle purposes."

It is good to engage now and then in self-examination. We should face up to the changes that need to be made, and then make plans for the way we're going to implement them. For example, if we realize that our devotional habits are weak and inconsistent, let's resolve to spend some time daily in focused fellowship with God. Let's ask the Spirit to help us in this consistent practice through all our tomorrows.

Today is a good day to start.
—VCG

God speaks to those who take time to listen,
and He listens to those who take time to pray.

WHAT WILL YOU WRITE?

January 4

You do not know what will happen tomorrow. For what is your life? It is even a vapor that appears for a little time and then vanishes away.
—James 4:14

In January 2006, a mine explosion in rural West Virginia threatened the lives of 13 coal miners. Having grown up in that state, I was among the millions riveted to the news for the next few days. Tragically, all but one of the miners were found dead. To compound the pain of that loss, the first reports given to the families said that all but one had been found alive. When the grim news of the deaths came, the grief was compounded with anger—and a desire to blame someone for the whole gut-wrenching event.

At one of the funerals, however, Rev. Wease Day asked the hurting to look in a different direction—within. During their last hours, some of the miners had written notes to their families, in some cases offering comfort and hope. In light of that, Pastor Day urged his congregation not to seek to fix blame. He instead challenged them to imagine what they would write in a farewell note if they had only hours to live.

In some ways we are like those miners. We are trapped in a dark world and are facing physical death. How we live our lives as followers of Christ becomes our "note" to the world. James wrote that life is "a vapor that appears for a little time and then vanishes away" (James 4:14). By God's grace, what will you write with your life today? —BC

Read: Psalm 90

Biblical Truth

Personal Application

Prayer Requests

Answers to Prayer

A Christlike life is a message of hope to a searching world.

January 5

Read: Deuteronomy 4:1–10

Biblical Truth

Personal Application

Prayer Requests

Answers to Prayer

GOING NOWHERE FAST

Only take heed to yourself, and diligently keep yourself, lest you forget the things your eyes have seen.
—DEUTERONOMY 4:9

I walked as fast as possible. Worked up quite a sweat, in fact. After about a mile, I broke into a jog and then ran as hard as I could. Finally, after about 25 minutes, I stopped. My heart was pounding. My shirt was soaked. But I had gone nowhere. I had just done 2.5 miles on the treadmill.

After I cooled off, I sat down with my Bible. I was following a reading schedule and the selection for the day was from the book of Numbers. I read some of it slowly and some faster, but I felt at times that I wasn't getting anywhere—like I was back on the treadmill. Censuses were taken. The long journey was recapped. The tribes were listed and relisted. The next day, I moved into Deuteronomy. More wanderings. More about the Israelites and their land.

But when I got to chapter 4, I was told why all that recapping was important. Moses told the people not to "forget the things your eyes have seen . . . Teach them to your children" (Numbers 4:9). The previous reading was not about Israel going nowhere fast. It was about training, about a lesson in using God's past workings as instruction for future godly living.

All Scripture is given by the inspiration of God. So even when it may seem unimportant—keep reading. Sometimes we have to be patient to realize its full purpose.
—DB

God speaks to us through His Word; take time to listen.

RIPPLE EFFECT

I pray . . . that you may approve the things that are excellent.
—Philippians 1:9–10

As a kid, one of my favorite pastimes was skipping stones across the surface of a smooth lake. Inevitably, ripples would flow from the impact of the stone.

It's like that with choices. Every choice we make creates a ripple effect on our lives as well as on the lives of others. The choices we have made throughout life determine where we are and what we are becoming.

Choices are also telling. What we really want, love, and think show up in the choices we make.

It's no wonder then that Paul urged us to make "excellent" choices—choices that emanate from a heart fully committed to Jesus. He stated that when our love abounds in knowledge and discernment, we are able to understand what is best, so that we may "approve the things that are excellent" (Philippians 1:9–10). Excellent choices are the proof of a life that is deeply committed to Jesus and His ways, and they have the ripple effect of filling our lives "with the fruits of righteousness which are by Jesus Christ, to the glory and praise of God" (Philippians 1:11).

As a friend of mine wisely told me, our lives are not made by the dreams we dream but by the choices we make. Let's make excellent ones! —JS

January 6

Read: Philippians 1:3–11

Biblical Truth

Personal Application

Prayer Requests

Answers to Prayer

Make an excellent choice and watch the ripple effect of blessing.

January 7

Read: Philippians 1:8–11

Biblical Truth

Personal Application

Prayer Requests

Answers to Prayer

BEWARE OF OPEN DOORS

Folly is joy to him who is destitute of discernment, but a man of understanding walks uprightly.
—Proverbs 15:21

Sometimes Christians follow an "open door" policy. When a door of opportunity opens, they assume that it's God's will to go through it.

Bestselling author Terri Blackstock knows this is untrue. She never openly rebelled against God, but she found herself far away from Him after walking through open doors of opportunity. "I had allowed myself to believe that God was blessing my career . . . because He had opened all the doors," she wrote in *Soul Restoration*. Although she got what she wanted—a successful career writing romance novels for Harlequin and Silhouette—she lost what she needed: a close relationship with God.

When she finally admitted that her career was keeping her from God, she turned her back on success and renewed her commitment to the Lord. Since then, her writing career has been revitalized, and she has become an award-winning author of Christian fiction.

Just because the Lord doesn't stop us from something doesn't mean He wants us to continue. To discern which opportunities to pursue, we need to "approve the things that are excellent" and to be "filled with the fruits of righteousness . . . to the glory and praise of God" (Philippians 1:10–11). —JAL

The best way to know God's will is to say "I will" to God.

WHEN LIFE GOES BAD

January 8

David strengthened himself in the Lord his God.
—1 Samuel 30:6

Read: 1 Samuel 30:1–6

Everything looked bleak to David and his men when they arrived at Ziklag (1 Samuel 30:1–6). The Amalekites had attacked the city and taken their wives and children captive. The men were so discouraged that they wept until they had no more energy. And David, their leader, was "greatly distressed" because the people were contemplating stoning him (v. 6).

In the end, David's army rescued their families and defeated the Amalekites. But the story takes a great turn even before that when "David strengthened himself in the Lord his God" (v. 6). Other translations use the words *encouraged* or *refreshed.*

The text doesn't say exactly how David did this. But it makes me wonder, *In what ways can we strengthen, encourage, or refresh ourselves in the Lord when we're feeling discouraged?*

First, we can remember what God has done. We can list the ways He has cared for us in the past, and how He has provided for us or answered a prayer request.

Second, we can remember what God has promised. "Be strong and of good courage . . . for the Lord your God is with you wherever you go" (Joshua 1:9).

Like David, let's learn to strengthen ourselves in the Lord, and then let's leave the rest with Him. —AC

Biblical Truth

Personal Application

Prayer Requests

Answers to Prayer

Our greatest strength is often shown in our ability to stand still and trust God.

January 9

Read: 2 Corinthians 1:1–7

Biblical Truth

Personal Application

Prayer Requests

Answers to Prayer

WOUNDS THAT HEAL

[God] comforts us . . .
that we may be able to comfort
those who are in any trouble.
—2 CORINTHIANS 1:4

Years ago I went through a time of painful emotional loss. A missionary friend who had experienced a similar situation comforted me and then offered these words: "In the future, Christ can use your emotional wounds to help heal others." Later, on a trip to visit a missionary training school, I lodged in a place where I saw a portrait of Jesus' nail-pierced hands. Below it, on a music stand, was the sheet music "He Touched Me."

Rarely have I experienced a string of circumstances that spoke so vividly to my situation. In His gracious providence, God used them to comfort and direct me. It became clear that healing flows from the wounded hands of Jesus and that our wounds can help others.

In hindsight, I have learned how God's comfort in suffering can build bridges to those in pain. Paul made this point clear: "Blessed be the God and Father of our Lord Jesus Christ, the Father of mercies and God of all comfort, who comforts us in all our tribulation, that we may be able to comfort those who are in any trouble, with the comfort with which we ourselves are comforted by God" (2 Corinthians 1:3–4).

Are you bringing your emotional pain to God? His spiritual healing can help you provide comfort to others, just as through Christ my friend comforted me. —DF

Christ was broken for us to comfort the broken among us.

APOLOGY HOTLINE

January 10

Leave your gift there before the altar, and go your way. First be reconciled to your brother, and then come and offer your gift.
—MATTHEW 5:24

Jesse Jacobs has created an apology hotline that makes it possible to apologize without actually talking to the person you've wronged. People who are unable or unwilling to unburden their conscience in person call the hotline and leave a message on an answering machine. Each week, 30 to 50 calls are logged, as people apologize for things from adultery to embezzlement. "The hotline offers participants a chance to alleviate their guilt and, to some degree, to own up to their misdeeds," said Jacobs.

The apology hotline may seem to offer some relief from guilt, but this is not how Jesus instructed His followers to handle conflict. In the Sermon on the Mount, Jesus told us to deal with conflict by taking the initiative and going to the offended brother to apologize for the offense (see also Matthew 18). In fact, Jesus taught that the problem of human estrangement is so serious that we should even interrupt our worship to go on a personal mission of reconciliation (Matthew 5:24). The Master encouraged His followers to be reconciled with one another eagerly, aggressively, quickly, and personally (Matthew 5:25).

Are any of your relationships broken or estranged because of something you said or did? Take the initiative. Go now and do all you can to be reconciled. —MW

Read: Matthew 5:21–26

Biblical Truth

Personal Application

Prayer Requests

Answers to Prayer

At the heart of all conflict is a selfish heart.

January 11

Read: John 13:3–15

Biblical Truth

Personal Application

Prayer Requests

Answers to Prayer

SCATTERED FRUIT

Imitate me, just as I also imitate Christ.
—1 Corinthians 11:1

The story is told of a Christian who was home on furlough from serving in the armed forces. He was rushing to catch his train when he ran into a fruit stand on the station platform, knocking most of the piled-up apples to the ground.

The young boy who operated the stand tried to pick up his scattered fruit but was having difficulty. The apologetic serviceman put down his luggage and started collecting the apples. He polished each one with his handkerchief and put it back on the counter. So impressed was the boy that he asked gratefully, "Soldier, are you Jesus?" With a smile the soldier replied, "No, but I'm trying to be like Him."

Sometimes, as we hurry about our own responsibilities, we become too busy to care about other people. But we must remember that Jesus urges us to show kindness and concern for our fellow travelers. He set the example for us in John 13 by being a servant. We need to take the time to be helpful also.

Would anyone ask of us, "Are you Jesus?" And could we honestly respond, "No, I'm not Jesus, but I'm trying to be like Him"? Christlike kindness can open the door for a heart-touching testimony. —VCG

Nothing is more attractive than being like Jesus.

GOD'S TEARS

Jesus wept.
—John 11:35

In C. S. Lewis's story *The Magician's Nephew,* Digory recalled his terminally ill mother and how his hopes were all dying away. With a lump in his throat and tears in his eyes, he blurted out to Aslan, the great lion who represents Christ, "Please, please—won't you—can't you give me something that will cure Mother?"

Then, in his despair, Digory looked up at Aslan's face. "Great shining tears stood in the Lion's eyes. They were such big, bright tears compared with Digory's own that for a moment he felt as if the Lion must really be sorrier about his Mother than he was himself. 'My son, my son,' said Aslan. 'I know. Grief is great. Only you and I in this land know that yet. Let us be good to one another.' "

I think of Jesus' tears at Lazarus' grave (John 11:35). I believe He wept for Lazarus as well as for Mary and Martha and their grief. Later, Jesus wept over Jerusalem (Luke 19:41–44). And He knows and shares our grief today. But as He promised, we will see Him again in the place He's preparing for us (John 14:3). In heaven, our grief will end. "God will wipe away every tear from [our] eyes; there shall be no more death, nor sorrow, nor crying" (Revelation 21:4).

Until then, know that God weeps with you. —DHR

January 12

Read: John 11:28–37

Biblical Truth

Personal Application

Prayer Requests

Answers to Prayer

If you doubt that Jesus cares, remember His tears.

January 13

Read: Colossians 3:15–17

Biblical Truth

Personal Application

Prayer Requests

Answers to Prayer

SCRIPTURAL SONGS

Let the word of Christ dwell in you richly . . . in psalms and hymns and spiritual songs, singing with grace in your hearts to the Lord.
—Colossians 3:16

John W. Peterson, the beloved songwriter, was a master at using Scripture in his songs. When I was a teenager in the church choir, we performed his cantata "Jesus Is Coming" and sang these words taken from 2 Timothy 3, verses 1 and 2: "In the last days perilous times shall come. Men shall be lovers of themselves." Then he wrote of the grim signs that we would recognize in the last days (vv. 2–7). The steady rhythm of his music helps me remember that list even today.

While some of us have trouble memorizing verses from God's Word, something in our brain helps us to remember words in songs. If we analyze some of our favorite Christian songs and choruses, we find that they have been derived from Scripture. Thus, we can use the memory boost of music to hide away God-breathed words in our hearts (2 Timothy 3:16). Songs such as "Open the Eyes of My Heart" (Isaiah 6:9–10; Ephesians 1:18), or favorites like "Thy Word Have I Hid in My Heart" (Psalm 119:11, 105), are taken from the Bible. With these words hidden in our memory, a song of praise comes quickly to our lips.

No matter what kind of voice you have, when you sing the words of Scripture back to God, it is sweet music to His ears.
—CHK

Hymns are the incense of a worshiping soul praising God!

REDISCOVERING THE PASSION

January 14

Remember therefore from where you have fallen; repent and do the first works.
—Revelation 2:5

Read: Revelation 2:1–7

A Major League baseball player announced his retirement, saying, "All of a sudden, that passion isn't there anymore. Physically, I think I could still do it. But something that I loved my whole life and had such a passion for became a major, major job for me. It's not like it used to be."

What can we do when something that once energized us has become a burden? A career can be changed, but the deepest matters of the heart, especially our relationship with Christ, cry out to recapture the fervor that fueled earlier days.

The risen Lord praised the church in Ephesus for their faithful service and perseverance, but added, "Nevertheless I have this against you, that you have left your first love. Remember therefore from where you have fallen; repent and do the first works" (Revelation 2:4–5).

Oswald Chambers reminds us that "the old writers used to speak of the Cross as the Passion of Our Lord. The Cross is the great opening through which all the blood of Christian service runs."

If our spiritual passion has grown cold, let us remember again the great sacrifice of Christ for our sin (Hebrews 12:3), turn away from grudging service and allow the wonder of His cross to rekindle our love for Him.
—DCM

Biblical Truth

Personal Application

Prayer Requests

Answers to Prayer

A passion for Jesus should become a passion for telling others about Jesus.

January 15

Read: Psalm 63:1–8

Biblical Truth

Personal Application

Prayer Requests

Answers to Prayer

CONNECTING WITH GOD

Because Your lovingkindness is better than life, my lips shall praise You.
—Psalm 63:3

In his book *Objects of His Affection*, Scotty Smith shares his journey of learning to personally experience the passionate love of God. As a young boy, he lost his mother suddenly in a car accident. Because of this, he closed off his wounded heart to others, including God. Several years later he received Jesus as his Savior and began to learn the truths of Christianity. Yet his relationship with the Lord in those days was, as he described, "side by side rather than face to face. Important, but not intimate."

Do you ever feel that way? You talk to the Lord a little bit, read His words in the Bible, but don't sense a passionate connection with Him like that expressed by the psalmist David in Psalm 63. Scotty suggests ways to overcome the obstacles to intimacy, from which we may glean these two ideas.

Live honestly. Open up to the Lord about the pain of your losses and admit your failures. "Draw near to God and He will draw near to you" (James 4:8; see also 1 John 1:9).

Ponder and believe the Scriptures about God's character and His longing for you. "Your lovingkindness is better than life" (Psalm 63:3; see also Psalm 139 and Ephesians 1:3–6).

Being close in a relationship takes time and effort—even when it's with the Lord. —AC

"God pursues us in our restlessness, receives us in our sinfulness, holds us in our brokenness." —Scotty Smith

WHAT ON EARTH ARE WE DOING?

January 16

Therefore, whether you eat or drink, or whatever you do, do all to the glory of God.
—1 CORINTHIANS 10:31

"What on earth are you doing?" You may have heard that phrase when your mom told you to clean your room and found you playing with your toys instead, or maybe when your teacher caught you passing notes in class.

But if God were to ask you this question, how would you respond?

Paul tells us that as followers of Jesus we have been put on this earth to bring glory to God in everything we do. So what should that look like?

God's glory is the manifestation of all that He is in His unsurpassed, stunning perfection. It is His amazing love, His wide mercy, His deep grace. His glory is seen in His truth, justice, wisdom, and power. To glorify Him means that we have the high privilege of showing Him off in a world that is totally unaware of what He is really like. Acts of mercy to the undeserving, grace to the needy, forgiveness to an offender, living wisely according to His will—all give glorious visibility to the character and quality of our God.

There are a lot of misconceptions floating around about God. It's our job to let others see what He is really like. And when they like what they see, let's be sure to let them know who taught us to live like that. It's not a good idea to steal God's glory! —JS

Read: 1 Corinthians 10:31–11:1

Biblical Truth

Personal Application

Prayer Requests

Answers to Prayer

May our lives be a "show and tell" for God's glory.

January 17

Read: Romans 12:3–8

Biblical Truth

Personal Application

Prayer Requests

Answers to Prayer

DESIGNED BY GOD

We have many members in one body, but all the members do not have the same function.
—Romans 12:4

Bison are made in such a way that their natural inclination is to look down; the design of their necks makes it difficult for them to look up. In contrast, giraffes are designed in a way that makes looking up easy; the way their necks are made makes it difficult for them to look down. Two creatures created by the same God but with distinctively different body parts and purposes. Giraffes eat leaves from branches above. Bison eat grass from the field below. God provides food for both, and neither has to become like the other to eat.

As we observe the animals and people around us, we're reminded that God made each of us unique for a purpose. One person's natural tendency is to look up and see the "big picture," while another looks down and focuses on details. Both are important. One is not better than the other. God gave us individual talents and spiritual gifts so that we can work together as a body.

Human beings are the crowning jewel of creation, and we shine the brightest not when we see our own likeness reflected in others but when each of us performs the unique functions that God designed for us to do. "Having then gifts differing according to the grace that is given to us, let us use them" (Romans 12:6).
—JAL

There are no unimportant members in the body of Christ.

THE HOSPITALITY MANAGER

Distributing to the needs of the saints, given to hospitality.
—Romans 12:13

Victoria's family refers to her as the "hospitality manager" of their home. She lives in Singapore with her daughter and son-in-law. He is the RBC Ministries international director, and they often have visitors. Victoria stays busy as a volunteer in the RBC office on that island nation, but her primary ministry is the gift of caring and hospitality. She makes their visitors feel welcome, loved, and cared for in their home.

The word *hospitality* means "love of strangers," and this is precisely what the apostle Paul was calling us to in Romans 12. In the midst of the practical challenges to believers about our relationship with God and one another, Paul said that we are to be "distributing to the needs of the saints, given to hospitality" (Romans 12:13). This may call us outside our comfort zone to show love and care to those the Lord brings across our path. Hebrews 13:2 adds this intriguing thought about hospitality: "Do not forget to entertain strangers, for by so doing some have unwittingly entertained angels."

Often overlooked and sometimes unappreciated, the ministry of the "hospitality manager" is a great gift, and it brings with it the added possibility of surprising blessings along the way! —BC

January 18

Read: Romans 12:9–21

Biblical Truth

Personal Application

Prayer Requests

Answers to Prayer

To stretch your soul, reach out with Jesus' love.

January 19

Read: Genesis 12:1–9

Biblical Truth

Personal Application

Prayer Requests

Answers to Prayer

SHENANDOAH

By faith Abraham obeyed when he was called to go.
—Hebrews 11:8

My grandfather grew up on the North American frontier and raised his family on a dairy farm. To pass the time, he often sang songs while he worked. "Shenandoah" was one of his favorites:

O Shenandoah, I long to hear you,
Away, you rolling river,
O Shenandoah, I long to hear you,
Away, I'm bound away,
'Cross the wide Missouri.

That song reflects the love the pioneer songwriter had for the Shenandoah River. Yet he felt compelled to leave its beauty and go west. His love for the familiar rooted him, but the pull of something better won his heart.

When Abraham was called out of Ur to follow God to the Promised Land, he had to leave everything that was familiar to him (Genesis 12:1). Despite the idolatry of that pagan city, Abraham had probably grown attached to the comfort of his home, the variety of the food, and the fellowship of his friends. But Abraham left the familiar to follow God's leading: "By faith Abraham obeyed when he was called to go" (Hebrews 11:8).

When we experience God's call to another place, it may mean leaving behind the people and the things we love. But when we're obedient to God, He will provide something even more fulfilling at our new destination.
—DF

You don't need to see the way if you follow the One who is the Way.

GREATLY VALUED

Mephibosheth . . . shall eat at my table like one of the king's sons.
—2 Samuel 9:11

A British factory worker and his wife were excited when, after many years of marriage, they discovered they were going to have their first child. According to author Jill Briscoe, who told this story, the man eagerly told his fellow workers that God had answered his prayers. But they made fun of him for asking God for a child.

When the baby was born, he was diagnosed with Down syndrome. As the father made his way to work for the first time after the birth, he wondered how to face his co-workers. "God, please give me wisdom," he prayed. Just as he feared, some mocked, "So, God gave you this child!" The new father stood for a long time, silently asking God for help. At last he said, "I'm glad the Lord gave this child to me and not to you."

As this man accepted his disabled son as God's gift to him, so David was pleased to show kindness to Jonathan's son, who was "lame in his feet" (2 Samuel 9:3). Some may have disregarded Mephibosheth because he was lame, or because he was from Saul's household, but David's action showed that he valued him greatly.

In God's eyes, every person is important. He sent His only Son to die for us. May we remember with gratitude how much He values each human life. —DB

January 20

Read: 2 Samuel 9

Biblical Truth

Personal Application

Prayer Requests

Answers to Prayer

Everyone is valuable to God.

January 21

Read: Psalm 31:1–8

Biblical Truth

Personal Application

Prayer Requests

Answers to Prayer

OUR BEST DEFENSE

Be my rock of refuge, a fortress of defense to save me.
—Psalm 31:2

In late January 1956, during the tense days of the Montgomery Boycott, civil rights leader Dr. Martin Luther King Jr. could not sleep. A threatening phone call had terrified him. So he prayed, "I am here taking a stand for what I believe is right. But Lord, I must confess that I'm weak now, I'm faltering. I'm losing my courage. Now, I am afraid . . . The people are looking to me for leadership, and if I stand before them without strength and courage, they too will falter. I am at the end of my powers . . . I can't face it alone."

Dr. King later wrote, "At that moment I experienced the presence of the Divine as I never experienced Him before. It seemed as though I could hear the quiet assurance of an inner voice saying, 'Stand up for righteousness, stand up for truth; and God will be at your side forever.' Almost at once my fears began to go. My uncertainty disappeared. I was ready to face anything."

The rest is history. Dr. King wanted to see people of all colors free of the damage done by racism and prejudice.

If we face opposition when we're trying to do what's right, we too must cry out to the Lord. He alone is our "rock of refuge, a fortress of defense" (Psalm 31:2). He is our reliable source of strength and protection. —DCE

When we trust the power of God, we experience peace, not panic.

ELIANA'S WORLD

January 22

Behold, children are a heritage from the Lord, the fruit of the womb is a reward.
—PSALM 127:3

On the day the US lost one of its most respected presidents, my wife and I celebrated the birth of our first grandchild. Gerald R. Ford died the day Eliana Ruth was born to our daughter Lisa and her husband, Todd. She came into the world in a hospital about a mile from where President Ford is now buried.

If Eliana lives to be the same age as President Ford when he died, she will live into the 22nd century! I wonder what mark this little girl will make on the world, and what kind of society she and her peers will experience.

Each child born into this world has potential for godliness and even greatness. The traits today's children need to guide a future society do not come by accident, but through diligent, godly parenting.

God's Word calls us to point children to Jesus (Mark 10:14–16). We are to instruct them in God's ways (Deuteronomy 6:4–9), discipline them toward godliness (Proverbs 19:18), and love them unconditionally (Luke 15:11–32). Imagine what Eliana's world can be like if the parents of her generation dedicate themselves to godly parenting.

Are you a parent? Teach your children godliness, faith, and uncommon love. Then, when they influence their world, they will reveal God to a new generation.
—DB

Read: Psalm 127

Biblical Truth

Personal Application

Prayer Requests

Answers to Prayer

To guide your children on the right way, you must go that way yourself.

January 23

Read: Colossians 1:3–14

Biblical Truth

Personal Application

Prayer Requests

Answers to Prayer

KINGDOM LIVING

He has delivered us from the power of darkness and conveyed us into the kingdom of the Son of His love.
—Colossians 1:13

I have a lot of friends who work in bad neighborhoods. One of these city warriors transplanted his family to the inner city. One day as he was walking down the hallway in his apartment building, he noticed two guys smoking crack cocaine. Not wanting his kids to see what they were doing, he asked the two to stop. The next thing he knew, one of their fists had found its way to his jaw. With a bleeding nose and mouth, he responded, "If Jesus shed His blood for me, I can shed my blood for you."

Shocked by the man's response, the two men fled. A few days later one of them returned, knocked on my friend's door, and said, "I have not forgotten your words. If your God is that real to you, then I want to know Him." That day, he was "delivered . . . from the power of darkness," and brought "into the kingdom of the Son of His love" (Colossians 1:13).

Those of us who have been rescued from the domain of darkness can bring a little bit of heaven to earth when we are willing to demonstrate the power of God's unique approach to life. Even in our moments of weakness and vulnerability, we are given opportunities to demonstrate the power and strength of God's forgiveness by showing His love for our enemies. —JS

A world in darkness needs the light of the gospel.

ABSOLUTE NEEDS

My God shall supply all your need according to His riches in glory by Christ Jesus.
—PHILIPPIANS 4:19

From our first breath until our last, we have few truly essential needs. Without oxygen, we would perish in minutes. We must have food and water. Our bodies, when exhausted, require rest. And in harsh weather, we must seek shelter. So, while we are needy creatures, our basic needs are few.

When it comes to our wants, however, there seems to be no limit. Indeed, the entire advertising industry is devoted to expanding our "needs."

But what about those basic needs we overlook? What about our need for the Bread of Life and the living water of God's truth? What about our need for spiritual fellowship that gives strength, hope, peace, and comfort? The vague dissatisfaction so many people experience is really spiritual malnutrition and thirst.

Jesus told a Samaritan woman about water that would become "a fountain of water springing up into everlasting life" (John 4:14). He had what she truly needed—what Peter later called "the words of eternal life" (John 6:68).

Have we been ignoring the words of Jesus: "Man shall not live by bread alone"? (Luke 4:4). Have we been failing to nourish our souls while pursuing our wants? "Seek first the kingdom of God and His righteousness, and all these things shall be added to you" (Matthew 6:33). —VCG

January 24

Read: John 4:7–15

Biblical Truth

Personal Application

Prayer Requests

Answers to Prayer

Just as our body needs daily food, so does our spirit.

January 25

Read: Exodus 6:1–9

Biblical Truth

Personal Application

Prayer Requests

Answers to Prayer

THE MOST DEPRESSING DAY

Be of good cheer! It is I; do not be afraid.
—Matthew 14:27

Scientists in the UK have calculated that the most depressing day of the year comes in the third week of January. Winter days are dark and cold, holiday excitement has worn off just as Christmas debts are coming due, and New Year's resolutions have all been broken. The celebrations, gift-giving, and good intentions that once made us feel happy now press us down and leave us feeling hopeless.

Long ago in Egypt, the Hebrew people had high hopes that Moses would rescue them from slavery. But their hopes were dashed when Moses' good intentions led to worse conditions for them. Instead of gaining freedom, the people were pressed even harder by slave drivers who demanded that they produce the same amount of bricks with fewer resources.

Moses cried out to the Lord, "Since I came to Pharaoh to speak in Your name, he has done evil to this people; neither have You delivered Your people at all" (Exodus 5:23). As Moses and the Hebrew people were about to learn, God's rescue plans sometimes don't kick in until all hope seems to be gone.

If the circumstances of your life seem to be going from bad to worse, sending you into depression and despair, remember that God always hears and answers our cries—but it's in His time, not ours. —JAL

When you feel hopeless, look to the God of hope.

JESUS' DIFFICULT WORDS

From that time many of His disciples went back and walked with Him no more.
—John 6:66

Recently, a company advertised a "huggable, washable, and talking" Jesus doll that recites "actual Scripture verses to introduce children of all ages to the wisdom of the Bible." Its sayings include, "I have an exciting plan for your life," and "Your life matters so much to me." Who wouldn't want to follow a Jesus like this?

Jesus does offer a wonderful plan for our lives. But He doesn't serve as a cosmic genie or cuddly doll to meet our every whim. John 6 gives us a picture of a Jesus who is not so cuddly—in fact, He's often offensive. Instead of fulfilling the selfish desires of His followers, He disturbed their expectations. He offered himself as spiritual bread from heaven and said, "Whoever eats My flesh and drinks My blood has eternal life" (John 6:54).

This message was offensive and difficult. The image of eating flesh and drinking blood did not give His hearers "warm fuzzies." Many stopped following Him (John 6:66). He wasn't the conquering Messiah-King they had expected.

Sometimes we want a Jesus who meets our selfish needs. But the wonderful life He offers is found only in radical obedience to His commands. Let's ask Jesus to show us what His words mean, and for the courage to act on His truth. —MW

January 26

Read: John 6:44–58

Biblical Truth

Personal Application

Prayer Requests

Answers to Prayer

The way of Jesus is not always easy.

January 27

Read: Psalm 37:1–11

Biblical Truth

Personal Application

Prayer Requests

Answers to Prayer

A SHEER DELIGHT

Delight yourself . . .
in the Lord, and He shall give you
the desires of your heart.
—Psalm 37:4

After finishing high school in 1941, Clair Hess anticipated serving his country by joining the army. But when he developed a heart murmur from a bout with scarlet fever, he was denied acceptance. He admits that he was envious of his fellow graduates and other servicemen in their uniforms, but he was helped by reading Psalm 37 and seeing how the psalmist David handled envy.

While Clair was wondering about God's direction for his life, his uncle suggested to him that the Lord might be calling him to *His* service. So Clair attended Moody Bible Institute and was led into a career of singing and later editing for RBC Ministries. He's been doing that for 50 years now and calls serving God "a sheer delight."

David encouraged us in Psalm 37 to delight in the Lord and not to envy others (vv. 1–4). Although he was talking about envying people who get away with evil, we can apply it to other types of envy. Instead of comparing ourselves with others, we need to delight ourselves in God. In His time, He'll fulfill the desires of our heart and affirm that we are in His will.

We're all in "God's service" as believers. And serving Him is a sheer delight. —AC

Contentment comes when God's will is more important than our wants.

ARMED AND EXTREMELY EFFECTIVE

January 28

We do not wrestle against flesh and blood, but against . . . spiritual hosts of wickedness.
—EPHESIANS 6:12

In January of 2007, the police officers in Tijuana, Mexico, had their guns confiscated. It was suspected that some of them had been in collusion with drug traffickers. At first, fearing for their safety, the police stopped patrolling. But eventually, some of them returned to work—carrying slingshots. Three weeks passed before their more effective weapons were returned to them.

Although we all remember a shepherd boy who used a sling and a single smooth stone with great success in his encounter with a giant (1 Samuel 17), few of us would have the courage to face violent threats armed with such puny protection. But every day, although we are often ill-prepared, we do face a threat. As believers, we fight against an enemy we cannot see. Our struggle is not "against flesh and blood, but against . . . spiritual hosts of wickedness" (Ephesians 6:12). The outcome of this battle is sure, however. Jesus is the Victor. And using the armor and weapons He supplies, we are able "to stand" (Ephesians 6:13). We fight in His power and strength.

Each day we must put on the armor of God—the breastplate of righteousness, the shield of faith, and the sword of the Spirit, God's Word (Ephesians 6:13–17). Preparation and protection are the key to winning spiritual battles.
—CHK

Read: Ephesians 6:10–18

Biblical Truth

Personal Application

Prayer Requests

Answers to Prayer

Spiritual victory comes only to those who are prepared for battle.

January 29

Read: Matthew 11:7–9

Biblical Truth

Personal Application

Prayer Requests

Answers to Prayer

SAYING GOOD-BYE

There has not risen one greater than John the Baptist; but he who is least in the kingdom of heaven is greater than he.
—MATTHEW 11:11

If you've ever been asked to say a few words at a memorial service, you know how difficult, yet important, it can be. Cyrus M. Copeland, compiler of two books of tributes to famous people, said: "A great eulogy is both art and architecture—a bridge between the living and the dead, memory and eternity."

The Bible contains little that corresponds to our modern eulogy. Yet Jesus paid a great tribute to John the Baptist when he faced the looming threat of execution by Herod. From prison, John sent his disciples to confirm the identity of Jesus the Messiah (Matthew 11:2–6). Jesus talked with them, then told the listening crowd, "Among those born of women there has not risen one greater than John the Baptist; but he who is least in the kingdom of heaven is greater than he" (Matthew 11:11).

Jesus' tribute captured the essence of the desert-dwelling, straight-preaching John, who was maligned and misunderstood as he prepared the way for the Son of God. John's greatness was more than personal; it was wrapped up in the kingdom of God. He wrote his own eulogy by his actions.

As we ponder what we might say about others at their passing, it's also good to ask, "What will people say about me when it's time to say good-bye?" —DCM

Living for the Lord today leaves a lasting legacy when we're gone.

WIPE AWAY TEARS

January 30

God will wipe away every tear from their eyes . . . There shall be no more pain, for the former things have passed away.
—Revelation 21:4

I had just finished preaching on the heartaches of life, when a couple approached me at the front of the church. The woman told me about the burden they bore as a family. Their young son had severe physical problems, and the strain of the constant care of this needy little guy, coupled with the heartache of knowing they couldn't improve his situation, sometimes felt unbearable.

As the couple shared, with tears in their eyes, their little daughter stood with them, listening and watching. Seeing the obvious hurt etched by tears on her mother's face, the girl reached up and gently wiped the tears from her mother's cheek. It was a simple gesture of love and compassion, and a profound display of concern from one so young.

Our tears often blur our sight and prevent us from seeing clearly. In those moments, it can be an encouragement to have a friend who cares enough to love us in our pain and walk with us in our struggles.

Even though friends can be a help, only Christ can reach beyond our tears and touch the deep hurts of our hearts. His comfort can carry us through the struggles of our lives until that day when God himself wipes away every tear from our eyes (Revelation 21:4). —BC

Read: Revelation 21:1–7

Biblical Truth

Personal Application

Prayer Requests

Answers to Prayer

The God who washed away our sins will also wipe away our tears.

January 31

Read: Exodus 18:13–24

Biblical Truth

Personal Application

Prayer Requests

Answers to Prayer

MINISTER MENTOR

Moses heeded the voice of his father-in-law and did all that he had said.
—Exodus 18:24

In 1959, when Lee Kuan Yew assumed the position of Prime Minister of Singapore, his leadership began a long process of national transformation. Initially, disagreements between ethnic groups and a weak economic base made the future of this tiny nation uncertain. By 1990, when Lee stepped down from his position, Singapore had become a model country for ethnic harmony and a thriving economy. After serving as Senior Minister, Lee became Minister Mentor in 2004. Since then he has been an invaluable resource to Singapore's cabinet and to other leaders around the world.

Insights from the older generation can greatly benefit the younger generation. Although Moses had been used by God to perform miracles and deliver Israel out of bondage in Egypt, he still listened to the advice of his father-in-law Jethro (Exodus 18:24). Jethro had watched his son-in-law care for the concerns of the people and observed: "Both you and these people who are with you will surely wear yourselves out. For this thing is too much for you" (Exodus 18:18). Moses followed Jethro's advice to select, train, and delegate others to share the workload (vv. 22–24).

Whom has God placed in your life to advise you as a "minister mentor"? —DF

Those who are mature in the faith can help others to mature in their faith.

February

February 1

Read: 2 Corinthians 5:12–21

Biblical Truth

Personal Application

Prayer Requests

Answers to Prayer

DARE TO BE DIFFERENT

Now then, we are ambassadors for Christ.
—2 Corinthians 5:20

Since my dad was a pastor, I got stuck with the label known to every pastor's kid: PK. But, much to the congregation's disappointment, the title didn't stop me from being my mischievous little self. I can't count the times I heard, "Little Joe, you're the pastor's son. You should be an example." But I didn't want to be an example! I was only five and wanted to have fun with my friends!

Let's face it, being an example is often about being different. But most of us don't want to be different. We want people to like us, and the safest way to do that is to blend in. But following Christ has never been about blending in. Following Him means to be like Him, to respond to life and relate to people as He did. It's a little risky and uncomfortable to be different. But that's what being an "ambassador for Christ" (2 Corinthians 5:20) is all about—bringing the wonderful difference of your King to bear on the territory you've been assigned: your home, your office, your friendships. Representing the King is not just our calling; it's a great honor.

In retrospect, I can see how my antics as a PK reflected poorly on my dad. It's motivating to remember that our non-Jesus attitudes and actions also reflect poorly on our King.

Make a difference by daring to be different! —JS

Dare to be different—for the Father's sake.

BEST IN SHOW?

February 2

Man looks at the outward appearance, but the Lord looks at the heart.
—1 Samuel 16:7

I enjoy watching dog shows on TV. The dog owners are impeccably dressed and trot along with their pedigreed pooches as they show off their unique canine beauty. The dogs have been trained to stand confidently with chins lifted high, their shiny coats carefully brushed and styled. To me, they *all* look like winners.

But I wonder sometimes, when their audience is gone, what are these dogs really like? Do they ever relax and let their sleek fur get so matted they're mistaken for mutts? Does their doggie breath start smelling foul?

More important, what are *we* really like when nobody's watching? In Matthew 23:2–7, Jesus rebuked those who were interested in how they looked in public rather than how they were seen by God. He wants us to be obedient, faithful, and committed to Him—even when nobody else sees. The Pharisees focused on the way they were perceived by other people. God's focus is on what we're like inside. His desire is for us to look like His Son.

We're not in a competition with other Christians. God will never ask us to compete for "best in show." He measures us by the perfect standard of His Son (Ephesians 4:13). And in love, He provides the righteousness we need so that we can be blameless before Him (Colossians 1:21–23). —CHK

Read: Matthew 23:1–12

Biblical Truth

Personal Application

Prayer Requests

Answers to Prayer

Living for God's approval is better than living for man's applause.

February 3

Read: Psalm 12

Biblical Truth

Personal Application

Prayer Requests

Answers to Prayer

IT LOOKS BAD

I will set him in the safety for which he yearns.
—Psalm 12:5

King David looked out at the world and was troubled. He didn't need the Internet to paint a bleak picture of society or the *New York Times* to remind him of crime and suffering. Even without a cable news show to give him all the bad news, he saw the evil.

He looked around and saw that "the godly man ceases." He noticed that "the faithful disappear." In his world, everyone spoke "idly" to his neighbor "with flattering lips and a double heart" (Psalm 12:1–2).

This description may sound like the theme of a TV show, but it was life, circa 1,000 BC. While we may view society's evils as much worse than anything that came before, David reminds us that evil is not a 21st-century innovation.

But David's words also give us hope. Notice his reaction to the bad news he bore. First, he turned to God and cried, "Help!" (v. 1). Then he implored God with specific needs. The response he got was positive. God promised that because He rules righteously, He would provide protection and safety (vv. 5–7).

When you are discouraged by all the bad news, cry out for God's help. Then bask in the confidence of His assurance. Three thousand years after David, God is still, and always will be, in control. —DB

We have nothing to fear, because God is in control.

UNLOCKING THE GATE

February 4

When a man or woman commits any sin . . . against the Lord . . . then he shall confess the sin which he has committed.
—NUMBERS 5:6–7

Researchers at the University of Toronto reported in 2006 that people who are suffering from a guilty conscience experience "a powerful urge to wash themselves." To study this effect, the researchers asked volunteers to recall past sins. They were then given an opportunity to wash their hands as a symbol of cleansing their conscience. Those who had recalled their sins washed their hands at "twice the rate of study subjects who had not imagined past transgressions."

The Bible proposes the only effective way of dealing with sin—confession. In the Old Testament, one of the ways the Israelites were supposed to cleanse themselves and maintain purity before God and in their community was by confessing their sins (Numbers 5:5–8). To *confess* means "to speak the same; to agree with; to admit the truth." When the people confessed to God, they were not telling Him anything He did not already know. But their confession was a demonstration of a change of heart. Refusing to confess their sins allowed sin to take deeper root within their lives and community.

Admitting our sin unlocks the gate so that we can have forgiveness, joy, and peace. If we confess our sins, God is faithful to forgive (1 John 1:9). —MW

Read: Numbers 5:5–8

Biblical Truth

Personal Application

Prayer Requests

Answers to Prayer

Confession is agreeing with God about our sin.

February 5

Read: Matthew 18:23–35

Biblical Truth

Personal Application

Prayer Requests

Answers to Prayer

THE ATROCIOUS MATHEMATICS OF THE GOSPEL

The master of that servant was moved with compassion, released him, and forgave him the debt.
—MATTHEW 18:27

From childhood we are taught how to succeed in the world of *ungrace*. "You get what you pay for." "The early bird gets the worm." "No pain, no gain." I know these rules well because I live by them. I work for what I earn. I like to win. I insist on my rights. I want people to get what they deserve.

But Jesus' parables about grace teach a radically different concept. In Matthew 18, no one could accumulate a debt as huge as the servant did (vv. 23–24). This underscores the point: The debt is unforgivable. Nevertheless, the master let the servant off scot-free.

The more I reflect on Jesus' parables proclaiming grace, the more tempted I am to apply the word *atrocious* to describe the mathematics of the gospel. I believe Jesus gave us these stories to call us to step completely outside our tit-for-tat world of ungrace and enter into God's realm of infinite grace.

If I care to listen, I hear a loud whisper from the gospel that I did not get what I deserved. I deserved punishment and got forgiveness. I deserved wrath and got love. I deserved debtor's prison and got instead a clean credit history. I deserved stern lectures and crawl-on-your-knees repentance. Instead, I got a banquet spread for me. —PY

Our sin is great; God's grace is greater.

PERIPHERAL VISION

Now it came to pass, when the time had come for [Jesus] to be received up, that He steadfastly set His face to go to Jerusalem.
—Luke 9:51

February 6

Read: Luke 9:51–62

Biblical Truth

Personal Application

Prayer Requests

Answers to Prayer

Peripheral vision enables us to be aware of our surroundings while remaining focused on our destination. What we see from "the corner of our eye" can be useful, unless it distracts us from our goal.

During the weeks leading to Easter, as we think about the cross, we may be struck by our Lord's purposeful approach to the city where He knew crucifixion and resurrection awaited Him. "Now it came to pass, when the time had come for Him to be received up, that He steadfastly set His face to go to Jerusalem" (Luke 9:51). From that moment on, Jesus' eyes were on the cross. Every obstacle to accomplishing His Father's will became part of His peripheral vision.

When a man professed an interest in following Him, Jesus told him: "No one, having put his hand to the plow, and looking back, is fit for the kingdom of God" (Luke 9:62). The issue was probably not the man's family (v. 61) but his focus. We can't move ahead while looking at what we've left behind.

Neither cries of "Hosanna" nor shouts of hatred could deter Jesus from His goal "to give His life a ransom for many" and to pay the price to set us free (Matthew 20:28).

Where is your focus today?
—DCM

You don't need to know where you're going if you know the One who does.

February 7

Read: Psalm 26

Biblical Truth

Personal Application

Prayer Requests

Answers to Prayer

CALLING MYSELF

Vindicate me, O Lord,
for I have walked in my integrity.
—Psalm 26:1

As I was moving my laptop, cell phone, and assorted books and papers from one room to another, the "regular" phone rang. I hurriedly set down my stuff and rushed to answer the call before the answering machine kicked in. "Hello," I said. No reply. I said hello again when I heard rustling, but still no response. So I hung up and went back to my stuff on the floor. When I picked up my cell phone I realized that I had accidentally speed-dialed my home phone number!

I laughed at myself, but then wondered: *How often are my prayers more like calling myself than calling on God?*

For example, when I am falsely accused, I plead with God for vindication. I want my name cleared and the guilty person held accountable for the harm done to my reputation. But then I get impatient with God and try to vindicate myself. I may as well be praying to myself.

Vindication does not come from self-defensive arguments; it stems from integrity (Psalm 26:1). It requires that I allow God to examine my mind and heart (v. 2) and that I walk in His truth (v. 3). This, of course, requires patient waiting (Psalm 25:21).

When we call on God, He will help us—but in His perfect time and in His perfect way. —JAL

The purpose of prayer is not to get what we want, but to become what God wants.

THE SECRET GARDEN

February 8

Keep your heart with all diligence, for out of it spring the issues of life.
—Proverbs 4:23

Read: Proverbs 4:20–27

The Secret Garden, a novel by Frances Hodgson Burnett, tells the story of Mary, a young girl who goes to live with her wealthy uncle Archibald on his estate in England. Mary gets to know Dickon, a working-class boy who loves nature. The two children discover a fenced-in garden that Mary's uncle has locked up because it reminds him of his deceased wife. The garden looks dead because of neglect, but Dickon assures Mary that, with proper tending, it will recover with new life. With the children's help, "the secret garden" eventually bursts forth with colorful, fragrant blooms.

All of us have a secret garden of the heart. How we tend it will determine what speech and behavior it produces. Proverbs wisely admonishes us: "Keep your heart with all diligence, for out of it spring the issues of life" (Proverbs 4:23). The word *keep* means "to watch or guard with fidelity." Guarding what we take into our hearts and monitoring our response will determine what takes root there. As we remove the thorns of resentment, weeds of lust, and roots of bitterness, we can replace them with the fruit of the Spirit: "love, joy, peace, longsuffering, kindness, goodness, faithfulness, gentleness, self-control" (Galatians 5:22–23).

Are you tending the garden of your heart? —DF

Biblical Truth

Personal Application

Prayer Requests

Answers to Prayer

God wants you to water the seed He's planted in your heart.

February 9

Read: Mark 1:16–20

Biblical Truth

Personal Application

Prayer Requests

Answers to Prayer

LIFE BEYOND THE RITUALS

They immediately left their nets and followed Him.
—Mark 1:18

A royal dignitary was greeting residents at a nursing home, when he was surprised by the unresponsiveness of one woman who just sat and stared at him. Finally, the dignitary asked, "Do you know who I am?"—to which the woman responded: "No. But that nurse over there helps us with those kinds of things."

Many people are confused about who Jesus is. But through His Word, God helps us know and enjoy the real Jesus. You will find Him wonderfully compelling. Tough fishermen, tax collectors, and zealots gave up everything to follow Him (Mark 1:18). Women felt safe with Him. Crowds stood in awe of His power and authority.

Jesus is not content to be just our "fire insurance," saving us from eternal punishment in hell. Rather, He wants us to know Him for who He really is, and He desires to connect with us on a deeper, more personal level.

If you are weary of a religion that is about rules and regulations, then welcome to life beyond the rituals. Welcome to a relationship in which you can find companionship, comfort, wisdom, and reality. Welcome to the wonderful privilege of getting to know Jesus and the joy of following Him.

Get to know Him—and you'll grow to love Him more and more each day. —JS

To know Jesus is to love Jesus.

ENDING ESCALATION

February 10

I tell you not to resist an evil person. But whoever slaps you on your right cheek, turn the other to him also.
—MATTHEW 5:39

The pastor of an inner-city church told his congregation: "Some people believe in 'an eye for an eye.' But in this neighborhood, it's *two* eyes for an eye. You can never even the score; you can only raise the stakes." The people nodded in solemn understanding of the reality they faced each day.

We've seen it happen on a school playground or in our own homes—a child bumps into another during a game. The one who was bumped pushes back, and the shoving quickly grows into a fight. It's the process of retaliation and escalation in which each act of revenge exceeds the one that provoked it.

In Matthew 5, Jesus tackled a number of key relational issues by raising the standard to the one that pleases God: "You have heard that it was said . . . But I tell you . . ." (vv. 38–39). His words about turning the other cheek, going the second mile, and giving to those who ask may sound as radical and unrealistic to us as they did to those who first heard them (vv. 38–42). Are we willing to ponder and pray about His teaching? Are we ready to apply it when we are wronged at home, at work, or at school?

The cycle of escalation can be broken when a courageous, faith-filled person refuses to strike back. —DCM

Read: Matthew 5:38–48

Biblical Truth

Personal Application

Prayer Requests

Answers to Prayer

To return good for good is natural;
to return good for evil is supernatural.

February 11

Read: 2 Samuel 12:1–13

Biblical Truth

Personal Application

Prayer Requests

Answers to Prayer

THE WOUNDS OF A FRIEND

Faithful are the wounds of a friend.
—PROVERBS 27:6

Not everyone appreciates correction, but David did. He felt indebted to those who corrected him and realized how much he owed them. "Let the righteous strike me; it shall be a kindness. Let him rebuke me; it shall be as excellent oil; let my head not refuse it" (Psalm 141:5).

Correction is a kindness, David insists, a word that suggests an act of loyalty. Loyal friends will correct one another, even when it's painful and disruptive to relationships to do so. It's one of the ways we show love and help one another to grow stronger. As Proverbs 27:6 states: "Faithful are the wounds of a friend."

It takes grace to give godly correction; it takes greater grace to receive it. Unlike David, who accepted Nathan's correction (2 Samuel 12:13), we're inclined to refuse it. We resent the interference; we do not want to be found out. But if we accept the reproof, we will find that it does indeed become "excellent oil" on our heads, an anointing that makes our lives a sweet aroma wherever we go.

Growth in grace sometimes comes through the kind but unpleasant correction of a loyal friend. Do not refuse it, for "he who receives correction is prudent" and "wise" (Proverbs 15:5; 9:8–9). —DHR

Correction from a loyal friend can help us change for the better.

DWELL WITH UNDERSTANDING

February 12

Husbands . . . dwell with [your wives] with understanding . . . that your prayers may not be hindered.
—1 Peter 3:7

My wife, Marlene, and I have been married for some 30 years, and have learned to appreciate each other and enjoy each other's unique qualities. But even after all these years she still surprises me from time to time. Recently, she reacted to a news report in a way that was opposite to what I expected. I told her, "Wow, that shocks me. I never would have thought you would land there on this issue." Her response? "Your job is to figure me out, and my job is to keep you guessing!" The responsibility to understand your spouse is what keeps married life interesting and stretching.

This is an ancient challenge. Peter wrote: "Husbands, likewise, dwell with them with understanding, giving honor to the wife, as to the weaker vessel, and as being heirs together of the grace of life, that your prayers may not be hindered" (1 Peter 3:7). He saw it as a priority for the husband to become a student of his wife—to know and understand her. Without that commitment to understanding his spouse, a husband is not capable of doing what comes next—honoring her.

As a husband, if I am to love my wife as Christ loves the church (Ephesians 5:25), it will begin with the intentional effort to grow in my understanding of her. —BC

Read: Ephesians 5:25–33

Biblical Truth

Personal Application

Prayer Requests

Answers to Prayer

Marriage thrives in a climate of love and respect.

February 13

Read: Psalm 51:8–13

Biblical Truth

Personal Application

Prayer Requests

Answers to Prayer

FRESH

Restore to me the joy of Your salvation.
—Psalm 51:12

What do you think of when you hear the word *fresh*? When the weather is nice, my husband and I enjoy going to the farmers market so we can buy produce that was picked that very morning. To me, fresh means just-harvested fruits and vegetables—not stale or spoiled, but crisp and full of exquisite flavor.

I need that kind of freshness in my relationship with God. I can have too many stale attitudes—impatience, criticism, and selfishness—and not enough "longsuffering, kindness . . . gentleness," which are "the fruit of the Spirit" (Galatians 5:22–23).

As David repented of the sin in his life, he prayed, "Create in me a clean heart." Then he petitioned God: "Restore to me the joy of Your salvation" (Psalm 51:10–12). Confession and repentance of our sin renews our fellowship with the Lord and allows us to joyously begin anew.

What better time than today to ask God to give you a newness of spirit, a freshness of faith, and a renewed appreciation of Him!

Lord, we want the fruit of our lives to always be "fresh and flourishing" (Psalm 92:14). *Help us to experience your love, compassion, and faithfulness that are "new every morning"* (Lamentations 3:22–23).
—CHK

To bear good fruit, clear out the weeds of sin.

THE BEST COMPANION

February 14

Behold what manner of love the Father has bestowed on us, that we should be called children of God!
—1 John 3:1

Read: 1 John 3:1–3

Some people looking for love have found help in an unusual place—a taxicab in New York City. Taxicab driver Ahmed Ibrahim loves to set up blind dates for his single passengers. His matchmaking services have been featured on the Fox News Channel, the *Wall Street Journal,* and NBC's *Today* show. He doesn't assist just anybody though; they have to be serious about looking to settle down with someone. Ahmed loves to help romance blossom, and he even hands out roses on Valentine's Day.

The best place to find love is not in another person but in a book, the Bible. The Bible tells of God's great love for us. This is expressed in what my friend called the best love note she had ever received. It's found in John 3:16:

For God so loVed the world,
That He gAve
His onLy
BegottEn
SoN
That whoever
Believes In Him
Should Not perish,
But have Everlasting life.

God loves us like no one else ever could. He showed that love when He sent His Son, Jesus, to be our Savior. He's also the best companion we'll ever have.

Open your Bible and learn more about Him. —AC

Biblical Truth

Personal Application

Prayer Requests

Answers to Prayer

The more you read the Bible, the more you'll love its Author.

February 15

Read: Psalm 119:65–80

Biblical Truth

Personal Application

Prayer Requests

Answers to Prayer

GROWING THROUGH GRIEF

It is good for me that I have been afflicted, that I may learn Your statutes.
—PSALM 119:71

A woman who lost her husband of 40 years to a sudden heart attack said that the resulting grief had caused her to value love more. When she heard couples arguing, she sometimes said to them, "You don't have time for this." She noted that the wasted moments in all our lives become more precious when they cannot be repeated.

Grief changes our perspective on life. It is trite but true that how we deal with sorrow will make us either bitter or better. In a remarkable statement, the psalmist actually thanked God for a difficult experience: "Before I was afflicted I went astray, but now I keep Your word . . . It is good for me that I have been afflicted, that I may learn Your statutes" (Psalm 119:67, 71).

We don't know the nature of the psalmist's affliction, but the positive outcome was a longing to obey the Lord and a hunger for His Word. Rarely can we use this truth to comfort those who hurt. Instead, it is the Lord's word to us from His compassionate heart and the touch from His healing hand.

When we grieve, it feels more like dying than growing. But as God wraps His loving arms around us, we have the assurance of His faithful care. —DCM

Precious in the sight of the Lord is the death of His saints.
—PSALM 116:15

IT'S A FACT

[I pray] that they all may be one,
as You, Father, are in Me,
and I in You.
—John 17:21

In doing research for his epic story *Roots,* Alex Haley embarked on the freighter *African Star,* sailing from Monrovia, Liberia, to Jacksonville, Florida. He did so to better understand the travails of his ancestors, who were brought in chains to America.

Haley descended into the ship's hold, stripped himself of protective clothing, and tried to sleep on some thick, rough-hewn bracing. After the third miserable night, he gave up and returned to his cabin. But he could now write with some small degree of empathy of the sufferings of his forebears.

It's one thing to *say* we believe that Jesus Christ, the second person of the Holy Trinity, identifies himself with us. It's quite another to *feel* the blessed experience of our identification with Him. But we need not resort to extreme measures to grasp the truth of that oneness, for Christ himself has endured the most extreme of all measures to identify with *us.* He went to the cross to reconcile a sinful human race to himself (Romans 5:10–11).

Reading Scripture, praying, and partaking of the Lord's Supper can help us gain at least some awareness of our identification with our Lord and Savior. But regardless of how we *feel*, our unity with Him is a fact that we must grasp in faith. —VCG

February 16

Read: Ephesians 4:1–6

Biblical Truth

Personal Application

Prayer Requests

Answers to Prayer

The just shall live by faith—not by feeling.

February 17

Read: Psalm 89:1–8

Biblical Truth

Personal Application

Prayer Requests

Answers to Prayer

JOIN THE CHOIR

I will sing of the mercies of the Lord forever; with my mouth will I make known Your faithfulness to all generations.
—Psalm 89:1

I'll never forget the first time I saw the Brooklyn Tabernacle Choir in concert. Nearly 200 people who had been redeemed out of the bowels of Brooklyn—former crack addicts and prostitutes included—sang their hearts out to God. Their faces glistened with tears running down their cheeks as they sang about God's work of redemption and forgiveness in their lives.

As I watched them, I felt somewhat shortchanged. Since I was saved when I was six, I didn't feel the same depth of gratefulness that they displayed as they sang about the dramatic rescue God had provided for them. I was saved from things like biting my sister—not exactly a significant testimony!

Then the Spirit reminded me that if He had not rescued me when I was young, who knows where my life would be today? What destructive paths would I have stumbled down if He had not been teaching me qualities like servanthood and self-control?

It became clear that I too am a great debtor to His grace. It's not only what we are saved "out of" but what we have been saved "from" that makes our hearts worthy of a spot in the chorus of the redeemed. Anyone who receives Jesus as Savior is welcome to join in the choir of praise: "I will sing of the mercies of the Lord forever" (Psalm 89:1). —JS

Praise flows freely from the choir of the redeemed.

LINCOLN'S TESTIMONY

February 18

Ought not the Christ to have suffered these things and to enter into His glory?
—Luke 24:26

Abraham Lincoln was a backwoodsman who rose from humble beginnings to the heights of political power. During the dark days of the US Civil War, he served as a compassionate and resolute president. Depression and mental pain were his frequent companions. Yet the terrible emotional suffering he endured drove him to receive Jesus Christ by faith.

Lincoln told a crowd in his hometown in Illinois: "When I left Springfield, I asked the people to pray for me; I was not a Christian. When I buried my son, the severest trial of my life, I was not a Christian. But when I saw the graves of thousands of our soldiers, I then and there consecrated myself to Christ. I do love Jesus." Life's most painful tragedies can bring us to a deeper understanding of the Savior.

When two men walked the road to Emmaus, they were dumbfounded by the senseless murder of Jesus of Nazareth. Then a stranger joined them and gave scriptural insight about the suffering Messiah (Luke 24:26–27). The stranger was Jesus himself, and His ministry to them brought comfort.

Heartache has a way of pointing us to the Lord Jesus, who has shared in our sufferings and can bring meaning to seemingly senseless pain. —DF

Read: Luke 24:13–27

Biblical Truth

Personal Application

Prayer Requests

Answers to Prayer

Suffering can teach us what we can't learn in any other way.

February 19

Read: 2 Timothy 1:6–12

Biblical Truth

Personal Application

Prayer Requests

Answers to Prayer

COURAGE: LIVE IT

God has not given us a spirit of fear, but of power.
—2 Timothy 1:7

Courage is one thing you need if you want to get God's work done. That's what I said when I spoke in a church service in Jamaica. I told the people that according to 2 Timothy 1:7, God did not give us a spirit of timidity but a spirit of power.

A couple of days later, I stood 35 feet above the water on the edge of the Caribbean Sea. Should I jump off the precipice into the waters below? The teenagers who were with me said, "Yes!" Most of them had already done so. One told me, "Mr. Branon, if you don't jump, you can't preach about courage again." I knew that sometimes the courageous thing is not to go along with the crowd. But this time, I jumped.

Courage makes a good theory, but sometimes we need help to practice it. We have many opportunities to step out of our comfort zone to serve God. When we don't have courage, we need to be reminded of God's promise in 2 Timothy, and we need others' encouragement to take the leap.

Perhaps you need someone to tell you: Volunteer for that job at church—they need you. Have lunch with your co-worker to discuss matters of faith. Or join that small group.

Be courageous for Jesus. Sometimes it takes just that first step of courage to serve our majestic God. —DB

Courage will follow when faith takes the lead.

THREATS AND WARNINGS

Keep His statutes and His commandments . . . that it may go well with you and with your children after you.
—Deuteronomy 4:40

"God never threatens; the devil never warns," declared Oswald Chambers. We sometimes use the words *threat* and *warning* interchangeably, but Chambers saw a principle that suggests a distinction. Threats are used to get people to do what is in *our* best interest. Warnings are issued to get people to do what is in *their* best interest. In other words, threats seek to preserve power, whereas warnings serve to protect people from danger.

Satan wants us to think of God's loving warnings as mean-spirited threats, but he is wrong. According to Chambers, "A warning is a great arresting statement of God's, inspired by His love and patience." The evidence of this is found in the many commands that are coupled with phrases like "that it may go well with you" (Deuteronomy 4:40; 12:28).

In loving relationships, people warn one another of the inevitable consequences of foolish behavior. In unhealthy relationships, people threaten one another with punishment if they fail to live up to unreasonable demands.

As we interact with others, it's good to consider the nature of our counsel and commands. Do we use ultimatums to preserve our own well-being? Or do we lovingly warn others to keep them from harm? —JAL

February 20

Read: Deuteronomy 4:32–40

Biblical Truth

Personal Application

Prayer Requests

Answers to Prayer

Warnings are an expression of love; threats are an expression of control.

February 21

Read: Hebrews 11:8–16

Biblical Truth

Personal Application

Prayer Requests

Answers to Prayer

BETWEEN THE ETERNITIES

These all died in faith,
not having received the promises,
but having seen them afar off
were assured of them.
—Hebrews 11:13

In the television western *Broken Trail,* cowboy Prentice Ritter must provide words of comfort at the funeral of a friend. Uncomfortable in the situation, he quietly says, "We are all travelers in this world. From the sweet grass to the packing house, birth till death, we travel between the eternities."

In a sense, he was right. We are travelers—pilgrims—in a world that offers no lasting peace or rest. And while there is only one eternity, we travel between eternity past and eternity future, waiting for promises of a home and a hope that will last forever—promises yet to be fulfilled.

In those times of struggle and despair when our pilgrimage of life is difficult, it is helpful to remember that though we are pilgrims who travel between the eternities, we have a Savior who is the Lord and Master of eternity. He has offered us the promise of life with Him forever and has secured that promise with His own sacrifice. This was the promise spoken of by the writer of Hebrews 11:13.

We are locked into the moments and hours and days of life, but we look ahead by faith in Christ. One day, we will experience the promises of eternity when faith will become sight as we see Him. That hope is what lifts us beyond life between the eternities to a joy that is eternal. —BC

For time and eternity, Jesus is all we need.

February 22

CARRIED IN HIS STRONG ARMS

I have made, and I will bear;
even I will carry,
and will deliver you.
—Isaiah 46:4

Missionary couple Ray and Sophie de le Haye served heroically in West Africa for more than 40 years. As she grew older, Sophie suffered from the loss of all motor control of her body. The once-strong servant of Christ, who had carried on a ministry of unimaginable stress, was suddenly reduced to helplessness, unable to button her clothes or lift a cup of water to her lips. But she refused to become bitter or self-pitying. In her moments of utter weakness, she would quietly remind herself, "For this you have Jesus."

Many centuries ago our heavenly Father gave a reassuring message to a burdened prophet of Israel—a message that we need today: "Listen to Me, O house of Jacob . . . who have been upheld by Me from birth, who have been carried from the womb: Even to your old age, I am He, and even to gray hairs I will carry you! I have made, and I will bear; even I will carry, and will deliver you" (Isaiah 46:3–4).

What an encouraging picture of divine grace! It calls to mind the Good Shepherd bearing a helpless lamb. Whether young or old, we can learn to let God carry us. Weak and burdened, we can lean on His everlasting arms and remind ourselves, "For *this* I have Jesus." —VCG

Read: Isaiah 46:1–11

Biblical Truth

Personal Application

Prayer Requests

Answers to Prayer

You can rest in the arms of Jesus—He'll never let you down.

February 23

Read: 2 Corinthians 2:14–17

Biblical Truth

Personal Application

Prayer Requests

Answers to Prayer

POSIES

We are to God
the fragrance of Christ.
—2 Corinthians 2:15

One morning I was looking at a bouquet of flowers in a vase on an old carpenter's bench in front of our "window on the world." I realized the bouquet was spent; its leaves had wilted and the blossoms were falling.

The same morning I also read George Herbert and quite by "accident" came across his poem titled "Life." In it Herbert talks about a "posy" (a bouquet of flowers) he gathered so that he could smell the fragrance. But, as he put it, "Time did beckon to the flowers, and they by noon most cunningly did steal away, and withered in my hand."

The loss of his flowers caused him at first to see "time's gentle admonition." Herbert wrote that it "[made] my mind to smell my fatal day; yet sugaring the suspicion." Yet even as the wilted flowers reminded him of his own death, he found in the metaphor something that sweetened the thought. Herbert concluded:

Farewell dear flowers, sweetly
your time ye spent,
Fit, while ye lived, for smell
or ornament,
And after death for cures.

What wisdom in this poem! Our time, however short, may be spent "sweetly"—a sweet fragrance of Christ to others (2 Corinthains 2:14–16). Should not this be our prayer each day as we arise? —DHR

A godly life is a fragrance that draws others to Christ.

GOD IS GOOD

February 24

Good and upright is the Lord;
therefore He teaches
sinners in the way.
—Psalm 25:8

The phrase "God is good, all the time; all the time, God is good" is repeated by many Christians almost like a mantra. I often wonder if they really believe it or even think about what they're saying. I sometimes doubt God's goodness—especially when it feels as though God isn't hearing or answering my prayers. I assume that if others were more honest, they'd admit they feel the same way.

The serpent planted a doubt in Eve's mind about whether God had been good to her and had her best interest at heart. He said, "God knows that in the day you eat of [the fruit] your eyes will be opened, and you will be like God, knowing good and evil" (Genesis 3:5). Satan tried to convince her to believe that God was holding out on her and not giving her something really good—more knowledge.

Do you feel as though God isn't answering your prayers? Are you tempted to doubt His goodness? When I feel this way, I have to remind myself that my circumstances aren't the barometer of God's love and goodness—the cross is. He has shown how good He is by giving His only Son Jesus to die for our sin. We can't rely on our feelings. But day by day as we choose to trust Him more, we learn to believe with confidence that God is good—all the time. —AC

Read: Genesis 3:1–7

Biblical Truth

Personal Application

Prayer Requests

Answers to Prayer

Circumstances aren't the barometer of God's love and goodness—the cross is.

February 25

Read: Philippians 2:1–8

Biblical Truth

Personal Application

Prayer Requests

Answers to Prayer

THE KINDNESS OF STRANGERS

Do not forget to entertain strangers, for by so doing some have unwittingly entertained angels.
—Hebrews 13:2

While I was taking a flight to Surabaya, Indonesia, for a Bible conference, the flight attendants brought meal service. I had just eaten in the Singapore airport, so I declined, asking only for a soft drink. The Indonesian man next to me, a stranger, was visibly concerned.

The man asked if I felt okay, and I assured him I was fine. He then asked if perhaps the meal didn't appeal to me. I responded that I just wasn't hungry. He then surprised me by offering his own meal to me, thinking that if I tried it I might actually enjoy it. It was done in such a gentle and genuine way that it was obviously an expression of his concern for my welfare.

In a self-centered world where we are conditioned to look out for our own interests above and beyond all else, such kindness was unexpected. The man's simple gesture showed a different kind of heart and a different set of values. As followers of Christ, we are called to model a similar counter-cultural attitude toward life (Philippians 2:1–8).

In Hebrews 13:2 we read, "Do not forget to entertain strangers, for by so doing some have unwittingly entertained angels." What better way to represent Christ than with kindness—even to strangers. —BC

Kindness is one gift anyone can give.

MAKING RESTITUTION

February 26

He shall make restitution for his trespass in full.
—Numbers 5:7

Read: Luke 19:1–9

During the compilation of the *Oxford English Dictionary*, managing editor James Murray received thousands of definitions from Dr. William Chester Minor. They were always sent in by mail and never brought in personally. Murray was curious about this brilliant man, so he went to visit him. He was shocked to find that Minor was incarcerated in an asylum for the criminally insane.

Years earlier, while in a delusional state, Minor had shot an innocent man whom he thought had been tormenting him. Later he was filled with remorse and began sending money to support the widow and her family. Minor was imprisoned for the rest of his life but he found practical ways of easing the pain of his victims and contributing to society through his work on the dictionary.

When the dishonest tax collector Zacchaeus heard Jesus' message of grace, he chose to return more than what he had extorted from others. "Look, Lord . . . if I have taken anything from anyone by false accusation, I restore fourfold" (Luke 19:8). The gospel of grace stirred Zacchaeus to help those he had harmed.

Have you wronged someone? What steps will you take to help make things right? —DF

Biblical Truth

Personal Application

Prayer Requests

Answers to Prayer

Making restitution reveals genuine repentance.

February 27

Read: Isaiah 55:1–5

Biblical Truth

Personal Application

Prayer Requests

Answers to Prayer

BUY WITHOUT MONEY

Incline your ear, and come to Me. Hear, and your soul shall live.
—Isaiah 55:3

A story was told of a wealthy man who felt his son needed to learn gratefulness. So he sent him to stay with a poor farmer's family. After one month, the son returned. The father asked, "Now don't you appreciate what we have?" The boy thought for a moment and said, "The family I stayed with is better off. With what they've planted, they enjoy meals together. And they always seem to have time for one another."

This story reminds us that money can't buy everything. Even though our bodies can live on what money can buy, money can't keep our souls from withering away. In Isaiah 55, we read: "Everyone who thirsts, come to the waters; and you who have no money, come, buy and eat" (v. 1).

Is it possible to buy what truly satisfies without money? Yes, the prophet Isaiah is pointing to the grace of God. This gift is so invaluable that no price tag is adequate. And the one who offers it—Jesus Christ—has paid the full price with His death. When we acknowledge our thirst for God, ask forgiveness for our sins, and accept the finished work of Christ on the cross, we will find spiritual food that satisfies and our soul will live forever!

He's calling, "Come to Me" (Isaiah 55:3). —AL

Only Jesus, the Living Water, satisfies the thirsty soul.

IDENTITY THEFT

February 28

Whoever is angry with his brother without a cause shall be in danger of the judgment.
—Matthew 5:22

Read: Matthew 5:21–26

Several years ago while I was having lunch with a friend, a white man called me "boy." Shock gave way to anger and hurt. My friend even shed tears. Why? The term *boy* was an insulting label used of black men in the US during slavery, an attempt to steal their identity by demoting them to less than men. As that ugly word recklessly barreled its way through my soul, I wanted to respond with an equally unkind name. But some ancient words from our Master about murder and anger changed my mind.

As Jesus was teaching His followers, He quoted the sixth commandment—"You shall not murder"—and the penalty for breaking it (Matthew 5:21). Then He gave a fuller interpretation. Taking someone's life was not limited to physical murder; you could show contempt for someone through name-calling and be just as guilty. In Jewish culture, to call someone "Raca" or "Fool" (v. 22) was the equivalent of calling someone empty-headed or an idiot. It was used to demean and demote another. What makes name-calling so damaging is that it insults the God who created that person in His image!

Jesus taught His followers that the weight of our neighbor's glory is a burden we carry daily. If we follow His teaching, we won't be guilty of identity theft. —MW

Biblical Truth

Personal Application

Prayer Requests

Answers to Prayer

To insult the creature is to insult the Creator.

February 29

Read: John 15:9–15

Biblical Truth

Personal Application

Prayer Requests

Answers to Prayer

THE BEST FRIEND

Greater love has no one than this, than to lay down one's life for his friends.
—John 15:13

It's an honor I cherish, and one I seek to live up to—but I don't always do it. It's the privilege of hearing my wife say, "You're my best friend," which she does often. As much as I love her, though, I occasionally do something that is not so "best friend-ish."

In reality, no matter how hard we try, we cannot live up to the high standard of being a friend who never lets others down. We all fail from time to time—forgetting to do what we should or simply allowing selfishness to build a barrier between us.

As believers, we take comfort in knowing that we are called a friend of God, and He is a true friend who will never falter. Michael Gungor's joyous song "Friend of God" captures the wonder of this relationship when it asks, "Who am I that You are mindful of me?"

Abraham was called "the friend of God," and that friendship was related to his faith (2 Chronicles 20:7; James 2:23). Jesus explained how we can receive that designation as well. He said to His disciples, "You are My friends if you do whatever I command you" (John 15:14). There is no better friend, for we know that He will never leave us nor forsake us (Hebrews 13:5).

Looking for the best friend ever? You can't do better than the Lord himself. —DB

Jesus is the only faultless Friend you'll ever find.

March

Read: Luke 1:67–80

Biblical Truth

Personal Application

Prayer Requests

Answers to Prayer

SONGBIRD IN THE DARK

The Dayspring from on high has visited us.
—Luke 1:78

Just before the sunrise, we often hear songbirds welcoming the dawn. Despite the darkness, we know that the radiant light of the sun will soon appear.

Fanny Crosby has been called "The Songbird in the Dark." Though blinded in infancy, she wrote hymns that inspirationally envision our future reunion with Christ. Early in her life, Fanny had a dream in which she saw the panorama of a glorious heaven, and many of her songs reflect that theme. By the time of her death, she had penned at least 8,000 hymns. Songs such as "Tell Me the Story of Jesus" and "To God Be the Glory" are still popular today.

When Zacharias praised God in anticipation of the Messiah, he also looked forward to a spiritual sunrise. Citing Malachi 4:2, he proclaimed: "The Dayspring [sunrise] from on high has visited us; to give light to those who sit in darkness" (Luke 1:78–79). That Messiah came to earth, died for our sins, rose again, ascended, and promised to return for us.

Do you feel surrounded by dark and confusing circumstances? You can still lift your praise to God for the bright future you will share with His Son. The words of Fanny Crosby's beloved hymn "Blessed Assurance" encourage us as we anticipate this glorious reunion with Christ: "Blessed assurance, Jesus is mine! O what a foretaste of glory divine!" —DF

For the Christian, the dark sorrows of earth will one day be changed into the bright songs of heaven.

WII AND MII

March 2

Let each one of you speak truth with his neighbor, for we are members of one another.
—EPHESIANS 4:25

Our grandsons introduced me to the amazing world of virtual bowling using the Nintendo Wii (pronounced we) video-game console. But before beginning, we had to create my look-alike character called Mii (me). From a selection of facial characteristics, they quickly created a person whose hair, nose, glasses, and mouth looked surprisingly like me. "Hey, Grandpa," they said. "It's you!" And so it was.

Much of our self-concept comes from others. The feedback of family and friends is vital in helping us discover our unique gifts. As followers of Christ, we are charged with making an honest, positive contribution to each other. We can apply the words of Paul to this critical process: "Let each one of you speak truth with his neighbor, for we are members of one another . . . Let no corrupt word proceed out of your mouth, but what is good for necessary edification, that it may impart grace to the hearers" (Ephesians 4:25, 29).

Between the extremes of hazardous flattery and destructive criticism, we should aim for beneficial reality in what we say to each other. In the "we" of Christian community, the "me" of personality is shaped. It's a great privilege and responsibility to help each other discover who we are in Christ. —DCM

Read: Ephesians 4:25–5:1

Biblical Truth

Personal Application

Prayer Requests

Answers to Prayer

True community is not organized but exercised.

Read: Numbers 14:1–5, 26–27

Biblical Truth

Personal Application

Prayer Requests

Answers to Prayer

AN IMPOSSIBLE CHALLENGE?

Do all things without complaining and disputing.
—Philippians 2:14

A pastor in Kansas City gave what seemed to be an impossible challenge to his congregation—to go 21 days without complaining (the amount of time some say it takes to develop a new habit). Special bracelets were distributed to participants as a reminder to live complaint-free lives. A movement was started, and millions of bracelets have been distributed all over the world.

The biblical principle "Do all things without complaining and disputing" (Philippians 2:14) is an important one. The ancient Israelites discovered this when, because of their constant complaining in the wilderness, they were judged by God and not allowed to enter the Promised Land (Numbers 14).

How can we learn to develop a noncomplaining, positive attitude that will please the Lord?

- By disciplining our thoughts (Romans 12:2). We need to meditate on Scripture and remember our blessings.
- By confessing our critical spirit and committing ourselves to obedience each time we fail (1 John 1:9).
- By enlisting God's help and the help of others. The Spirit will empower us as we depend on Him (John 14:26).

Because God helps us, doing all things without complaining is not an impossible challenge. —AC

A complaining Christian is a contradiction in terms.

THE MIRACLE OF RESTRAINT

March 4

We love Him because He first loved us.
—1 John 4:19

In Dostoevsky's novel *The Brothers Karamazov,* Ivan Karamazov refers to "the miracle of restraint"—God's choice to curb His own power. The more I get to know Jesus, the more that observation impresses me.

The miracles Satan suggested to Jesus (Luke 4:3, 9–11), the signs the Pharisees demanded (Matthew 12:38; 16:1), the final proofs I yearn for offer no obstacle to an omnipotent God. More amazing is His refusal to perform, to overwhelm. God's terrible insistence on human freedom is so absolute that He granted us the power to live as though He does not exist. Jesus must have known this as He faced the tempter in the desert, focusing His power on the energy of restraint.

I believe God insists on such restraint because no pyrotechnic displays of omnipotence will achieve the response He desires. Only love can summon a response of love. "I, if I am lifted up from the earth, will draw all peoples to Myself," Jesus said (John 12:32). He said this to show the kind of death He would die. God's nature is self-giving.

Why does God content himself with the slow, mysterious way of making righteousness grow rather than avenging it? That's how love is. Love has its own power—the only power capable of conquering the human heart.
—PY

Read: Luke 4:1–13

Biblical Truth

Personal Application

Prayer Requests

Answers to Prayer

Revenge restrained is a victory gained.

March 5

Read: Joshua 22:10–16, 21–29

Biblical Truth

Personal Application

Prayer Requests

Answers to Prayer

URGE TO JUMP

If you hear someone . . .
saying, "Corrupt men have gone
out from among you and
enticed the inhabitants," . . .
then you shall inquire,
search out, and ask diligently.
—DEUTERONOMY 13:12–14

In April 2006, a stuntman tried to jump from the top of the Empire State Building. At the last minute, authorities restrained him and charged him with reckless endangerment. After a judge had looked carefully at all the facts, he dismissed the charges, noting that the accused had taken steps to ensure the safety of others. With a parachute strapped to his back, Jeb Corliss had safely made 3,000 previous jumps, including leaps from the 1,483-foot Petronas Towers in Kuala Lumpur and the Eiffel Tower.

As extreme as Corliss's sport is, it is safer than the kind of leap that almost took place in Joshua 22. Israel had just engaged in a seven-year conquest of Canaan. Suddenly, an alarming rumor raised the possibility of civil war. Word spread that the families who settled east of the Jordan River had built an idolatrous altar (v. 10).

A national catastrophe was averted that day, only because someone took time to investigate the facts and listen to both sides of the issue (vv. 16–29). A terrible, costly misunderstanding was avoided. The wisdom of God was honored (v. 31). Our loving Lord taught His people that the cost of listening is not nearly as great as the cost of jumping to wrong conclusions. —MD

Jumping to wrong conclusions is one of the greatest of all dangers.

FROM NOTHING

In the beginning God created the heavens and the earth.
—GENESIS 1:1

March 6

Read: Genesis 1:1–13

Nothing. Absolutely nothing. No light. No sky. No land. It's incomprehensible to our finite thinking—the barren nothingness that existed before Genesis 1:1.

Then suddenly, through the work of the Almighty, God supplanted nothingness with "the heavens and the earth." The divine hand reached through the void and produced a place, a world, a universe. Through the magnificent convergence of the workings of the Godhead—with the Son enacting the will of the Father as the agent of creation, and the Holy Spirit as the hovering presence—nothing became something. History began its long march toward today.

The first verse of Genesis provides us with sufficient concepts to contemplate for a lifetime. That introductory statement speaks of enough glory, enough majesty, enough awe to leave us speechless before God. Just as today we would have no life, no breath, no existence without His sustaining action, neither would we have the cosmos without His mighty act at the moment of creation.

In awe we wonder what went on before "the beginning." With breathless praise we marvel at the words "God created the heavens and the earth." We read—and we stand in adoration. "Nothing" has never been so fascinating! —DB

Biblical Truth

Personal Application

Prayer Requests

Answers to Prayer

Nature is but a name for an effect whose cause is God.

March 7

Read: Matthew 4:18–22

Biblical Truth

Personal Application

Prayer Requests

Answers to Prayer

A NEW CAREER

Immediately they left the boat and their father, and followed Him.
—Matthew 4:22

For some guys, the annual fishing trip is the highlight of their calendar. They stay in cozy cabins and spend long days fishing just for the fun of it. You can be sure it wasn't that way for the disciples. They weren't on vacation when they met Jesus. Fishing was their career.

Our careers often demand much of our time and attention. But Jesus has an interesting way of interrupting our business-as-usual agenda. In fact, He invites us to join His business.

Notice the sequence of His statement to the fishermen: "Follow Me, and I will make you fishers of men" (Matthew 4:19). We are tempted to think that we should make something of our lives and at the same time follow Jesus. Wrong! He calls us first to follow Him, and then He makes something of our lives. He leads us to prioritize so that we see the needs of people and their eternity as the goal of all our endeavors.

And while God may not require you to give up your career, following Him will guarantee that you will never see your career in the same way again. *Where* you "fish" is not important. But if you follow, you must fish.

What are you waiting for? Drop your nets, follow Him, and let Him make something of your life.
—JS

Drop your nets and follow Jesus.

A TO-DO LIST

The fruit of the Spirit is love, joy, peace, longsuffering, kindness, goodness, faithfulness.
—GALATIANS 5:22

What's on your to-do list today? Cleaning out an overstuffed closet? Calculating a financial report at work? Paying your monthly bills?

We all have things we need to get done today, whether we've written them down or not. They're important for us to accomplish.

While a to-do list is helpful, another type of list is even more valuable: a "to be" list. Albert Einstein said, "Try not to become a man of success but rather to become a man of value."

The apostle Paul encouraged the Galatian believers, and now tells us, to be concerned with our character. He said that if we're controlled by the Holy Spirit, God will produce in us the characteristics of "love, joy, peace, longsuffering, kindness, goodness, faithfulness, gentleness, self-control" (Galatians 5:22–23).

As you look at those character traits, which are you needing most in your life? More patience with a co-worker or a child? A little more gentleness and kindness toward a neighbor? As you draw near to God, He will enable you to be the person He wants you to be.

Perhaps at the top of your to-do list today you could put: Spend time praying and reading God's Word. That would be a good start in helping with your "to be" list. —AC

March 8

Read: Galatians 5:16–26

Biblical Truth

Personal Application

Prayer Requests

Answers to Prayer

It's not what you do but who you are that's most important.

March 9

Read: Psalm 27

Biblical Truth

Personal Application

Prayer Requests

Answers to Prayer

WAIT ON THE LORD

Wait on the Lord; be of good courage, and He shall strengthen your heart; wait, I say, on the Lord!
—Psalm 27:14

In Cantonese, a Chinese dialect, the word for *wait* sounds like the word for *class*. Making a pun on this word, some senior folks in Hong Kong identify themselves as "third-class citizens," which also means "people of three waits." They *wait* for their children to return home from work late at night. They *wait* for the morning sun to dispel their sleepless nights. And with a sigh of resignation, they *wait* for death.

In the Bible, the word *wait* is more an attitude than an activity. To "wait on the Lord" is to trust Him. Psalm 27 is David's exuberant declaration of faith in God. He sees the Lord as his salvation (v. 1). In times of danger, he knows for certain that God will hide him (v. 5). He remembers that God has asked him to seek His face, so he asks God not to hide from him. For, like a child, he longs to see God's approving face (vv. 8–10). In his darkest moments, David declares: "I would have lost heart, unless I had believed that I would see the goodness of the Lord in the land of the living" (v. 13).

Though no one knows how life will unfold, we can decide to trust God and to focus our mind on Him. For to those who wait on the Lord, the promise is given: Our heart will be strengthened (v. 14). —AL

Those who wait on the Lord shall renew their strength.
—Isaiah 40:31

FAST FEET

The Lord God is my strength; He will make my feet like deer's feet, and He will make me walk on my high hills.
—Habakkuk 3:19

While in Chile for a Bible conference, I was resting at the hotel when a rugby match came on the television. Though I don't fully understand rugby, I enjoy it and admire the courage it takes to play such a dangerous sport.

During the match, one of the French players was injured and had to be taken to the sidelines. As the trainers attended to him, the camera showed a closeup of his shoes, where, with a black marker, the player had written the words: "Habakkuk 3:19" and "Jesus is the way." Those expressions of faith and hope were a strong testimony of that young athlete's priorities and values.

The verse cited on that rugby player's shoes is not just one of heavenly hope and persevering faith. It is one of practical value—especially to an athlete dependent on speed for success. It says, "The Lord God is my strength; He will make my feet like deer's feet, and He will make me walk on my high hills."

In all of life, we need the strength and supply of our God. He alone can give us "feet" that are swift and strong. He alone can equip us for all of the uncertainties of life, for He alone is our strength. With Paul, we can be assured: "My God shall supply all your need" (Philippians 4:19).
—BC

March 10

Read: Philippians 4:10–19

Biblical Truth

Personal Application

Prayer Requests

Answers to Prayer

We always have enough when God is our supply.

March 11

Read: Luke 15:11–24

Biblical Truth

Personal Application

Prayer Requests

Answers to Prayer

AGENTS OF GRACE

When he was still a great way off, his father saw him and had compassion, and ran and fell on his neck and kissed him.
—Luke 15:20

Jesus' most memorable story, the Prodigal Son, ends with a banquet scene, featuring as its hero a good-for-nothing who has soiled the family reputation. Those judged undesirable by everyone else—like the Prodigal Son—are infinitely desirable to God. When one of them turns to God, a party breaks out (Luke 15:22–24).

In the Old Testament, Levitical laws guarded against contagion. Among the things that would contaminate a person was contact with certain animals, carcasses, or the sick. But Jesus reversed the process. Rather than becoming contaminated by what was unclean, He made the unclean whole.

I sense in Jesus a fulfillment, not an abolition, of the Old Testament laws. God had hallowed creation by separating the sacred from the profane, the clean from the unclean. Jesus did not cancel out this hallowing principle; rather He changed its source.

Because of God's great grace, we can be agents of His holiness, for He now dwells within us. We can seek, as Jesus did, for ways to be a source of holiness. The sick and the maimed are not hot spots of contamination but potential reservoirs of God's mercy. We are called to extend that mercy, to be conveyers of grace, not avoiders of contagion. Like Jesus, we can help make the "unclean" clean.
—PY

No one is beyond the reach of God's grace.

JOHNSTOWN FLOOD

Your people shall be my people, and your God, my God.
—RUTH 1:16

On May 31, 1889, a massive rainstorm filled Lake Conemaugh in Pennsylvania until its dam finally gave way. A wall of water 40 feet high traveling at 40 mph rushed down the valley toward the town of Johnstown. The torrent picked up buildings, animals, and human beings and sent them crashing down the spillway. When the lake had emptied itself, debris covered 30 acres, and 2,209 people were dead.

At first, stunned by the loss of loved ones and property, survivors felt hopeless. But later, community leaders gave speeches about how local industry and homes could be rebuilt. This acted like a healing balm, and the survivors energetically got to work. Johnstown was rebuilt and today is a thriving town with a population of approximately 28,000.

The Bible tells us that when Naomi despaired over the loss of her husband and sons, her daughter-in-law Ruth refused to leave her. Instead, Ruth focused on God, her relationships, and the future. God rewarded her faith by providing for them and making Ruth an ancestor of Jesus Christ (Matthew 1:5–16).

After a tragic loss, we should look at the resources and relationships that remain and trust God to use them. This can inspire the hope of rebuilding a new life. —DF

March 12

Read: Ruth 1:8–17

Biblical Truth

Personal Application

Prayer Requests

Answers to Prayer

No one is hopeless whose hope is in God.

March 13

Read: Acts 5:1–11

Biblical Truth

Personal Application

Prayer Requests

Answers to Prayer

COMPLETE HONESTY

Why have you conceived this thing in your heart? You have not lied to men but to God.
—Acts 5:4

Ask the families and friends of six people buried in a collapsed subway tunnel about complete honesty. The rescue of their loved ones was delayed for hours because the contractor didn't report the disaster to the authorities immediately. Instead, the company sealed the site and confiscated cell phones. It wasn't an outright *lie*, but it *was* a cover-up. This dishonest act showed disregard for life.

In the book of Acts, God gives us a sobering example of how He views dishonesty (4:32–5:11). Some believers had sold their land and shared all the proceeds with the church. Ananias and Sapphira decided to do likewise. But the couple kept some money back, despite declaring that they had given the whole amount. Expecting commendation, they were struck dead instead.

Was their punishment too harsh? After all, their "slight" lie wasn't life-threatening. "Whoever falsely boasts of giving is like clouds and wind without rain," warns Proverbs 25:14. The apostle Peter asked Ananias, "Why has Satan filled your heart to lie to the Holy Spirit?" (Acts 5:3), adding, "You have not lied to men, but to God" (v. 4).

If we are completely honest with ourselves, can we say that we are completely honest before God? —AL

There are no degrees of honesty.

SANCTUARY

Be my strong refuge, to which I may resort continually; You have given the commandment to save me.
—Psalm 71:3

A professional athlete built a palatial eight-bedroom home where he lives by himself. His secluded house includes a movie theater, a gymnasium, a swimming pool, and a five-car garage.

The athlete told the *New York Times* that he doesn't view the eight-million-dollar estate as a monument to success. Instead, he considers it to be a sanctuary from his painful childhood memories of poverty and abuse. The young man is seeking something much deeper than luxury and entertainment. "Got to get my peace," he says.

All of us know the feeling of being overwhelmed. When the present is daunting and the past is haunting, where can we turn for release? To whom do we go for comfort and peace?

The psalmist wrote: "Deliver me in Your righteousness, and cause me to escape; incline Your ear to me, and save me. Be my strong refuge, to which I may resort continually" (Psalm 71:2–3). God was his hope, his trust, and his hiding place in the storms of life (vv. 5–8).

Few people can afford a mansion, but everyone who knows the Lord can find refuge and peace in His abiding presence.
—DCM

March 14

Read: Psalm 71:1–16

Biblical Truth

Personal Application

Prayer Requests

Answers to Prayer

*When we put our problems in God's hands,
He puts His peace in our hearts.*

March 15

Read: Luke 19:29–40

Biblical Truth

Personal Application

Prayer Requests

Answers to Prayer

WANTED!

The Lord has need of him.
—Luke 19:34

As Jesus approached Jerusalem for the last time, He sent two disciples into the city to bring Him a donkey. He told them, "If anyone asks you, 'Why are you loosing it?' thus you shall say to him, 'Because the Lord has need of it'" (Luke 19:31).

As we approach our sunset years, we may ask ourselves, "Can I still be useful to God? Is there some service I can render that will fill my days with significance? Am I needed?"

Of course you are! God needs you just as He needed the donkey to carry Him through the streets of Jerusalem. He has always needed something or someone to get His work done. He still has useful work for you to do.

Perhaps your work will be one brief task, like the donkey's single act of service. Or it may be some activity that will fully occupy your years until your Master calls you home. It may be an opportunity to share your faith with someone, to intercede for someone, or to love someone through quiet acts of mercy, friendly visits, or to extend some small courtesy. There will always be something for you to do.

In the meantime, you and I must stand and wait, preparing ourselves through prayer, Bible reading, and quiet listening—ready for the moment that our Lord has need of us.

Will you be ready when He needs you? —DHR

God has work for all His children, regardless of age or ability.

WHAT CHANGED?

Behold, your King is coming to you.
—MATTHEW 21:5

Jesus put a damper on His own party. On Sunday, He entered Jerusalem as the triumphant king, welcomed into the city by throngs of worshipers shouting, "Hosanna!" and honoring Him by waving palm branches. The healer of the sick and the giver of great wisdom had come, and the masses adored Him.

What went wrong that week? What changed the "Hosannas" to "Crucify Him"? It started to go bad when Jesus told the people what they didn't want to hear. Look at what He did. He threw the money changers out of the temple area (Matthew 21:12). He taught that tax collectors and prostitutes could enter the kingdom of heaven before the religious (21:31). He told the people to pay taxes (22:21). Then He pronounced a series of woes against the religious leaders: "Woe to you, scribes and Pharisees" (23:13–31).

But this was Jesus. The righteous One. The only perfect Man. God in the flesh. He was not in town for a popularity contest. His task was to proclaim the truth and provide salvation. And it cost Him His life.

Think about Jesus' up-and-down week in Jerusalem. Then praise Him for His perfection and His love—love that took Him all the way to the cross. —DB

March 16

Read: Matthew 21:1–11

Biblical Truth

Personal Application

Prayer Requests

Answers to Prayer

The nail-pierced hands of Jesus reveal the love-filled heart of God.

March 17

Read: Mark 7:9–23

Biblical Truth

Personal Application

Prayer Requests

Answers to Prayer

INSIDE OUT

Out of the heart of men proceed evil thoughts, adulteries, fornications, murders, thefts, covetousness, wickedness, deceit . . . blasphemy, pride, foolishness.
—Mark 7:21-22

Shopping for a melon is a tough assignment. No matter how good it looks, it's hard to tell! So I tap it, thump it, and, if no one is looking, squeeze it—and then take it home, only to discover that it's bad on the inside.

When the Pharisees were irritated that Jesus' disciples did not wash their hands before eating—a violation of one of their traditions—Jesus immediately challenged them: "All too well you reject the commandment of God, that you may keep your tradition" (Mark 7:9). He even called them "hypocrites" and explained that what comes from the inside of a person is what "defiles" him, not the other way around.

If we're not careful, we can become absorbed with looking good on the outside and forget what really counts. In fact, when we get to the place where we are keeping all the "right" rules, we may become proud of ourselves and judgmental toward others. But harboring bitterness, clinging to critical attitudes, and thinking too highly of ourselves are the kind of defiling stuff that make us guilty of Jesus' charge of "hypocrite."

So don't miss the point. Remember, it's the things on the inside—your heart, your thoughts, your attitudes—that really matter. —JS

What matters to Jesus is what's on the inside.

March 18

SO OTHERS MAY LIVE

I could wish that I myself were accursed from Christ for my brethren, my countrymen according to the flesh.
—Romans 9:3

In the film *The Guardian,* the viewer is taken into the world of United States Coast Guard rescue swimmers. Eighteen weeks of intense training prepares these courageous men and women for the task of jumping from helicopters to rescue those in danger at sea. The challenges they face include hypothermia and death by drowning. Why would people risk so much for strangers? The answer is found in the rescue swimmer's motto: "So Others May Live."

In *Foxe's Book of Martyrs,* we read of a different kind of rescue that demanded extreme commitment and sacrifice. John Foxe records the stories of believers who suffered and died because they proclaimed the love of Jesus. Knowing it could cost them their lives, these believers made the Savior known to a world in desperate need of Him.

The apostle Paul, himself a martyr for Christ, expressed his passion for the hearts of people this way: "I could wish that I myself were accursed from Christ for my brethren, my countrymen according to the flesh" (Romans 9:3). Paul so longed for his fellow Jews to come to Christ that he was willing to sacrifice all, "so others may live."

May we likewise embrace this passion for the eternal souls of men and women. —BC

Read: Romans 9:1–5

Biblical Truth

Personal Application

Prayer Requests

Answers to Prayer

The cross reveals God's heart for the lost.

March 19

Read: 1 Corinthians 11:23–26

Biblical Truth

Personal Application

Prayer Requests

Answers to Prayer

A FRAGILE LAMB

He was wounded for our transgressions, He was bruised for our iniquities.
—Isaiah 53:5

After the Easter eggs were located and the Easter baskets had been opened, Uncle Jay felt compelled to find out whether the white chocolate lamb was hollow or solid. Without thinking of the potential consequences, he squeezed the lamb. Suddenly Jay's whole body stiffened, as if he'd ingested some paralyzing poison. Finally his eyes moved to see if anyone had witnessed the deed. His thumb, however, remained stuck in the side of the lamb.

We waited for the reaction. A wail. A howl. A cry of anguish over the crushed chocolate candy. As the adults in the room scrambled for words that would soothe the sorrow of three-year-old Jenna, she calmly spoke words that soothed us. "That's okay, Uncle Jay. The lamb would have been broken when I ate him anyway."

While we adults tried to make sacred memories out of Easter traditions, a three-year-old made a sacred moment for us. She reminded us that Easter is about the perfect Lamb of God, broken so that we can be whole. Her youthful wisdom reminds me of the words we recall at communion: "This is My body which is broken for you." May we taste and see that the life He offers is sweeter than anything we concoct for ourselves. —JAL

Nothing speaks more clearly of God's love than the cross.

WHO HOLDS THE CUP?

Shall I not drink the cup which My Father has given Me?
—John 18:11

Are you being called to taste some bitter cup of pain or loss? Are you tempted to push it away? You may be wondering, *Is God in this situation?* If so, recall the dark and distressing experience of Jesus and His example on the night of His betrayal.

We must never forget that Jesus was the God-Man, with both divine and human natures. He therefore recoiled from the prospect of agonizing crucifixion and the ordeal of having the world's sin heaped on His sinless soul. And worst of all, He shuddered at the thought of being abandoned by His Father. So He pleaded, "If it is possible, let this cup pass from Me" (Matthew 26:39). Yet after that He said in trustful submission, "Shall I not drink the cup which My Father has given Me?" (John 18:11). He knew that the hand, which would for our redemption hold the cup to His lips, was not the hand of Judas or Caiaphas or Pilate. It was the hand of His loving Father intent on redeeming our lost human race.

Baffled by the mystery of such love, we take our stand on Calvary and believe that any cup we drink is held to our lips by the Father of fathomless love and wisdom. Our prayer is that of trustful submission because we believe that even life's most bitter cup is held in the Father's hand.
—VCG

March 20

Read: Matthew 26:36–46

Biblical Truth

Personal Application

Prayer Requests

Answers to Prayer

We learn the lesson of trust in the school of trial.

March 21

Read: Luke 23:39–43

Biblical Truth

Personal Application

Prayer Requests

Answers to Prayer

REMEMBER ME

Remember me when
You come into Your kingdom.
—Luke 23:42

Matthew Henshaw got his name into the *Guinness Book of World Records* in an unusual way. After swallowing a 15.9-inch sword, Henshaw attached a 40-pound sack of potatoes to the handle of the sword and held it for 5 seconds. (This is not recommended.)

Henshaw and others like him have gone to extraordinary lengths to have their names memorialized in the world's most famous record book. The longing for immortality compels people to do many things—some remarkable and some bizarre.

The immortality Jesus offers has nothing to do with anything we *do*. In fact, after giving His disciples the authority to do truly remarkable things (Luke 10:17–19), Jesus said, "Do not rejoice . . . that the spirits are subject to you, but rather rejoice because your names are written in heaven" (v. 20).

At Golgotha, an unnamed thief believed that message just in time (Luke 23:40–42). He understood that eternal life had nothing to do with what he had done—good or bad. It had to do with what Jesus was doing—giving His own life so that even the undeserving could be welcomed into heaven by God. The important thing is being remembered not by others, but by God. —JAL

Our lives matter because God loves us.

A VIRTUOSO IGNORED

March 22

Since the creation of the world His invisible attributes are clearly seen.
—Romans 1:20

Read: Romans 1:18–23

A man wearing jeans, a T-shirt, and a baseball cap positioned himself against a wall beside a trash can at the L'Enfant Plaza station in Washington, DC. He pulled out a violin and began to play. In the next forty-three minutes, as he performed six classical pieces, 1,097 people passed by, ignoring him.

No one knew it, but the man playing outside the Metro was Joshua Bell, one of the finest classical musicians in the world, playing some of the most elegant music ever written on a $3.5 million Stradivarius. But no crowd gathered for the virtuoso. "It was a strange feeling, that people were actually . . . ignoring me," said Bell.

God also knows what it feels like to be ignored. The apostle Paul said that God has sovereignly planted evidence of His existence in the very nature of man. And creation delivers an unmistakable message about His creativity, beauty, power, and character. Although God has revealed His majesty, many refuse to acknowledge and thank Him. But God will hold everyone responsible for ignoring who He is and what He has revealed: "They are without excuse, because, although they knew God, they did not glorify Him as God, nor were thankful" (Romans 1:20–21).

Let us acknowledge and thank the Virtuoso of heaven, who has wonderfully revealed himself to us. —MW

Biblical Truth

Personal Application

Prayer Requests

Answers to Prayer

All creation is an outstretched finger pointing toward God.

March 23

Read: Romans 8:11–18

Biblical Truth

Personal Application

Prayer Requests

Answers to Prayer

WE BELIEVE

Blessed be the God and Father of our Lord Jesus Christ, who . . . has begotten us again to a living hope through the resurrection of Jesus Christ.
—1 Peter 1:3

In 2005, Hurricane Katrina put New Orleans underwater. But an unlikely event gave the city a new lease on life just seventeen months later. The New Orleans Saints, a perennially woeful football team, made a run at the Super Bowl championship. The whole region grasped the excitement. Signs saying "We Believe" reflected a new day.

Commenting on the phenomenon, producer Quint Davis said, "When the season is over, the miles of devastation are still going to be devastated." But, he added, "If this can happen for New Orleans, this miracle, then anything can happen for New Orleans."

The Saints fell one game short, but the idea remained enticing. An "impossibility" had so captured the hearts of the people of that city that they began thinking anything was possible.

In an infinitely more important way, this is what we have in Jesus' bodily resurrection from the dead. Christ defeated death on mortality's own turf, declaring the power of God to give us new life and hope. Paul wrote, "He who raised Christ from the dead will also give life to your mortal bodies through His Spirit who dwells in you" (Romans 8:11).

No other event in human history is more significant. No other event is so full of immediate hope and ultimate victory for the saints in Christ Jesus. —MD

Christ's resurrection is the bud of promise; our resurrection is the flower of fulfillment!

JUST JEWELRY?

God forbid that I should boast except in the cross of our Lord Jesus Christ.
—GALATIANS 6:14

Some Christians make it a habit to wear a cross. It may be on a necklace or a lapel pin. It may be worn thoughtlessly as a decoration or prayerfully to let people know of the wearer's personal faith.

In April 2006, a Methodist church in the city of Dudley, England, found out that it would have to pay a fee to put a cross on its new building. Yes, a fee was required because under British law the cross is an advertisement. It proclaims to the world, whether on a person or a building, that the blood-stained cross of Calvary is our only hope of forgiveness and salvation.

Our Bible reading today tells us of the cross—the instrument of execution used on our Savior (Matthew 27:22–26). The crowd in anger shouted, "Let Him be crucified!" The cross is a sign of His death and must not be taken lightly. This should cause us to examine what the cross means to us. Is it a witness to our eternal hope in the saving death of Jesus on Calvary?

While wearing the cross may be a challenging mark of discipleship, far more challenging is our Lord's command that we "take up [our] cross daily" and learn what it means to follow in His footsteps (Luke 9:23). And that includes a willingness to practice costly discipleship. —VCG

March 24

Read: Matthew 27:22–26

Biblical Truth

Personal Application

Prayer Requests

Answers to Prayer

Because Jesus bore the cross for us, we should be willing to take it up for Him.

March 25

Read: Luke 24:1–12

Biblical Truth

Personal Application

Prayer Requests

Answers to Prayer

THE TOMB OF JESUS

He is not here, but is risen!
—Luke 24:6

In his documentary *The Lost Tomb of Jesus,* Simcha Jacobovici claims archaeological evidence that disproves the resurrection of Christ. He says that the words "Jesus son of Joseph" found on a burial container near Jerusalem refer to Jesus of Nazareth. He also claims to have identified Jesus' DNA.

How valid are these conclusions? The Israel Antiquities Authority calls them "nonsense." Other secular and religious scholars agree. Jesus and Joseph were common names in first-century Judea. And Jacobovici needs DNA samples from Jesus to compare with the bones in the tomb. Obviously, that's impossible!

But there are strong arguments in favor of Jesus' resurrection. Most compelling is the fact that every disciple except John died a martyr's death. Central to their message was Jesus' resurrection (Acts 2:29–32). If Christ had not been raised from the dead, why did the disciples choose to die rather than deny it?

Assaults on our faith and on the Scriptures come and go. Don't be shaken by these baseless attacks. Two thousand years ago, the disciples were eyewitnesses to the real tomb of Jesus. The angels told them, "Why do you seek the living among the dead? He is not here, but is risen!" (Luke 24:5–6). —DF

The resurrection is a fact of history that demands a response of faith.

HONEST DOUBTS

When they saw [Jesus], they worshiped Him; but some doubted.
—MATTHEW 28:17

March 26

Read: Matthew 28

Our experience tells us that people do not return from the grave. At the heart of our desolation when death strikes is the awful certainty that in this life we will not see our loved ones again. We attend funerals to honor their memory and grieve our loss, but we do not expect to be greeted at the door by the person who has died.

In light of this, it should not seem surprising that Jesus' disciples were reluctant to believe that He had risen from the dead. Following the testimony of the women who had seen an angel, an empty tomb, and Jesus himself (Matthew 28:1–10), "the eleven disciples went away into Galilee, to the mountain which Jesus had appointed for them. When they saw Him, they worshiped Him; but some doubted" (vv. 16–17).

Among those who were closest to the Lord and had heard His remarkable teaching and witnessed His powerful miracles, some doubted that Jesus was actually alive again. But the honest doubts of the disciples soon turned to joy and hope as they embraced the reality of their risen Lord.

What do we doubt about Jesus today? Does our experience tell us that our past mistakes, present struggles, or future prospects can't be changed? Remembering what happened that first Easter, let's trust that He can do all things. —DCM

Biblical Truth

Personal Application

Prayer Requests

Answers to Prayer

One look to Calvary can dispel your doubts.

March 27

Read: Psalm 146

Biblical Truth

Personal Application

Prayer Requests

Answers to Prayer

CREATE YOUR OWN GOD

That they may know You, the only true God, and Jesus Christ whom You have sent.
—John 17:3

I've built a bathroom. I've wired an addition to my house. I've finished an entire basement. I enjoy do-it-yourself projects—as long as there's a good hardware store nearby.

But some people take this do-it-yourself thing too far. They create their own God. A report in *Newsweek* magazine said a youth pastor asked his teens who they think God is. One said He was like his grandfather: "He's there, but I never see him." Another suggested He is "an evil being who wants to punish me all the time." The last teen to comment concluded that everyone is right because that's what they really believe.

Do we decide who God is by taking a poll? Is He a being we can make up as we go along? This create-your-own-deity idea is increasingly popular today. And it is extremely dangerous. It robs us of knowing who our heavenly Father really is—as Scripture describes Him. He is, after all, the One "who made heaven and earth" (Psalm 146:6) and "the only true God" (John 17:3).

One historical confession of faith says: "God is a spirit, infinite, eternal, and unchangeable in His being, wisdom, power, holiness, justice, and truth." Examine the Scriptures. Find out who God really is and establish a relationship through Jesus. Then trust and obey the one true God.
—DB

The infinite God cannot be measured by finite man.

NIC AT NITE

I have come as a light into the world, that whoever believes in Me should not abide in darkness.
—JOHN 12:46

According to the apostle John, Nicodemus "came to Jesus by night" (John 3:2). Was this Pharisee skulking under cover of darkness, embarrassed or ashamed that he, as one of the ruling class, was curious about Jesus?

Some have suggested that rather than come in the heat of the day he came at night because it was cooler. Others have said that evening was a better time to ask Jesus questions because it was quieter and there were fewer distractions.

We really don't know the reason Nicodemus went to Jesus at night, but John seemed determined to make a point of that specific fact. Every time he mentioned Nicodemus, he identified him by saying something like: "You know who I'm talking about—the guy who came to Jesus by night" (see John 7:50; 19:39).

Nicodemus, no doubt, was quite moral and lived according to Mosaic law. People probably thought he was a pretty good person. Yet none of that mattered. He was in the dark about who Jesus really was, and he wanted to know the truth. So he was drawn from the darkness into the presence of "the light of the world" (John 8:12).

Jesus calls us "out of darkness" too (1 Peter 2:9) and promises that whoever believes in Him will not stay in the dark (John 12:46).
—CHK

March 28

Read: John 3:1–21

Biblical Truth

Personal Application

Prayer Requests

Answers to Prayer

Faith in Christ is not a leap into the dark; it's a step into the Light.

March 29

Read: Ephesians 5:1–17

Biblical Truth

Personal Application

Prayer Requests

Answers to Prayer

SEE ALL EVIL

It is shameful even to speak of those things which are done by them in secret.
—Ephesians 5:12

While waiting at the doctor's office, I read an article about the importance of freedom of speech. The writer suggested that producing obscene movies and pornography is good because it helps us to see our own potential for evil. He believes that naively thinking we are innocent is worse than knowing about and watching evil.

This rationale for evil is disturbing, especially for those of us who follow Christ. God doesn't expect us to avoid all contact with wickedness. Jesus—God in the flesh—loves sinners. But in the book of Ephesians, Paul said: "Have no fellowship with the unfruitful works of darkness, but rather expose them. For it is shameful even to speak of those things which are done by them in secret" (5:11–12).

Our responsibility is to expose evil by living a life of "goodness, righteousness, and truth" (v. 9), and by not taking part in "the unfruitful works of darkness" (v. 11). Hendriksen's *New Testament Commentary* says that the conduct of believers as children of light exposes the deeds of those in darkness and reveals the vast contrast between the two.

It's not realistic or wise to hide in a "holy cocoon." But we don't need to see evil to understand our propensity to sin. Expose the darkness by living in the Light.
—AC

Children of the light will not be comfortable in the dark.

THE RICHNESS OF HUMILITY

Neither he who plants is anything, nor he who waters, but God who gives the increase.
—1 CORINTHIANS 3:7

She lived out spiritual humility, yet she had much on a human level to be proud of. As an author of over seventy books and a translator of many others into Afrikaans, Annalou Marais had much cause to brag; but she was more concerned about honoring Christ than advancing herself. She worked behind the scenes of the Bible conference, doing a servant's tasks with a smiling face and a joyful heart. It would have been natural for her to desire, and even deserve, the spotlight. Instead, she quietly served, joyfully weeping as God worked in people's hearts. It was an impressive humility, because it was completely genuine.

I have heard it said, "It is amazing what can be accomplished when we don't care who gets the credit." This is certainly true of Christian service. Paul told the church at Corinth, "I planted, Apollos watered, but God gave the increase. So then neither he who plants is anything, nor he who waters, but God who gives the increase" (1 Corinthians 3:6–7). Paul had learned that great lesson of the servant's heart, as Annalou has learned—it's entirely about God. What we do is accomplished by His power and grace, and all the glory must go to Him.

It was a lesson in humility watching Annalou, and one that reminded me of the richness of serving God. —BC

Read: 1 Corinthians 3:1–10

Biblical Truth

Personal Application

Prayer Requests

Answers to Prayer

Pride and grace cannot dwell in the same place.

March 31

Read: Revelation 3:14–22

Biblical Truth

Personal Application

Prayer Requests

Answers to Prayer

FINDING JESUS

Behold, I stand at the door and knock. If anyone hears My voice and opens the door, I will come in to him and dine with him, and he with Me.
—REVELATION 3:20

If I asked the question, "Where's Waldo?" you might recall those popular children's picture books from the 1980s. That little guy in the red-and-white-striped shirt and hat loved to hide in the pages amid a busy blur of images that made it nearly impossible to find him.

Thankfully, finding Jesus is a lot easier than finding Waldo. Jesus doesn't play hide-and-seek. He says, "Behold, I stand at the door and knock" (Revelation 3:20). You can find Him at the door of your heart—the core of your existence—waiting to come in. He doesn't just want to meet you at church, or to be kept at bay on the outer edges of your life. Rather, He longs to be in the center of your dreams, deliberations, and desires. He wants a real relationship with the real you.

And as wonderful as that is, I need to warn you that it may be a little unsettling. Your heart is no doubt harboring a few things that He will want to deal with. But there is nothing that is more valuable than intimacy with Him. Welcome Jesus in and He will clear out the clutter until the air is fragrant and fresh with the purity, power, and pleasure of His presence.

Who's knocking at your heart's door? It's Jesus! How wonderful is that! —JS

Jesus is standing at the door of your heart—welcome Him in!

April

April 1

Read: Matthew 5:13–16

Biblical Truth

Personal Application

Prayer Requests

Answers to Prayer

IN THE DRIVER'S SEAT

Let your light so shine before men, that they may see your good works and glorify your Father in heaven.
—Matthew 5:16

I love the story of the stressed-out woman who was tailgating a man as they drove on a busy boulevard. When he slowed to a stop at a yellow light, the woman hit the horn, cussing and screaming in frustration and gesturing angrily. As she was still in mid-rant, she heard a tap on her window and looked up into the face of a police officer who ordered her to exit the car with her hands up. He took her to the police station and placed her in a holding cell.

An hour later, the officer returned and said, "I'm sorry, Ma'am. This has been a big mistake. When I pulled up behind you, I noticed your 'What Would Jesus Do?' license plate holder and your 'Follow Me to Sunday School' bumper sticker. I assumed the car was stolen!"

Satan doesn't care so much if you're a Christian as long as you don't act like one. If he can get you to live by his signals, he can damage and disarm you every time and dishonor the name of Christ in the process.

Instead, Jesus calls believers to be "salt" and to "Let your light so shine before men, that they may see your good works and glorify your Father in heaven" (Matthew 5:16).

With Jesus in the driver's seat of our lives, we can show off the love and glory of God. —JS

Don't let Satan manage the details of your life.

MICHAEL CARDINAL

Look at the birds of the air . . .
—Matthew 6:26

Twig by twig a cardinal constructed a bowl-shaped home in the bush outside my office window. Soon she laid an egg and kept it warm until it hatched. I named the little bird Michael. Although he was tiny, he had a huge appetite. His parents worked hard to keep him fed and safe. In a few months, Michael was ready to leave, and I was there to witness the amazing event.

When Michael left, so did mom and dad. The nest remained empty until the next spring. When mama cardinal returned, I was happy to see her but also sad. We had sold our house and I was concerned that the new owners might chop down the bush. But my concern soon turned to amazement. As I dismantled my office, mama cardinal dismantled her nest. By the time we left, so had the cardinal family. Mama cardinal's God-given instincts had told her to move.

This brought to mind another nature lesson. Using birds and lilies as examples, Jesus urged people not to worry. Since God takes care of birds, surely He will take care of His people (Matthew 6:26–34).

When concern for our own well-being leads to anxious thoughts, we can look at the birds and be assured of our value to God and of His care for us.
—JAL

April 2

Read: Matthew 6:25–34

Biblical Truth

Personal Application

Prayer Requests

Answers to Prayer

We need not fear the perils around us because the eye of the Lord is always upon us.

April 3

Read: Proverbs 16:1–9

Biblical Truth

Personal Application

Prayer Requests

Answers to Prayer

RIGHT PLACE

A man's heart plans his way, but the Lord directs his steps.
—Proverbs 16:9

They were in the right place—on the wrong day. Or so it would seem.

The Dayspring Chorale, a traveling high school singing group, arrived at a nursing home for a Thursday concert. However, the folks at the home were expecting them on Friday. But they said if the group could get set up fast, they could sing for twenty minutes. Then they'd have to stop for a memorial service for one of the residents.

The chorale hurriedly got ready and sang, and as they did, the son of the man who had died heard them. When they were done, he asked if they could sing at his dad's service. They gladly agreed and ministered hope and truth to all who attended. God used these young people in a special way—all because of a secretarial error. But was it a mistake?

We carefully make schedules so we can be where we think we should be. But we always need to keep in mind the words of Solomon: "A man's heart plans his way, but the Lord directs his steps" (Proverbs 16:9).

Do we seek ministry in life's unplanned schedule changes? Do we turn detours into guided tours of what He wants to do through us? If we're doing God's will, we'll be in the right place. Then, wherever we are, we can point people to Him. —DB

Unexpected changes are opportunities in disguise.

WHAT SHOULD I DO?

The Lord gives wisdom;
from His mouth come knowledge
and understanding.
—Proverbs 2:6

My friend Krista is struggling with a decision: Should she keep her old car with its continual maintenance problems or buy a newer model? She wants to be a good steward of her finances, and she desires to make a wise decision. And most of all, she wants to honor God.

Financial decisions can be tough to make. Billy Graham even says, "If a person gets his attitude toward money straight, it will help straighten out almost every other area in his life."

Here are a few ideas to consider about wisdom in decisions about money matters:

Do a checkup to be sure you're following God's priorities. Are you giving to Him and to others? (1 Corinthians 16:2). Taking care of family needs? (1 Timothy 5:8). Not letting money control you? (Luke 16:13).

Research the topic. Consider all the options and the pros and cons of each one.

Ask God for wisdom. Pray, pray, and pray some more. He will direct you (Proverbs 2:6).

Trust God and make the decision. Use the knowledge and wisdom you've gained, and commit your decision to Him.

Obedience to God nurtures a growing love-and-trust relationship with Him. What's most important is that we see each decision as an opportunity to draw closer to Him. —AC

April 4

Read: Proverbs 2:1–9

Biblical Truth

Personal Application

Prayer Requests

Answers to Prayer

The closer we walk with God, the clearer we see His guidance.

April 5

Read: John 6:60–71

Biblical Truth

Personal Application

Prayer Requests

Answers to Prayer

WORDS OF LIFE

Lord, to whom shall we go? You have the words of eternal life.
—John 6:68

In his book *Amusing Ourselves to Death: Public Discourse in the Age of Show Business,* Neil Postman warns us of the danger of a world of information overload. He reminds us of a chilling futuristic vision: Aldous Huxley's *Brave New World,* which describes a world thoroughly flooded with information, but with data that is manipulated so that none of it has any significance.

A glance at the Internet or a magazine rack hints that we are living in just such a culture. We're drowning in a sea of information, often marketed by the unscrupulous. We need discernment to choose wisely whom we will listen to.

In John 6, Jesus delivered His "I am the bread of life" message (v. 35). It was a sermon so controversial that, at its conclusion, many of His followers went away and stopped following Him (v. 66). They chose to stop listening to the voice of Christ. When Jesus challenged His disciples as to whether they would also walk away, Peter wisely responded, "Lord, to whom shall we go? You have the words of eternal life" (v. 68).

In a world swamped with confusing and contradictory information, we can, like Peter, turn to Christ for wisdom. He cuts through the words of confusion with words of life. —BC

If you want to be wise, listen to Jesus.

NEST IN THE GREATNESS

April 6

The Lord God . . .
put him in the garden of Eden
to tend and keep it.
—Genesis 2:15

In his historical novel *Chesapeake*, James Michener tells the story of multiple generations living near a marsh. One character, Chris Pflaum, is introduced as a restless thirteen-year-old sitting in class waiting for summer break. But when the teacher reads a poem by Sidney Lanier, the boy's heart is stirred.

As the marsh-hen secretly builds
on the watery sod,
Behold I will build me a nest on
the greatness of God:
I will fly in the greatness of God
as the marsh-hen flies
In the freedom that fills all the space
'twixt the marsh and the skies.

When Chris grew up, this poem motivated him to work tirelessly to preserve the precious wetlands and the wildlife he loved.

The poem's words stir the heart because they use nature as a springboard of praise to the Creator. But, unfortunately, our living planet can be neglected and exploited. God's mandate to Adam has been passed on to all believers: "The Lord God . . . put him in the garden of Eden to tend and keep it" (Genesis 2:15). The words *tend* and *keep* mean "to cultivate as servants."

We are to care for and guard God's creation as responsible stewards. —DF

Read: Genesis 2:1–15

Biblical Truth

Personal Application

Prayer Requests

Answers to Prayer

To mistreat God's creation is to offend the Creator.

April 7

Read: Proverbs 3:1–12

Biblical Truth

Personal Application

Prayer Requests

Answers to Prayer

WHY? WHY? OH, WHY?

If you endure chastening, God deals with you as with sons.
—Hebrews 12:7

Why must I suffer disappointment, sorrow, and tribulation? What have I done that God should send me trials? Is He displeased with me? These questions are constantly asked by God's dear children.

Much of this fear and questioning is due to our misunderstanding of God's dealings with His own. He has His good reasons. And one of those reasons is for our spiritual discipline. We should be far more afraid of being left alone than of God's chastening, for He wastes no time on worthless objects that give no promise of fruitfulness.

On the shores of Lake Michigan are great barren sand dunes that have never felt the point of a plow. But in the rich lowlands beyond them, the farmer is constantly cultivating the soil. The farmer knows what he is doing, so he keeps on breaking up the soil. The deeper the plow works and the more the sharp harrow, the more precious the crop will be when harvest time comes.

God's plow goes deep, but it is only that in the end we may forget the plowing and rejoice in the blessing of bearing much fruit for Him. "No chastening seems to be joyful for the present, but painful; nevertheless, afterward it yields the peaceable fruit of righteousness to those who have been trained by it" (Hebrews 12:11).
—MRD

All sunshine and no rain make a desert.

INTEGRITY—IS IT POSSIBLE?

April 8

Give me understanding, that I may know Your testimonies.
—PSALM 119:125

Read: Psalm 119:121–128

Samuel DiPiazza, CEO of a major public accounting firm, co-authored a book on building trust in the business world. The book proposes a spirit of transparency, a culture of accountability, and a people of integrity. But in an interview in Singapore, he noted there is one thing the book cannot teach—integrity. "Either you have it or you don't," he said.

Is he right? In our world of shifting standards, can integrity be acquired by those who don't have it? The answer is found in our unchanging standard—God's Word, the Bible.

David the psalmist did not head a multinational corporation. But he did rule over a kingdom, and he was serious about doing what was right. He recognized how easy it is to slide down the slippery path of unethical behavior simply because it seems advantageous.

So David asked God, "Teach me Your statutes" (Psalm 119:124). "Give me understanding," he said, "that I may know Your testimonies" (v. 125). David hated "every false way" and based his life on the principle that "all Your precepts concerning all things I consider to be right" (v. 128).

No one is born with godly character. But by studying God's Word and listening to His Holy Spirit, we can learn to hate falsehood and love integrity. —CPH

Biblical Truth

Personal Application

Prayer Requests

Answers to Prayer

The measure of a man's character is what he would do if he knew he never would be found out. —MACAULEY

April 9

Read: 2 Corinthians 4:1–7

Biblical Truth

Personal Application

Prayer Requests

Answers to Prayer

THE OYSTER MAN

That the excellence of the power may be of God and not of us.
—2 Corinthians 4:7

In the days of John Wesley, lay preachers with limited education would sometimes conduct the church services. One man used Luke 19:21 as his text: "Lord, I feared Thee, because Thou art an austere man" (KJV). Not knowing the word *austere,* he thought the text spoke of "an oyster man."

He explained how a diver must grope in dark, freezing water to retrieve oysters. In his attempt, he cuts his hands on the sharp edges of the shells. After he obtains an oyster, he rises to the surface, clutching it "in his torn and bleeding hands." The preacher added, "Christ descended from the glory of heaven into . . . sinful human society in order to retrieve humans and bring them back up with Him to the glory of heaven. His torn and bleeding hands are a sign of the value He has placed on the object of His quest."

Afterward, twelve men received Christ. Later that night someone came to Wesley to complain about unschooled preachers who were too ignorant even to know the meaning of the texts they were preaching on. The Oxford-educated Wesley simply said, "Never mind. The Lord got a dozen oysters tonight."

Our best may not always measure up to the standards of others. But God takes our inadequacies and humble efforts and uses them for His glory. —CHK

Do what you can where you are with what you have.

THE CHALLENGE OF FORGIVENESS

April 10

If you forgive men their trespasses, your heavenly Father will also forgive you.
—Matthew 6:14

In the heat of an argument, my wife came up with an acute theological insight. We were discussing my shortcomings in a rather spirited way when she said, "I think it's pretty amazing that I forgive you for some of the dastardly things you've done!"

What struck me about her comment was its sharp perception into the nature of forgiveness. It is not a sweet platonic ideal to be dispersed in the world like air-freshener sprayed from a can. Forgiveness is achingly difficult, and long after you've forgiven, the wound lives on in memory. Forgiveness is an unnatural act, and my wife was protesting its blatant unfairness.

A story from Genesis captures much the same sentiment. The brothers that Joseph struggled to forgive were the very ones who had bullied him, had cooked up schemes to murder him, had sold him into slavery. Though he went on to triumph over adversity, and though with all his heart he now wanted to forgive these brothers, he could not bring himself to that point—not yet.

I view Genesis 42–45 as Joseph's way of saying, "I think it's pretty amazing that I forgive you for the dastardly things you've done!" When grace finally broke through, the sound of Joseph's grief and love echoed through the palace. What was that wail? It was the sound of a man forgiving. —PY

Read: Genesis 45:1–15

Biblical Truth

Personal Application

Prayer Requests

Answers to Prayer

We can stop forgiving others when Christ stops forgiving us.

April 11

Read: Acts 16:6–10

Biblical Truth

Personal Application

Prayer Requests

Answers to Prayer

LISTEN TO HIS PROMPTINGS

After they had come to Mysia, they tried to go into Bithynia, but the Spirit did not permit them.
—Acts 16:7

On Friday, my day of rest as a pastor, the Holy Spirit prompted me to call a young single mother in our faith community to see if her car had been repaired. I had some reservations about making the call, but I obeyed.

Little did I know that my obedience would help save her life. She said later: "Friday at work I was planning on taking my life; but in a time of need, I believe God was there for me. He had Pastor Williams call me, and just by listening to his voice, I knew that God loved me."

The apostle Paul must have had reservations when the Holy Spirit prompted him and his team not to go into the provinces of Asia and Bithynia. Instead, they felt the Spirit's call to go into Macedonia to preach the good news. In each situation they obeyed the Spirit's promptings. As a result, Paul and his team were instrumental in giving birth to a new faith community in Philippi (Acts 16:11–15).

As believers in Christ who are indwelt by the Holy Spirit (Ephesians 2:22), our desire should be to please Him. May we not grieve the Holy Spirit (Ephesians 4:30) by ignoring His gentle promptings. When we obey Him, we might be used by God to lead someone to Christ, to disciple new believers—or even to help save somebody's life. —MW

Make the right choice: Obey the Spirit's voice.

WHAT DID HE SAY?

April 12

Your words were found, and I ate them, and Your word was to me the joy and rejoicing of my heart.
—Jeremiah 15:16

Read: Psalm 19:7–14

Because our son Steve spent most of his teen years connected to a cell phone, it was a bit of a shock for us when we couldn't talk with him for long periods of time after he joined the US Navy. First at boot camp and later while he trained as a hospital corpsman, we endured long periods of time without any communication. So it was a treat whenever we finally did hear from him.

After one of us would get his call, the first question from the other was always, "What did he say?" We hung on every word to hear how he was doing, what he was thinking, and what the Navy was planning for him.

It's natural to respond like this to the words of those who are important to us. We eagerly anticipate hearing from them.

Are we like that with the Word of God? Are we eager to communicate with Him—to look carefully into His Book to ask, "What did He say?" Unlike the infrequent calls from a son in the military, God's words of encouragement and guidance are always available to us. We just have to listen.

The prophet Jeremiah prayed, "Your words were found, and I ate them, and Your word was to me the joy and rejoicing of my heart" (Jeremiah 15:16). Do you have that same longing to hear God speak to you through His Word? —DB

Biblical Truth

Personal Application

Prayer Requests

Answers to Prayer

We cannot know the heart of God unless we have a heart for God.

April 13

Read: Hebrews 10:19–25

Biblical Truth

Personal Application

Prayer Requests

Answers to Prayer

CHEERING EACH OTHER ON

Let us consider one another in order to stir up love and good works.
—Hebrews 10:24

A mile from the finish line of the London Marathon, thousands of onlookers holding signs lined the route. When spectators spotted a family member or friend coming into view, they shouted the person's name, waved, and yelled encouragement: "Just a little farther! Keep going! You're almost there." After running 25 miles, many competitors were barely walking and ready to quit. It was amazing to watch exhausted runners brighten and pick up the pace when they saw someone they knew or heard their name called out.

Encouragement! We all need it, especially in our walk of faith. The book of Hebrews tells us to keep urging each other on. "Let us consider one another in order to stir up love and good works, not forsaking the assembling of ourselves together . . . but exhorting one another, and so much the more as you see the Day approaching" (10:24–25).

The New Testament is filled with the certainty that Christ will return soon. "The Lord is at hand" (Philippians 4:5). "The coming of the Lord is at hand" (James 5:8). "Behold, I am coming quickly" (Revelation 22:12).

As we "see the Day approaching," let's keep cheering each other on in the faith. "Keep going! You're almost there! The finish line is in sight." —DCM

Even if you have nothing else to give, you can give encouragement.

WHEN IN DOUBT

Are you the Coming One,
or do we look for another?
—Matthew 11:3

John the Baptist was languishing in prison and questioning his faith. He may well have wondered: Is Jesus the Messiah? Is His word true? Have I believed and labored in vain for my Master? Is this dark place my final reward for answering God's call?

Perhaps countless questions make their way through your mind as well: Is Jesus really the Savior? Have my sins been forgiven? Can I trust the Bible? Will I be raised from the dead? Does heaven lie ahead? Is all that I believe a cruel illusion?

Most of us ask questions like these from time to time. I do—especially on those dark days when circumstances bring sorrow and bitter disappointment.

These questionings are not *failures* of faith but *tests* of faith, and they can be answered in John the Baptist's way: We must take our doubts to Jesus. In His time, and in His own wise way, He will restore the confidence our hearts desire.

Jesus didn't abandon John to his doubt. He sent word of the miracles He performed and the hope He preached (Matthew 11:4–6). As George MacDonald said of God's faithfulness: "You might as well say that a mother would go away from her little child lying moaning in the dark."
—DHR

April 14

Read: Matthew 11:1–6

Biblical Truth

Personal Application

Prayer Requests

Answers to Prayer

Never doubt in the dark what God has shown you in the light.

April 15

Read: Mark 12:12–17, 41–44

Biblical Truth

Personal Application

Prayer Requests

Answers to Prayer

THE ALICE TAX

Having food and clothing,
with these we shall be content.
—1 Timothy 6:8

Author Calvin Trillin's wife, Alice, held a unique view of income tax. She believed that "after a certain level of income, the government would simply take everything." She thought there should be a limit on how much money people were allowed to keep for themselves. Writing in the *New Yorker,* Trillin said of his wife, "She believed in the principle of enoughness."

In Mark 12, Jesus avoided a carefully laid trap by telling His questioners to "render to Caesar the things that are Caesar's, and to God the things that are God's" (v. 17). When Jesus watched people making their offerings to the temple treasury, He commended a woman who would have been considered foolish for her extravagance. "This poor widow has put in more than all those who have given to the treasury; for they all put in out of their abundance, but she out of her poverty put in all that she had, her whole livelihood" (vv. 43–44).

Jesus placed more importance on wholehearted love for God than on wholesale concern over material needs. His tranquil attitude toward money and possessions was based on trusting His Father to supply each day's needs. "Your Father knows the things you have need of" (Matthew 6:8).

Enoughness. What a concept!
—DCM

Contentment is not getting what we want
but being satisfied with what we have.

April 16

DEFINING MOMENT

You meant evil against me;
but God meant it for good . . .
to save many people alive.
—Genesis 50:20

On this date in 2007, people around the world were stunned by a shooting rampage that left 32 victims dead on the campus of Virginia Tech University. In the aftermath, the mother of one critically wounded student who survived said she did not want the ordeal to become the defining moment in her son's life. Instead, she hoped it could be "something positive, some great celebration of his life."

When the unthinkable happens, it may seem impossible to believe that anything can overcome the emotional scars. Yet, the life of Joseph offers a powerful illustration of God's transforming power (Genesis 37–50). The brothers who sold Joseph into slavery were sure he would take revenge on them (50:15–17). But Joseph told them, "You meant evil against me; but God meant it for good, in order to bring it about as it is this day, to save many people alive" (v. 20).

When we place our desire for revenge in God's hands, we become participants in the remarkable process described by Paul: "Do not be overcome by evil, but overcome evil with good" (Romans 12:21).

The defining moments of our lives are not determined by the evil done to us, but by our response through the grace and power of God. —DCM

Read: Genesis 50:15–21

Biblical Truth

Personal Application

Prayer Requests

Answers to Prayer

Let danger drive you to Jesus.

April 17

Read: James 1:2–18

Biblical Truth

Personal Application

Prayer Requests

Answers to Prayer

IMPERFECT GIFTS

Every good gift and every perfect gift is from above, and comes down from the Father of lights.
—JAMES 1:17

When I was a child, I wondered why I had to thank God for food I didn't want to eat. In my immature mind, gratitude was a response to receiving something I wanted—like a hamburger and French fries, not asparagus. So why did I have to be thankful for something I didn't want?

In the human realm, my thinking was logical. Not everything people give us is for our good. And of course not everything we want is good.

But the situation with God is different. As Christ reminded us, loving parents do not give their children a stone rather than bread, a snake instead of a fish. And God is far more loving than our earthly parents (Matthew 7:9–11).

This doesn't mean that God's children can expect a pain-free, stress-free life. James tells us not only that every good gift comes from our heavenly Father (1:17), but also that we are to "count it all joy" when we "fall into various trials." The testing of our "faith produces patience," and the work of patience makes us "perfect and complete, lacking nothing" (vv. 2–4).

Even when we receive something that doesn't seem good, we can be grateful because we know there is more to it than we can see. What seems like an imperfect gift may be the means by which God perfects us. —JAL

A trial may be God's good gift in disguise.

FORGIVEN!

Blessed is he whose transgression is forgiven, whose sin is covered.
—Psalm 32:1

A little boy had just been tucked into bed by his mother, who was waiting to hear his prayers. But he had been naughty that day, and now it was bothering him. So he said, "Mama, I wish you'd go now and leave me alone. I want to pray by myself."

Sensing that something was wrong, she asked, "Bobby, is there anything you ought to tell me?" "No, Mommy," he replied. "You would just scold me, but God will forgive me and forget about it."

That little boy understood one of the greatest salvation benefits of all—the reality of sins forgiven. The Bible indicates that in Christ "we have redemption through His blood, the forgiveness of sins" (Colossians 1:14). We who have received the Lord Jesus as Savior enjoy freedom from sin's eternal condemnation (Romans 8:1), and we can also have daily forgiveness and cleansing (1 John 1:9).

The apostle Paul said that salvation provides these added benefits: we are justified (Romans 3:24), and we are at peace with God (5:1).

We should never get the idea that our sins are taken lightly by the Lord. But when we acknowledge our guilt with true repentance, God is ready to forgive because of what Jesus did on the cross. It's up to us to accept it.
—RDH

April 18

Read: Psalm 103:1–12

Biblical Truth

Personal Application

Prayer Requests

Answers to Prayer

When God forgives a sin, He never brings it up again.

April 19

Read: John 17:6–19

Biblical Truth

Personal Application

Prayer Requests

Answers to Prayer

PRETEND

When I was a child, I spoke as a child, I understood as a child . . . but when I became a man, I put away childish things.
—1 Corinthians 13:11

Our four-year-old grandson loves to play pretend games with grandma. He comes over to our home once a week, and Ma-Ma (that's what he calls her) takes him to the supermarket, to the botanical gardens to feed fish and turtles, and to ride the underground train—all without leaving our home! He guards this game of pretend so jealously as something between him and Ma-Ma that one day when we rode the real train, he asked, "Why are there other people in our train?"

Pretending is normal for a young child. But some carry the habit of pretending into adulthood when they attend church. What they do in church has no bearing on what they do the rest of the week. On Sunday they praise God heartily, but on Monday they become different people. What they express in worship is not seen in their behavior.

Our Lord Jesus Christ knows that we can fall into this trap easily. That is why in His prayer to His Father, He said, "I do not pray that You should take them out of the world, but that You should keep them from the evil one" (John 17:15).

God has placed us here to make a difference in our world. As He protects us from falling for the wiles of the evil one, He wants us to live by the same consistent standards in every aspect of our lives—not just on Sunday.
—CPH

Some people have heaven on their tongues but the world in their hearts.

THE ENDURING WORD

April 20

Heaven and earth will pass away,
but My words will
by no means pass away.
—Mark 13:31

At Dublin Castle in Ireland is the Chester Beatty Library, named for an industrialist who gave generously to charity. The beautiful library includes a quaint coffee shop and a variety of exhibits.

The exhibit that grabbed my attention was the ancient manuscripts. I slowly walked through the area and viewed fragments of the New Testament Gospels dating back to the third century AD. These scrolls were among the oldest known biblical texts until the discovery of the Dead Sea Scrolls in the mid-20th century. God's Word, preserved through the years!

As I looked at those portions of inspired text, I was moved by the permanence of the Word of God. It is because of the enduring nature of God's Word that we can have confidence in the message it contains. Jesus said, "Heaven and earth will pass away, but My words will by no means pass away" (Mark 13:31). Later, Jesus' disciple Peter would write, "All flesh is as grass, and all the glory of man as the flower of the grass. The grass withers, and its flower falls away, but the Word of the Lord endures forever" (1 Peter 1:24–25).

God's Word, enduring through the ages, is still the most trusted guide for living. —BC

Read: 1 Peter 1:17–25

Biblical Truth

Personal Application

Prayer Requests

Answers to Prayer

Like a compass, the Bible always points you in the right direction.

April 21

Read: 1 Corinthians 6:12–20

Biblical Truth

Personal Application

Prayer Requests

Answers to Prayer

RETURN ON INVESTMENT

You were bought at a price; therefore glorify God in your body and in your spirit.
—1 Corinthians 6:20

Long before the US professional baseball season begins each spring, team owners and managers are busy negotiating trades and contracts. They'll pay large sums of money to get the athlete who will help them win the championship. When the season starts, all eyes are on the newly acquired talent to see if he was worth the cost. The ultimate measure of the player's success is whether his contribution to the team is a good return on the investment.

In 1 Corinthians 6:20, Paul reminds us that we too have been "bought at a price." The context paints a compelling picture of Christ's great sacrifice. He liberated us from the cruel slavemaster of sin by buying us with the high price of His own life.

Getting a grip on God's great and loving investment in us should motivate us to gladly consider making His sacrifice rich in dividends. How is that return on His investment measured? By living to bring glory to Him! Our eyes, hands, feet, thoughts, dreams, and desires have been purchased to reflect the wondrous glory of God's will and wisdom. In other words, we are no longer our own.

Paul concluded, "Therefore glorify God in your body and in your spirit" (1 Corinthians 6:20). Living to reflect His glory is the return on investment that makes the Owner of our lives look good! —JS

Our choice to bring glory to God yields a great return on Christ's investment.

HAPPY EARTH DAY

April 22

His name alone is exalted;
His glory is above the
earth and heaven.
—Psalm 148:13

Read: Psalm 148

You don't have to tour Resurrection Bay in Alaska to appreciate the natural marvels of our earth, but it helps. You don't have to snorkel the warm waters of Jamaica to be impressed with the hidden beauty of our planet's seas, but it helps. You don't have to view the Rockies, experience the Rock of Gibraltar, or gaze at Mount Fuji to realize how awe-inspiring are the vistas of our globe, but it helps.

Experiencing firsthand the majesty of the mountains and the glory of the oceans can leave us breathless as we ponder how spectacular our big blue marble really is.

Today is Earth Day, a commemoration of our global home and a reminder of our responsibility to be careful stewards of this orb. But celebrating the greatness of our unique home among the planets can take on a dangerous slant if we leave out one key element. Contemplating the grandeur of earth should remind us that we are merely "the people of His pasture" (Psalm 95:7), and we must worship "our Maker" (v. 6).

The creation was flung into space to point to God and His greatness, power, and majesty. He alone deserves our praise and worship (Psalm 148:5). —DB

Biblical Truth

Personal Application

Prayer Requests

Answers to Prayer

How foolish to worship the creation,
when the Creator is so much greater.

April 23

Read: Acts 20:22–24

Biblical Truth

Personal Application

Prayer Requests

Answers to Prayer

DRIVEN BY GRATITUDE

Be steadfast, immovable, always abounding in the work of the Lord, knowing that your labor is not in vain in the Lord.
—1 Corinthians 15:58

What's the greatest novel ever written? Many readers would vote for Leo Tolstoy's *War and Peace,* which, depending on the edition, can run well over 1,000 pages. Even after his novel was finished, Tolstoy continued to write, often until he was on the brink of exhaustion, unable to sleep, and on the verge of a breakdown.

One day a friend asked him why he kept writing and driving himself to the edge of exhaustion. He reminded Tolstoy that he was a wealthy Russian count with servants at his beck and call, and that he had a secure future.

Tolstoy explained that he kept writing because he was the slave of an inner compulsion and had a consuming desire deep within his bones. He felt that he had to keep writing or he would go mad.

The apostle Paul experienced a similar compulsion, except that his drive was God-motivated. As he explained to his friends in Corinth, "the love of Christ compels us" (2 Corinthians 5:14). His was a burning passion, an emotional fire, a spiritual force that made him share the good news of Jesus and His death and resurrection.

Such dedicated zeal has characterized many of our Lord's followers throughout the years. May a spark of that fire burn in our own hearts. —VCG

The good news is too good to keep to yourself.

A SAILING SHIP

We are confident, yes, well pleased rather to be absent from the body and to be present with the Lord.
—2 CORINTHIANS 5:8

Dorothy, an elderly woman, was near death. She loved the Lord and longed to be with Him. The nurse told her family that Dorothy would probably hold on until she could see her daughter, who was on her way to say good-bye. The nurse said, "It's as if Dorothy has one foot here and the other in heaven. She wants to take that last step soon."

That reminds me of the following beautiful description of dying by Henry van Dyke: "I am standing at the seashore. A ship at my side spreads her white sails to the morning breeze and starts for the blue ocean. I stand and watch her until, at length, she hangs like a speck of white cloud, just where the sea and sky come to mingle with each other . . . And just at the moment when someone at my side says: 'There, she is gone!' there are other eyes watching her coming, and other voices ready to take up the glad shout: 'Here she comes!' And that is dying."

Even more comforting for the loved ones of a believer who dies are the words of the apostle Paul: "If our earthly house, this tent, is destroyed, we have a building from God, a house not made with hands, eternal in the heavens" (2 Corinthians 5:1). We can rejoice in our sorrow knowing our departed loved ones are now present with the Lord (v. 8).
—AC

April 24

Read: 2 Corinthians 5:1–10

Biblical Truth

Personal Application

Prayer Requests

Answers to Prayer

Because Christ lives, death is not tragedy but triumph.

April 25

Read: Mark 8:31–38

Biblical Truth

Personal Application

Prayer Requests

Answers to Prayer

IT'S NOT A GAME

Whoever desires to come after Me, let him deny himself, and take up his cross, and follow Me.
—Mark 8:34

My former neighbor often talked about "the game of life," and I can understand why he did. It's part of human nature to approach life as one big game made up of a lot of little games. Competing can be fun, exciting, and stimulating.

But life is a whole lot more than a game, especially for a follower of Jesus Christ. When a believer needs to own the biggest house, drive the largest SUV, get the promotion first, and win every argument, something's terribly wrong from God's point of view. It's not right to run over people's feelings, bend or break the rules, and gloat over victories.

To approach life as one big game that you always have to win is to live in hopeless delusion and fantasy. While material possessions, professional success, and personal victories are enjoyable, they last only for this life. Then they're all left behind.

Jesus instructed His disciples to deny themselves, identify with His cross, and follow Him in self-denial, and for some that even meant death (Mark 8:34–35). He made it clear to His disciples that artificial victories in "the game of life" don't count for much. What really counts is what's done for the Lord. —DCE

Those who live for God are the real winners in life.

RESPECT

You have made him a little lower than the angels, and You have crowned him with glory and honor.
—Psalm 8:5

In 1967, American vocalist Aretha Franklin topped the charts with her hit single "Respect." The song became an inspirational anthem for the civil rights movement and for others who demanded to be treated with respect.

Long before Aretha's hit record, Queen Vashti topped the Persian charts with her own version of "Respect." The book of Esther begins with King Ahasuerus hosting a great celebration. In addition to displaying his wealth and power, he also wanted to showcase his wife's beauty. So he commanded that Queen Vashti be brought before him and his guests.

If Queen Vashti obeyed, she would allow the king to degrade and disrespect her. If she refused, she risked losing her life. She refused. What courage! Vashti didn't want to compromise her character by being reduced to a piece of property. Her desire for respect led to her banishment. We have no record that Vashti feared the Lord. But her courage shows that she understood the God-given dignity accorded to every human being.

God created us in His image and crowned us with glory and honor, having made us "a little lower than the angels" (Psalm 8:5). Out of love and reverence for Him, let us treat ourselves and others with honor, dignity, and respect. —MW

April 26

Read: Esther 1:1–5, 9–12

Biblical Truth

Personal Application

Prayer Requests

Answers to Prayer

Even the most difficult people we know bear the image of God.

April 27

Read: Isaiah 55:8–11

Biblical Truth

Personal Application

Prayer Requests

Answers to Prayer

GOD'S REFRESHING WORD

My word . . . shall not return to Me void.
—Isaiah 55:11

When I was a boy, our family would occasionally travel across Nevada. We loved the desert thunderstorms. Accompanied by lightning bolts and claps of thunder, huge sheets of rain would blanket the hot sand as far as the eye could see. The cooling water refreshed the earth—and us.

Water produces marvelous changes in arid regions. For example, the pincushion cactus is completely dormant during the dry season. But after the first summer rains, cactuses burst into bloom, displaying delicate petals of pink, gold, and white.

Likewise, in the Holy Land after a rainstorm, dry ground can seemingly sprout vegetation overnight. Isaiah used rain's renewal to illustrate God's refreshing Word: "As the rain comes down, and the snow from heaven, and do not return there, but water the earth, and make it bring forth and bud, that it may give seed to the sower and bread to the eater, so shall My word be that goes forth from My mouth; it shall not return to Me void, but it shall accomplish what I please, and it shall prosper in the thing for which I sent it" (Isaiah 55:10–11).

Scripture carries spiritual vitality. That's why it doesn't return void. Wherever it encounters an open heart, it brings refreshment, nourishment, and new life. —DF

The Bible is to a thirsty soul what water is to a barren land.

THE GREATEST GIFT

April 28

They sat down with him on the ground seven days and seven nights, and no one spoke a word to him.
—Job 2:13

We rightly disparage Job's three friends for their insensitive response to his suffering. Yet when they came, they sat in silence beside Job for seven days before speaking. As it turned out, those were the most eloquent moments they spent with him.

Instinctively, I shrink back from people who are in pain. Who can know whether they want to talk about their predicament or not? Do they want to be consoled or cheered up? What good can my presence possibly do?

Tony Campolo tells of going to a funeral. By mistake he ended up in the wrong parlor. It held the body of an elderly man, and his widow was the only mourner present. She seemed so lonely that Campolo decided to stay for the funeral. He even drove with her to the cemetery.

At the conclusion of the graveside service, Campolo finally confessed that he had not known her husband. "I thought as much," said the widow. "But it doesn't really matter. You'll never, ever, know what this means to me."

Most often those who suffer remember the quiet, unassuming person. Someone who was there when needed, who listened, who didn't keep glancing at a watch, who hugged, touched, and cried. In short, someone who was available and came on the sufferer's terms, not their own. —PY

Read: Job 2

Biblical Truth

Personal Application

Prayer Requests

Answers to Prayer

Often, the best comfort is just being there.

April 29

Read: Psalm 23

Biblical Truth

Personal Application

Prayer Requests

Answers to Prayer

THE LAMB IS MY SHEPHERD

The Lamb who is in the midst of the throne will shepherd them.
—Revelation 7:17

The writers of the Old and New Testaments used many different metaphors for the Lord Jesus Christ. These word pictures vividly describe the marvelous aspects of Jesus' life and ministry.

While visiting a friend, hymn writer Albert Simpson Reitz saw the following motto hanging on a wall: "The Lamb Is My Shepherd." How foolish, he thought. Then he realized that a smudge on his glasses had distorted the second word of the motto. Actually it read: "The Lord Is My Shepherd."

His mistake started him thinking. He remembered that the Scriptures present Jesus both as the Good Shepherd and as the Lamb of God. Reitz said to his friend, "I've just seen the glorious gospel of our Lord in a new light. I'm reminded that the apostle John on the island of Patmos saw a vision, assuring him that the resurrected 'Lamb who is in the midst of the throne' will guide His people even when they get to heaven. Misreading that motto on your wall has given me a rich blessing. It could actually read, 'The Lamb Is My Shepherd.'"

It's reassuring to know that our Shepherd will guide us safely through this life, and that He will continue to feed and lead us throughout eternity. —HGB

The Lamb who died to save us is the Shepherd who lives to lead us.

A PERSONAL GOSPEL

Go into all the world and preach the gospel to every creature.
—Mark 16:15

In John 3:16 we read, "For God so loved the world." But what about His love for individuals? The rest of the verse reveals the central purpose behind God's sacrifice of His Son: "That whoever believes in Him should not perish but have everlasting life." Therefore, without exception, every person may interpret John 3:16 like this: "For God so loved me!"

A. B. Simpson, a great missionary of the past, often hugged a globe to his chest and wept over the world's lostness. Yet his global vision was marked by compassion for individuals. You and I also must feel the responsibility to take the gospel to our world—by sharing the good news with one person at a time.

Unfortunately, we often think of the Great Commission in terms of "foreign missions" only. "World missions" is perhaps a better term, for that includes our nearest neighbors, who are part of the world to which God has called us. And we are already there!

Like A. B. Simpson, embrace your smaller world through earnest prayer as you consider lost individuals in your family, neighborhood, and workplace. Then, as you seek to live and give the good news, expect God to open doors of opportunity. —JY

April 30

Read: Romans 10:13–17

Biblical Truth

Personal Application

Prayer Requests

Answers to Prayer

The light that shines farthest, shines brightest at home.

May

Read: Psalm 34:1–15

Biblical Truth

Personal Application

Prayer Requests

Answers to Prayer

HE'S WAITING

I sought the Lord,
and He heard me.
—Psalm 34:4

Jane Welsh, secretary to Scottish essayist Thomas Carlyle (1795–1881), married him and devoted her life to him and his work. He loved her deeply but was so busy with his writing and speaking that he often neglected her. Some time into their marriage, she became ill and suddenly died.

In a new book by John Ortberg, I read that after the funeral Thomas went alone to Jane's room and looked at her diary. He found these words she had written about him: "Yesterday he spent an hour with me and it was like heaven. I love him so." On another day, she wrote, "I have listened all day to hear his steps in the hall, but now it is late. I guess he will not come today." He wept brokenly, realizing his neglect of her and her desire just to talk with him.

As I read that, I couldn't help but think, *God loves me dearly and waits for me to fellowship with Him. How many days do I forget Him?*

The Lord welcomes our worship, our prayer, our praise. He has told us in His Word to pray all the time (1 Thessalonians 5:17). As He did with the church in Laodicea (see Revelation 3), Christ knocks on the door of our heart and patiently waits (v. 20). He listens attentively for our call, our cry, our prayer. How often does He wait in vain? —DCE

Talk with God—He longs to hear from you.

NO GOOD DEED

Blessed be the Lord, who has pleaded the cause of my reproach.
—1 Samuel 25:39

May 2

Read: 1 Samuel 25:32–39

Playwright and US Congresswoman Clare Boothe Luce (1903–1987) once said, "No good deed goes unpunished." Sadly, it sometimes seems as if this aphorism is true.

David, soon to be king of Israel, had an experience that corroborates this idea. While hiding from Saul, David and his men watched over the property of a rich landowner named Nabal. But later, when David asked a favor of Nabal, he was met with scorn. "Surely in vain I have protected all that this fellow has," said David. "He has repaid me evil for good" (1 Samuel 25:21).

Before David could carry out revenge, Nabal's wife intervened and kept David from acting rashly. Soon, God struck Nabal dead (v. 38). Then David praised God for keeping him from evil and for returning "the wickedness of Nabal on his own head" (v. 39).

Perhaps you've had an experience when kindness was repaid with ingratitude, a generous gift was treated as an entitlement, kind actions were interpreted as an attempt to control, or well-intended advice was received with scorn.

David's story reminds us that even when it seems as if we're being repaid with evil for doing good, we don't have to take matters into our own hands; we can trust God with the outcome.
—JAL

Biblical Truth

Personal Application

Prayer Requests

Answers to Prayer

One day God will right every wrong.

May 3

Read: Philippians 3:1–11

Biblical Truth

Personal Application

Prayer Requests

Answers to Prayer

CHINA'S BILLY GRAHAM

What things were gain to me, these I have counted loss for Christ.
—Philippians 3:7

In 1927, John Sung boarded a ship from the US bound for Shanghai. He had been in the States for more than seven years, earning three degrees in that time, including a Ph.D.

As the ship neared its destination, Sung threw all his diplomas, medals, and fraternity keys overboard, keeping only his doctorate diploma to show his father. He had received Jesus Christ and was determined that for the rest of his life he would live only for what counted for eternity.

Many older Christians still living in East and Southeast Asia came to know Christ through the ministry of John Sung, who has been called China's Billy Graham for his evangelistic work. His actions demonstrate what Paul wrote in Philippians 3:7: "What things were gain to me, these I have counted loss for Christ."

Not everyone can do what John Sung did. But, like Paul, we all should regard the things of this life "as rubbish" (v. 8) and live our lives so that they will count for eternity.

There are people within your sphere of influence whose lives you can impact for God. He has placed them there for you to point them to Jesus. Think of someone you can speak to about Jesus Christ and what He has done for you. —CPH

Only one life, 'twill soon be past; only what's done for Christ will last.

THE ASCENSION

*I go to prepare a place for you. . . .
I will come again and receive you
to Myself; that where I am,
there you may be also.*
—John 14:2–3

The repeated appearances of Jesus after His death and resurrection brought His followers so much joy that they must have wanted the visits to continue indefinitely. But on the 40th day after His resurrection, having given His disciples final instructions, Jesus slowly ascended and a cloud hid Him from view.

Jesus could have vanished instantly, as He had done previously (Luke 24:31). But He chose to ascend visibly to impress on His followers that this was the end of His visits. His bodily presence would soon be replaced by "another Helper," the Holy Spirit promised in John 14:16. Jesus' ascension marked the dawn of a new era.

In His glorified human body, the Lord Jesus ascended, entered heaven, sat down at the right hand of God, sent the Holy Spirit (John 14:16–18; Acts 2:33), and now intercedes for us (Romans 8:34; Hebrews 7:25). He permeates the whole universe with His spiritual presence and power (Colossians 1:15–23; Ephesians 4:10).

An ancient writing says that Jesus ascended bodily into heaven "our entrance to secure, and our abode to prepare." That's true. But it's also true that, as God, He is always spiritually present with us and will be "to the end of the age" (Matthews 28:20). What a wonderful Savior we have! —HVL

May 4

Read: Acts 1:1–11

Biblical Truth

Personal Application

Prayer Requests

Answers to Prayer

Jesus went away so the Holy Spirit could come to stay.

May 5

Read: Psalm 86

Biblical Truth

Personal Application

Prayer Requests

Answers to Prayer

THE DEBT OF LEADERSHIP

Save Your servant who trusts in You!
—Psalm 86:2

Examine the words of Psalm 86 and you might forget that you are reading the musings of a good leader. King David prayed, "O Lord, hear me; for I am poor and needy" (v. 1). Then the king of Israel refers to himself as a "servant" and pleads for mercy. Think of it! This was the man God had chosen to lead His people, pleading for God's help. Wow!

As we think about the role of leaders—whether centuries ago or today—it's vital that we review what leadership means. According to businessman and author Max De Pree, whose leadership moved his company near the top of the Fortune 500: "The first responsibility of a leader is to define reality. The last is to say thank you. In between the two, the leader must become a *servant* and a *debtor.* That sums up the progress of an artful leader." Those two words, *servant* and *debtor*, describe David's view of himself as he asked God for help during his time of leadership.

All of us who are in a leadership position—whether leading a family, a church, a classroom, or a business—need the humble words of Psalm 86 as our guide. The "poor and needy" servant-leader who trusts God is the one who, in the end, can say as David did, "You, Lord, have helped me and comforted me" (v. 17). —DB

The only leaders qualified to lead are those who have learned to serve.

ANTI-AGING POWER

Those who wait on the Lord shall renew their strength.
—Isaiah 40:31

May 6

Read: Isaiah 40:25–41:1

Americans spend more than $20 billion annually on various anti-aging products that claim to cure baldness, remove wrinkles, build muscle, and renew the powers of youth. Can those products deliver what they promise? Dr. Thomas Perls of Boston University School of Medicine says there is "absolutely no scientific proof that any commercially available product will stop or reverse aging."

But there is a promise of spiritual vitality that defies the ravages of time. "Even the youths shall faint and be weary, and the young men shall utterly fall, but those who wait on the Lord shall renew their strength; they shall mount up with wings like eagles, they shall run and not be weary, they shall walk and not faint" (Isaiah 40:30–31).

Isaiah used the eagle as a symbol of freedom and endurance, held aloft by a source of power outside itself. As we put our hope and trust in the Lord, we are carried along by His strength and not our own. The psalmist said it is the Lord who nourishes us so that our "youth is renewed like the eagle's" (Psalm 103:5).

Are we taking advantage of God's anti-aging power? It's promised to all who put their trust in Him for strength of heart, vigor of spirit, and energy of soul.
—DCM

Biblical Truth

Personal Application

Prayer Requests

Answers to Prayer

Growing old is a blessing when you're growing closer to God.

May 7

Read: Matthew 7:7–12

Biblical Truth

Personal Application

Prayer Requests

Answers to Prayer

DO UNTO OTHERS

Whatever you want men to do to you, do also to them, for this is the Law and the Prophets.
—Matthew 7:12

In May 2006, a man set out from base camp to make his third attempt on Mount Everest. He actually reached the summit, but on his way down he ran out of oxygen. As he lay on the side of the mountain dying, 40 climbers passed him by.

Some say that at such oxygen-deprived altitudes, rescues are too perilous. But others say that climbers are too eager to reach the top and too selfish to help those in trouble.

I wonder what would have happened if someone who passed that stricken climber had said, "I will treat him the way I want to be treated."

In Matthew 7:12, the golden rule, Jesus gave His disciples the secret to fulfilling the entire Old Testament relational regulations—love others and live for their benefit. He said this in the larger context of all the radical principles that He had taught up to this point in His sermon (Matthew 5:17–7:11).

As difficult as it is to live for the benefit of others, Jesus knew His followers could consistently live out this ethic as they drew strength from a righteousness that went beyond duty and outward conformity to rules (5:20). It is a righteousness that can come only from God himself.

If we are Jesus-followers, let's walk in His steps—loving others and living for their benefit.
—MW

Love is the debt we owe one another.

MOODY ARTWORK

May 8

Be tenderhearted, be courteous.
—1 Peter 3:8

Read: 1 Peter 3:8–12

British and American computer scientists have created artwork that changes according to how the viewer feels. The computer program analyzes the position and shape of the mouth, the angle of the brows, the openness of the eyes, and five other facial features to determine the viewer's emotional state. The artwork then alters, based on the viewer's mood. If joy is seen on the face, the artwork will show up in bright colors. If there's a scowl, the image will become dark and somber.

Our moods can also affect the people around us—our family, friends, co-workers, and acquaintances. Our life touches people, whether for good or bad. Each person is responsible for his or her own reaction to us, of course. Yet the way we behave makes a difference in others' lives.

The apostle Peter encouraged us to have compassion for others, to love, to be tenderhearted and courteous, and not to return evil for evil but rather blessing (1 Peter 3:8–9). Following his instructions may be difficult for us on a day when we feel cranky. By depending on the Holy Spirit, we can have a positive impact on everyone we meet—even if all we do is smile or listen.

Let's paint our world in bright colors today. —AC

Biblical Truth

Personal Application

Prayer Requests

Answers to Prayer

A heart touched by grace brings joy to the face.

May 9

Read: Jeremiah 6:16–21

Biblical Truth

Personal Application

Prayer Requests

Answers to Prayer

HORSEPOWER

Ask for the old paths, where the good way is, and walk in it; then you will find rest for your souls.
—Jeremiah 6:16

On a cold winter day in Michigan, a woman in labor was being rushed to the hospital when the unthinkable happened. The ambulance slid off an icy road into a ditch. A passing four-wheel-drive truck stopped and tried to haul the emergency vehicle out but couldn't get a grip.

That's when help arrived. An Amish man driving a two-horse team stopped to offer help. He told the ambulance service that the horses' shoes had been sharpened so they would bite into the ice. Once he hooked up the horses to the ambulance, they walked it right out of the ditch.

By today's standards, this young mother received help from a source of strength that was old-fashioned and outmoded. But on that day, old ways helped to ensure the safe arrival of new life into the world.

Most of us wouldn't want to return to the old-fashioned ways. But more than 2,500 years ago, Jeremiah reminded us that there is nothing more relevant than the truth of the past. Even though he was regarded as a relic of his time, he urged his neighbors to walk in the old paths of truth so that they would find peace and rest for their souls (Jeremiah 6:16). Today, we can still find rest and peace in Jesus, our eternal source of truth (Matthew 11:28).
—MD

The old truth of God's Word is ever new.

THE POWER OF PENTECOST

May 10

You shall receive power when the Holy Spirit has come upon you; and you shall be witnesses to Me.
—Acts 1:8

A pastor I know and love is discouraged. Although he is diligent in prayer and works hard, his church remains small while a new congregation nearby is rapidly developing into a megachurch. Yet when I think of the alcoholics, drug addicts, and sexually immoral people he has led to the Savior and a new way of life, I see him as one who witnesses in the power of the Holy Spirit.

Because of what happened on the day of Pentecost (described in Acts 2), we tend to associate the Holy Spirit's presence and power with amazing phenomena and large numbers. We forget that a little later the same people filled with the same Holy Spirit were rejected, flogged, imprisoned, and even executed. But through it all they were powerful witnesses!

The Holy Spirit's presence and power can be evidenced in a dynamic preacher who attracts great audiences. But it is seen as well in the volunteer who carries on a one-on-one prison ministry, in the person who witnesses to a co-worker or a neighbor, and in the Sunday school teacher who faithfully teaches week after week.

The power of Pentecost is not especially reserved for the highly gifted. Rather, it is available to all believers in Christ who want to serve Him. —HVL

Read: Acts 2:1–17

Biblical Truth

Personal Application

Prayer Requests

Answers to Prayer

The power of God's Spirit gives power to our witness.

May 11

Read: Proverbs 31:10–12, 28–31

Biblical Truth

Personal Application

Prayer Requests

Answers to Prayer

BEST MUM

Her children rise up and call her blessed; her husband also, and he praises her.
—Proverbs 31:28

On Mother's Day, 2007, British national television ran an intriguing story. Peggy Bush's daughter had died, so Peggy absorbed the responsibility of caring for her daughter's three children while her son-in-law worked. Then, tragically, her son-in-law also died. With both parents gone, Peggy took her three grandchildren in and raised them as if they were her own.

In a world where wrong is glamorized and the lurid is presented as appealing, we seldom hear of the good things that happen. Yet this woman's love and sacrifice were recognized, acknowledged, and honored as the nation took note of her as Britain's "Best Mum" for 2007.

Most of the efforts, sacrifices, and expressions of love our mothers have given us will never be the lead story on the news. Their recognition will be more personal. But what matters is not the scope of the appreciation but its genuineness.

May we remember to thank God for the mothers who have molded our hearts. As we honor them, we fulfill the truth of Proverbs 31:28: "Her children rise up and call her blessed; her husband also, and he praises her." —BC

Nothing touches a child like a mother's love.

A CHILD'S WONDER

That they may arise and declare [God's law] to their children, that they may set their hope in God.
—Psalm 78:6–7

In 19th-century Scotland, a young mother observed her three-year-old son's inquisitive nature. It seemed he was curious about everything that moved or made a noise. James Clerk Maxwell would carry his boyhood wonder with him into a remarkable career in science. He went on to do groundbreaking work in electricity and magnetism. Years later, Albert Einstein would say of Maxwell's work that it was "the most fruitful that physics has experienced since the time of Newton."

From early childhood, religion touched all aspects of Maxwell's life. As a committed Christian, he prayed: "Teach us to study the works of Thy hands . . . and strengthen our reason for Thy service." The boyhood cultivation of Maxwell's spiritual life and curiosity resulted in a lifetime of using science in service to the Creator.

The community of faith has always had the responsibility to nurture the talent of the younger generation and to orient their lives to the Lord, "that they may arise and declare [God's law] to their children, that they may set their hope in God" (Psalm 78:6–7).

Finding ways to encourage children's love for learning while establishing them in the faith is an important investment in the future. —DF

May 12

Read: Psalm 78:1–8

Biblical Truth

Personal Application

Prayer Requests

Answers to Prayer

We shape tomorrow's world by what we teach our children today.

May 13

Read: Deuteronomy 32:7–12

Biblical Truth

Personal Application

Prayer Requests

Answers to Prayer

REFRAMING THE PICTURE

As an eagle stirs up its nest,
hovers over its young,
spreading out its wings . . .
so the Lord alone led [Jacob].
—Deuteronomy 32:11–12

For three months I had a ringside seat—or should I say a bird's-eye view—of God's amazing handiwork. Ninety feet above the floor of Norfolk Botanical Garden, workers installed a webcam focused on the nest of a family of bald eagles, and online viewers were allowed to watch.

When the eggs hatched, Mama and Papa Eagle were attentive to their offspring, taking turns hunting for food and guarding the nest. But one day when the eaglets still looked like fuzzballs with beaks, both parents disappeared. I worried that harm had come to them.

My concern was unfounded. The webcam operator enlarged the camera angle, and there was Mama Eagle perched on a nearby branch.

As I pondered this "reframed" picture, I thought of times when I have feared that God had abandoned me. The view in the forest heights of Virginia reminded me that my vision is limited. I see only a small part of the entire scene.

Moses used eagle imagery to describe God. As eagles carry their young, God carries His people (Deuteronomy 32:11–12). Despite how it may seem, the Lord "is not far from each one of us" (Acts 17:27). This is true even when we feel abandoned. —JAL

Because the Lord is watching over us,
we don't have to fear the dangers around us.

May 14

TRUE TRUST

Neither this man nor his parents sinned, but that the works of God should be revealed in him.
—John 9:3

If you didn't know him, you might think Nick Vujicic has everything going for him. Nick has never had a sore arm. He's never had knee problems. He's never smashed his finger in a door, stubbed his toe, or banged his shin against a table leg.

But that's because Nick doesn't have a shin. Or a toe. Or a finger. Or a knee. Or an arm. Nick was born with no arms and no legs. Before you begin to feel sorry for Nick, however, read his words: "God won't let anything happen to us in our life unless He has a good purpose for it all. I completely gave my life to Christ at the age of fifteen after reading John 9. Jesus said that the reason the man was born blind was 'so that the works of God may be revealed through him.' . . . I now see that glory revealed as He is using me just the way I am and in ways others can't be used." Nick travels the world to spread the gospel and love of Jesus.

Nick says: "If I can trust in God with my circumstances, then you can trust in God with your circumstances . . . The greatest joy of all is having Jesus Christ in my life and living the godly purpose He has for me."

Can we say that? Can we look beyond our limitations and have the same trust in God that transformed a man with no arms or legs into a missionary for Jesus?
—DB

Read: John 9:1–11

Biblical Truth

Personal Application

Prayer Requests

Answers to Prayer

Trusting God turns problems into opportunities.

May 15

Read: Ephesians 3:14–21

Biblical Truth

Personal Application

Prayer Requests

Answers to Prayer

SURPRISE ME!

"My thoughts are not your thoughts, nor are your ways My ways," says the Lord.
—Isaiah 55:8

When our family went out for an ice cream cone, my dad would ask my mother what flavor she'd like. Often she would reply, "Surprise me!" She told me she was rarely disappointed in his choice.

Do you like surprises? Would you ever dare say "Surprise me!" to God? A lot of us are a little scared to do that. Yes, we have faith that God is good and that He loves us. Yet we're afraid we won't like what He chooses for us.

Throughout the Bible we read that God delights in doing the unexpected. Sometimes it's folding back the waters for His people to cross a sea on dry ground (Exodus 14:21–22). Or forgiving and embracing those who repent of their sin (Psalm 130:1–4). Jesus' time on earth was filled with amazing events that pointed people to His Father. He turned water into wine, calmed storms, healed the sick, and raised the dead.

What kind of God do we serve? One who is not confined by our finite imagination (Ephesians 3:20). God's thoughts and ways are not like ours (Isaiah 55:8), and He wants to bless us with far more than a special flavor of ice cream. He delights in His children who trust Him and are willing to say, "Surprise me, Lord!" —CHK

Those who let God provide will always be satisfied.

DRAGON SKIN

Put on the new man which was created according to God, in true righteousness and holiness.
—Ephesians 4:24

In the fifth Chronicle of Narnia, *The Voyage of the Dawn Treader,* Edmund, Lucy, and their spoiled cousin Eustace are summoned to help on a quest in the Eastern Sea. Along the way, Eustace is tempted by enchanted treasure and turned into a dragon. The desperate dragon accepts the help of the great lion Aslan, king of Narnia. But Eustace can only be freed by allowing Aslan's claws to painfully tear off the dragon's flesh. Grateful for his deliverance, Eustace chooses to become a better boy.

Receiving God's gift of salvation through Christ is a one-time event, but to become like Him often requires suffering and struggle. It involves putting off old sinful habits and replacing them with new godly ones. Paul wrote: "Put off, concerning your former conduct, the old man which grows corrupt . . . [and] put on the new man which was created according to God, in true righteousness and holiness" (Ephesians 4:22–24).

What is troubling you today? God may be using the kind rebuke of a friend or a painful trial to prompt you to get rid of a sinful habit and to replace it with godly character (Romans 8:29; 1 Peter 4:1–2).

The process of becoming like Christ is sometimes painful, but it's always worth it. —DF

May 16

Read: Ephesians 4:17–24

Biblical Truth

Personal Application

Prayer Requests

Answers to Prayer

The conversion of a soul is the miracle of a moment; the growth of a saint is the work of a lifetime.

May 17

Read: Hebrews 3:7–15

Biblical Truth

Personal Application

Prayer Requests

Answers to Prayer

SEIZE THE DAY

My times are in Your hand.
—Psalm 31:15

Before entering the broadcasting field, Jim Valvano led the North Carolina State University basketball team to a national championship. Then cancer developed in his lower back. Invited to address the Duke University squad, Jim had this to say: "Life changes when you least expect it to. The future is uncertain. So, seize this day, seize this moment, and make the most of it."

God gives us an urgent directive in Hebrews 3:13: "Exhort one another daily, while it is called 'Today,' lest any of you be hardened through the deceitfulness of sin." Why is there such a strong insistence on *today*?

It may be that *today*, this very day, could be the last one in our time here on earth. Today may be your last opportunity to accept God's gift of salvation, or if you know the Lord already, to share His love with a friend or loved one.

James has this warning about presuming upon our tomorrows: "You do not know what will happen tomorrow. For what is your life? It is even a vapor that appears for a little time and then vanishes away" (4:14).

Seize the opportunities that God gives you today. That's sound advice—not just for basketball players, but for all of us.
—VCG

Plan as though you'll be living for a century;
live as though you'll be leaving today.

May 18

GOD'S STRONG HANDS

Jacob was left alone;
and a Man wrestled with him
until the breaking of day.
—Genesis 32:24

In Genesis, it seems that almost every person and family mentioned is dysfunctional. The text is filled with accounts of jealousy, anger, violence, and deception that leave a trail of damaged relationships. Even Noah, Abraham, Isaac, and Jacob—lauded as heroes of faith in Hebrews 11—display flawed character and spiritual lapses. But God never leaves them that way.

Jacob defrauded his older twin Esau, who swore to kill him (Genesis 27:41). Then, before the estranged brothers would face each other after twenty years, Jacob wrestled with God. When asked his name, the conniving younger brother finally admitted who he was: Jacob—the deceiver (Genesis 32:24–27). That marked a spiritual turning point.

Noted preacher Carlyle Marney said that because God doesn't give up on us, we should not give up on ourselves. "The last person on earth you will forgive a weakness is yourself," Dr. Marney wrote. "Only in the gospel can men go on loving themselves. Wait on God! See what His strong hands will fashion out of your defection."

When we have turned back, God can turn us around. When we have destroyed, God can rebuild. "Christ in the strong hands of God conquering my defection. This is the gospel."
—DCM

Read: Genesis 32:22–30

Biblical Truth

Personal Application

Prayer Requests

Answers to Prayer

There is victory in surrender when we are conquered by Christ.

May 19

Read: Hebrews 4:11–16

Biblical Truth

Personal Application

Prayer Requests

Answers to Prayer

A QUESTION OF MOTIVE

The Word of God is living and powerful, and sharper than any two-edged sword . . . and is a discerner of the thoughts and intents of the heart.
—Hebrews 4:12

My wife and I were stopped at a railroad crossing to allow a train to pass. As we waited in the line of cars, the driver next to us suddenly darted through a nearby parking lot and headed in the direction of the next available railroad crossing.

I turned to Marlene and said, with some righteous indignation, "Look at that guy. He's trying to get around the train instead of waiting like the rest of us." As soon as I said those words, the man, camera in hand, hopped from his car to take pictures of the oncoming train. I had judged his motives, and I was dead wrong.

Although we can observe behavior and outward appearance, only God can see what's in the heart. That is one reason we all need the Word of God so desperately. Hebrews 4:12 says: "The Word of God is living and powerful, and sharper than any two-edged sword, piercing even to the division of soul and spirit, and of joints and marrow, and is a discerner of the thoughts and intents of the heart."

When we find ourselves ready to judge another person's motives, let's pause and remember—only God can see the heart, and only His Word can expose its motives. Our responsibility is to let the Lord and His Word convict us about our own hearts. —BC

People will be judged by the way God sees them not by the way we see them.

PRODUCTIVE PAIN

All things work together for good to those who love God, to those who are the called according to His purpose.
—Romans 8:28

I'll never forget when our youngest child Matthew fell and broke his wrist. It was grotesque! His arm took a sharp left turn at his wrist and then turned again to resume its normal journey to his hand.

We rushed him to the hospital where the doctor began to set his wrist. I watched as the physician pulled and twisted Matthew's arm. I wanted to jump up and pull him away from my son! But I simply sat and watched, knowing that the agony was necessary to make Matt whole again.

If we trust earthly doctors to do that for our children, how much more we should be willing to trust God, the Great Physician, to reset our broken lives "to be conformed to the image of His Son" (Romans 8:29). One of God's purposes in pain is to brand the image of Jesus in our hearts. Can we weep with those who weep? God may need to stain our cheeks with our own tears so that we can genuinely empathize with others as Jesus did. Are we self-sufficient? God may need to strip away our security to conform us to the God-sufficiency that Christ displayed. Are we faithless? It may require a tragedy to teach us to trust the Father as Jesus did.

Next time you feel broken, don't panic—praise Him! God is at work! —JS

May 20

Read: Romans 8:18–30

Biblical Truth

Personal Application

Prayer Requests

Answers to Prayer

God's purpose in pain is to brand His image in our hearts.

Read: Psalm 119:9–16

Biblical Truth

Personal Application

Prayer Requests

Answers to Prayer

SPELLING BEE

Your Word I have hidden in my heart.
—PSALM 119:11

My wife and I stayed up late to watch a TV program we found exciting—the Scripps National Spelling Bee. It was fascinating to watch middle-school children as they recited the correct spelling for some of the most difficult words imaginable.

Anticipation grew as one contestant after another was disqualified. Finally, only thirteen-year-old Katharine Close remained. One word stood between her and the world championship. With little hesitation, Katharine correctly spelled the word *ursprache*.

Obviously, Katharine can spell. But it's possible to know how to spell a word, yet not understand its meaning.

As believers in Jesus Christ, it's vital for us to know God's Word, the Bible. Our goal is not to accumulate knowledge but to internalize His Word so that we can be equipped in our walk of faith. When we know God's Word, it keeps our spiritual walk from slipping (Psalm 37:31). It satisfies the hunger of our souls (Jeremiah 15:16). And it is a key weapon in facing temptations and trials (Matthew 4:1–11; Ephesians 6:10–18).

Let's make it our aim to know the Word. Then, when facing life's challenges, we can be ready for any situation (2 Timothy 3:16–17). —DF

To the wise, God's Word is sufficient.

May 22

THE NEXT GENERATION

The things that you have heard from me . . . commit these to faithful men who will be able to teach others also.
—2 Timothy 2:2

A man who played double-bass in the Mexico City Philharmonic told me that the finest instruments are made of wood that has been allowed to age naturally to remove the moisture. "You must age the wood for 80 years, then play the instrument for 80 years before it reaches its best sound," said Luis Antonio Rojas. "A craftsman must use wood cut and aged by someone else, and he will never see any instrument reach its peak during his own lifetime."

Many important things in life are "next generation" matters—teaching, training, and parenting are among them. The apostle Paul invested himself in people whose spiritual influence would continue long after he was gone. He wrote to Timothy: "The things that you have heard from me among many witnesses, commit these to faithful men who will be able to teach others also" (2 Timothy 2:2). Paul, Timothy, "faithful men," and "others" represent four spiritual generations built on the enduring foundation of the gospel of Jesus Christ.

Are we living only for today and the short term, or are we giving ourselves to others who will continue the faith after our race is run? Living for Christ and making disciples are all about the next generation. —DCM

Read: 2 Timothy 2:1–13

Biblical Truth

Personal Application

Prayer Requests

Answers to Prayer

We influence future generations by living for Christ today.

May 23

Read: Zechariah 7:8–14

Biblical Truth

Personal Application

Prayer Requests

Answers to Prayer

HEART DISEASE

Do not harden your hearts.
—PSALM 95:8

Pharmaceutical companies make billions of dollars selling drugs that prevent hardening of the arteries, a condition that can lead to heart attacks, which kill thousands of people every year.

A more serious condition than hardening of the arteries, however, is hardening of the heart, and it cannot be prevented by any wonder drug. The prophet Zechariah warned the Israelites about it. They had hardened their hearts and refused to listen to the words of the Lord. Symptoms of this deadly condition were their refusal to execute true justice and their failure to show mercy and compassion (Zechariah 7:9). As a result, the Lord became angry and stopped listening to them (v. 13).

While it's important to keep plaque from forming in our arteries, it's even more important to keep our hearts from becoming callous to people who are important to God: widows, orphans, aliens, and the poor (v. 10).

It's crucial to follow our doctor's orders to keep our arteries from hardening. But it's even more crucial to obey God to keep our hearts from becoming hardened to the needs of others.

Ask God to bring to mind a person who needs the help of someone with a soft heart. —JAL

To love Christ is to have a heart for others.

GETTING WHAT YOU WANT

One's life does not consist in the abundance of the things he possesses.
—Luke 12:15

There's a popular idea floating around about how to get whatever you want. It's called "the law of attraction." Just think and feel what you want to attract and "the law will use people, circumstances, and events to magnetize what you want to you, and magnetize you to it." This positive-thinking philosophy teaches that the "energy" of your dominant thoughts "attracts" your circumstances.

You won't find that idea anywhere in the Bible! As believers, we have good reason to be positive in our thinking, but it's because our heavenly Father understands our needs and meets them. Because He cares for us, we don't have to be anxious (Luke 12:29–30). Life doesn't consist "in the abundance of the things [we possess]" (v. 15), so we make it our aim instead to be "rich toward God" (v. 21). We do that by seeking His kingdom and purpose (v. 31) and by laying up treasures in heaven, not for ourselves in this life.

Jesus said, "Take heed and beware of covetousness" (v. 15) because one day, like the rich fool in the parable in Luke 12, we will leave it all behind. That's when we'll have more than we ever dreamed of. In the meantime, God promises to care for our needs, no matter what the circumstances. And that's no secret.
—AC

May 24

Read: Luke 12:15, 22–34

Biblical Truth

Personal Application

Prayer Requests

Answers to Prayer

God has promised to supply all our needs, not all our wants.

May 25

Read: Acts 9:17–27

Biblical Truth

Personal Application

Prayer Requests

Answers to Prayer

BUILDING BRIDGES

Barnabas took him and brought him to the apostles.
—Acts 9:27

A new believer recently attended our worship service. He had long, multicolored, spiked hair. He dressed in dark clothes and had multiple piercings and tattoos. Some gaped; others just gave him that "It's good to see you in church, but please don't sit next to me" smile. Yet there were some during the greeting time who went out of their way to welcome and accept him. They were bridge builders.

Barnabas was that bridge builder for Saul (also called Paul). When Saul arrived in Jerusalem three years after his conversion, many disciples were afraid of him and doubted his transformation (Acts 9:26). He didn't receive a warm welcome from the Jerusalem church greeters—for good reason. Saul had a terrible reputation for persecuting Christians! But Barnabas, a Jewish convert, believed God's work of grace in Saul's life and became a bridge between him and the apostles (v. 27).

Saul needed someone to come alongside him to encourage and teach him, and to introduce him to other believers. Barnabas was that bridge. As a result, Saul was brought into deeper fellowship with the disciples in Jerusalem and was able to preach the gospel there freely and boldly.

New believers need a Barnabas in their lives. We are to be a bridge in the lives of others.
—MW

Be a bridge of encouragement to someone today.

May 26

GONE THE SUN

Your sun shall no longer go down . . . for the Lord will be your everlasting light, and the days of your mourning shall be ended.
—Isaiah 60:20

In 1862, during the US Civil War, General Daniel Butterfield wanted a new melody for "lights out." And so, without any musical training, he composed one in his head.

Years later, the general wrote: "I called in someone who could write music, and practiced a change in the call of 'Taps' until I had it suit my ear, and then . . . got it to my taste without being able to write music or knowing the technical name of any note, but, simply by ear, arranged it." General Butterfield gave the music to the brigade bugler, and the rest is history.

While there are no official lyrics to the hauntingly familiar strains of "Taps," here is a commonly accepted version of one verse:

Day is done, gone the sun,
From the hills, from the lake,
from the sky;
All is well, safely rest, God is nigh.

What a comforting lyric as faithful members of the military are laid to rest! And what hope in the acknowledgment that God is near, even—especially—in death!

The prophet Isaiah anticipated a day when death itself would die. "Your sun shall no longer go down . . . for the Lord will be Your everlasting light" (60:20).

For those who follow Jesus, the strains of "Taps" are not a funeral dirge but a song of hope. All is well. God is nigh. —TG

Read: Isaiah 60:17–22

Biblical Truth

Personal Application

Prayer Requests

Answers to Prayer

Sunset in one land is sunrise in another.

May 27

Read: 1 Kings 19:9–12

Biblical Truth

Personal Application

Prayer Requests

Answers to Prayer

CAN WE REALLY HEAR FROM GOD?

Be still, and know that I am God.
—Psalm 46:10

A friend of mine who leads spiritual retreats once told me that not one person who has followed his regimen of a silent retreat has failed to hear from God. Intrigued and a bit skeptical, I signed up for a five-day retreat. We had much free time and just a few requirements, such as the assignment to spend two hours praying each day.

I doubt I had devoted more than thirty minutes to prayer at any one session in my life. The first day I wandered to a meadow and sat against a tree. How long will I stay awake? I wondered. To my great fortune, a herd of 147 elk wandered into the very field where I was sitting. To watch 147 elk in their natural habitat is enthralling and, eventually, boring. Yet after a while the very placidity of the scene began to affect me. Over the next few days I said many words to God. I was turning fifty, and I asked for guidance on how I should prepare my soul for the rest of life. Many things came to mind while sitting in a field for hours at a time. I had to agree that I had indeed heard from God.

When Elijah stood before the Lord on Mount Horeb, he didn't meet Him in the wind, earthquake, or fire. Rather, God spoke in a "still small voice" (1 Kings 19:11–12).

I'm more convinced than ever that God finds ways to communicate to those who truly seek Him—especially when we lower the volume of the surrounding static. —PY

God speaks to those who are quiet before Him.

ARE WE LISTENING?

Be doers of the Word, and not hearers only, deceiving yourselves.
—James 1:22

Read: Psalm 119:41–48

A fascinating film made in 1950, *The Next Voice You Hear,* tells a story of a family with a typical amount of trials and tensions. Then, one night, the voice of God speaks on the radio. But not just their radio—God's voice is heard throughout the world on every radio, saying the same thing at the same time.

At first people react with disbelief, then fear. After several days of hearing "The Voice," however, people's attitudes, actions, and priorities begin to change. The impact of what God is saying directly affects how they live their lives.

I have heard people say, "If only God would talk to me! If He would just tell me what to do, I would do it." The simple fact is that God has already spoken to us through His Word, the Bible. Do we listen to Him as He speaks?

The psalmist desired to obey God's Word "continually, forever and ever" (119:44). And James warned about ignoring it when he said, "Be doers of the Word, and not hearers only, deceiving yourselves" (James 1:22).

We can be thankful that God does speak to us—not on the radio but in the Scriptures. May we be wise enough to listen and obey. —BC

Biblical Truth

Personal Application

Prayer Requests

Answers to Prayer

In God's works we see His hand; in His Word we hear His heart.

May 29

Read: John 14:1–6

Biblical Truth

Personal Application

Prayer Requests

Answers to Prayer

FINALLY HOME

If I go and prepare a place for you, I will come again and receive you to Myself; that where I am, there you may be also.
—JOHN 14:3

Jan and Hendrikje Kasper sailed into United States waters in January 1957. Their family of twelve, along with other Dutch immigrants on board the *Grote Beer,* crowded on deck to catch their first glimpse of the Statue of Liberty in New York Harbor.

That initial view of Lady Liberty was exciting—and emotional. They had just endured an arduous eleven-day journey across the sea on a no-frills voyage. They had left many friends and family members behind in The Netherlands. They had experienced rough seas brought on by a hurricane and had dealt with seemingly endless seasickness. But now—finally—they had arrived. They were home!

Someday those of us who have trusted Jesus Christ as our personal Savior will leave this life and go to the place He has prepared for us (John 14:3). The journey may be difficult or uncomfortable, but we certainly look forward to the final destination.

When we see Jesus face to face for the first time, we will be "finally home." —CHK

Those who love and serve God on earth will be right at home in heaven.

FROM HERE TO HEAVEN

May 30

We are His workmanship, created in Christ Jesus for good works.
—Ephesians 2:10

Read: Ephesians 2:1–10

Pro athletes and coaches sometimes get something for nothing. Let's say a coach signs a three-year contract and the team agrees to pay him $1 million a year. But in his first season the team is terrible and management fires him. So, the coach leaves but still has two more years of pay coming to him. He gets the next $2 million without doing a thing.

We as Christians have to be careful that we don't view our saving faith like that. We must never think, "Hey, I'm saved. I've got eternal riches coming my way. I don't have to do anything for God."

That's partially right but very wrong. In one regard, our journey from here to heaven is paid for in full by Jesus' sacrifice. There's nothing we can do to earn salvation. But there's another part of this that we must consider.

In Ephesians 2:8–9, after Paul clearly says that we do not have to "do" anything and that salvation is a "gift of God," he goes on to say that we indeed have a job to do (v. 10). As believers, we are "created in Christ Jesus for good works." God has tasks planned for us to do while we are on this earth—not to pay our debt but to honor our Savior.

Life from here to heaven is not a vacation cruise. It's a wonderful privilege and calling to serve God. —DB

Biblical Truth

Personal Application

Prayer Requests

Answers to Prayer

We are not saved by good works but for good works.

May 31

Read: Romans 3:9–20

Biblical Truth

Personal Application

Prayer Requests

Answers to Prayer

SPEEDING TICKET

There is none righteous,
no, not one.
—Romans 3:10

I had been driving in Singapore for thirty-four years when I received my first summons for speeding! It was not the first time I had exceeded the speed limit, but it was the first time I had been fined for doing so.

My first reaction was one of disgust. But as I contemplated the spiritual lesson, I realized that no matter how long I had been driving without a ticket, I was still accountable.

If I can break such a clearly defined law as a speed limit, think how easy it is to break God's perfect law, which covers every aspect of life. No one, no matter how moral or religiously fervent, can keep it perfectly.

Paul wrote: "By the deeds of the law no flesh will be justified in His sight, for by the law is the knowledge of sin" (Romans 3:20). Keeping the law can't save us; rather, through the law we become aware of our sin (3:7–12). That's why God sent His Son to save us. We need the righteousness of Jesus because we can't be justified through our good deeds. "Therefore," Paul said, "we conclude that a man is justified by faith apart from the deeds of the law" (v. 28).

If you have put your faith in Christ, you can say with Paul, "Blessed are those whose lawless deeds are forgiven, and whose sins are covered; blessed is the man to whom the Lord shall not impute sin" (Romans 4:7–8).
—CPH

God's law shows us a need that only God's grace can supply.

June

Read: Colossians 1:3–8

Biblical Truth

Personal Application

Prayer Requests

Answers to Prayer

CHUMS

We give thanks to the God and Father of our Lord Jesus Christ, praying always for you.
—Colossians 1:3

In 19th-century England, debtors' prison housed those unfortunate souls who couldn't pay their bills. Since the people were not there for violent crimes, a spirit of trust and camaraderie soon developed. They played games together and had plenty to eat. Some were even allowed private rooms.

New prisoners were escorted to the "chummage," a prison dormitory. In time, the prisoners began to refer to each other as "chums." Later, the word caught on outside the prison walls and took on the meaning of "a cordial friend."

Deep bonds of friendship also develop in Christian ministry. Those who worked alongside Paul were not strangers to persecution and imprisonment. But a common mission created a deep sense of connectedness. In his letter to the believers in Colosse, Paul called Epaphras a "fellow servant" (Colossians 1:7). The term can be paraphrased as "together slave" or "one who serves the same master with another."

When believers live under the lordship of Christ, they can see their lives intertwined in service. By serving as slaves to Christ, a spiritual camaraderie results that transcends being "chums." And that special relationship will continue on into eternity! —DF

Christians stand strong when they stand together.

RISKY BUSINESS

He said to them, "Why are you fearful, O you of little faith?" Then He arose and rebuked the winds and the sea, and there was a great calm.
—Matthew 8:26

Denis Boyles knew it would be challenging to interview a man on a roller coaster, especially when the interview took place *during* an attempt to set a world's record for continuous riding. After several times around the track, Denis was so overcome with fear he could hardly talk.

Then the man showed him how to use his body and feet to lean into the loops, twists, and turns. Writing in *AARP Magazine*, Boyles explained how that took away the terror. It also taught him a lesson about risk and fear. The roller coaster *felt* risky though it was quite safe. But driving his car to the amusement park posed a far greater risk of injury. Risk and fear are easily confused.

As Jesus and His disciples crossed the Sea of Galilee, a storm came up and waves swept over their boat. Incredibly, Jesus fell asleep in the midst of the storm. The disciples woke Him and said, "Lord, save us! We are perishing!" (Matthew 8:25). In a gentle rebuke, Jesus asked, "'Why are you fearful, O you of little faith?' Then He arose and rebuked the winds and the sea, and there was a great calm" (v. 26).

Like the disciples, the more we learn about Jesus, the more we trust Him. Our greatest risk is failing to depend on Him when life seems out of control. —DCM

June 2

Read: Matthew 8:23–27

Biblical Truth

Personal Application

Prayer Requests

Answers to Prayer

Keep your eyes on Jesus and you'll soon lose sight of your fears.

June 3

Read: Ecclesiastes 3:14–22

Biblical Truth

Personal Application

Prayer Requests

Answers to Prayer

THE SEARCH FOR JUSTICE

I saw under the sun: In the place of judgment, wickedness was there; and in the place of righteousness, iniquity was there.
—ECCLESIASTES 3:16

A trial has just ended, and the reactions to the verdict could not be more different. The family of the alleged murderer celebrates the declaration of a mistrial due to a legal technicality. Meanwhile, the grieving parents whose daughter has died wonder about a justice system that would allow such a decision. As they stand weeping before a mass of microphones and cameras, they exclaim: "Where is the justice in this? Where is the justice?"

We've seen this scenario played out in the news or on TV crime dramas. We instinctively long for justice but cannot seem to find it. The wisest man of his day, Solomon, faced a similar frustration and disappointment. He saw that imperfect human beings could never administer perfect justice. He wrote: "I saw under the sun: In the place of judgment, wickedness was there; and in the place of righteousness, iniquity was there" (Ecclesiastes 3:16).

If all we trusted in were imperfect people, we would lose all hope. But Solomon wisely added in verse 17: "God shall judge the righteous and the wicked, for there is a time there for every purpose and for every work."

The search for justice can be satisfied only by trusting the God who is always just. —BC

Someday the scales of justice will be perfectly balanced.

DON'T GO DOWN THERE

June 4

This is love, that we walk according to His commandments.
—2 John 1:6

In his book *Lessons Learned Early,* Jerry Jenkins tells a story about his freshman year in college. It was 1968, a year of tremendous political and social upheaval in the US. Riots had broken out in many major cities. From the rooftop of his dorm in Chicago, Jerry heard sirens and saw fires burning. Students had been told to stay on campus, but Jerry wanted to see what was happening.

As he ran toward a store that was blazing a few blocks away, a police car pulled up beside him. "Don't go down there," the officer warned.

Jerry waited till the car pulled away and then kept walking. The officer returned. This time he made it more clear as he repeated, "Don't go down there"—and leveled a shotgun out the window.

Our rebellious or willful streaks often lead to unhappy outcomes. In anger Moses struck the rock to get water, rather than just speaking to it as God had commanded. As a result, he forfeited the privilege of entering the Promised Land with his people (Numbers 20:7–12). Jonah disobeyed an order to go to Nineveh and was given three days to think about his choice—inside a big fish (Jonah 1).

What does it take for us to obey Him? Will we obey simply because we love Him? (John 14:15, 21). —CHK

Read: John 14:15–24

Biblical Truth

Personal Application

Prayer Requests

Answers to Prayer

Obedience is another word for love and loyalty.

June 5

Read: Psalm 42

Biblical Truth

Personal Application

Prayer Requests

Answers to Prayer

A GRADUATION WISH

***Why are you cast down,
O my soul? . . . Hope in God;
for I shall yet praise Him.***
—Psalm 42:5

The high school commencement speaker was the president of a large corporation. He was chosen for the occasion because of his success. Yet his speech came with a most unusual wish for the graduates.

The speaker told the students sitting before him in their graduation gowns: "If I could have one hope for you as you go out into the world, it would be this: I hope you fail. I hope that you fail at something that is important to you." He went on to tell them how his own early life had been one failure after another until he learned to see failure as an effective teacher.

Many of the songs of Israel were born in seasons of failure. Out of desperation came the cry, "As the deer pants for the water brooks, so pants my soul for You, O God. My soul thirsts for God, for the living God" (Psalm 42:1–2).

Sometimes we are not ready to see the wonder of God's wisdom and strength until we are gasping for breath in the exhaustion of our own strength.

A recurring story of the Bible is that mountains of faith rise from the valleys of failure. Before discovering the high ground we are looking for, we may need to see the failure of the dreams we hold in our hearts and trust instead in the love, wisdom, and guidance of our God. —MD

Learn from your failures, or you will fail to learn.

LINKED HEARTS

Beloved, if God so loved us, we also ought to love one another.
—1 John 4:11

Each new day, it seems, brings new ways our family sees the body of Christ at work. One demonstration of the fellowship of Christians sits on my desk as I write. It's a basket overflowing with letters from people I have never met. Since the time *Our Daily Bread* readers first learned of the car accident that ushered our daughter Melissa into heaven six years ago, we've received hundreds of messages from our brothers and sisters in the faith.

They've said things such as: "I grieve with you, my brother, and I will keep you and your family in my prayers." "I weep at your loss." "I hurt with you." Many have recommended books to read. Others have sent poems or articles of comfort and hope. Some have shared their own stories of bereavement, and we've discovered new partners on the path of pain. They demonstrate the principle of love among the family of God that's commanded in 1 John 4:11.

Each of those gracious notes is different from the others, but they contain a common thread: Because of our shared faith in Christ, I find my heart joined to the hearts of the writers of these messages.

Hearts linked by Jesus create a chain of love that can encourage even the most grieving heart. —DB

June 6

Read: 1 John 4:7–14

Biblical Truth

Personal Application

Prayer Requests

Answers to Prayer

Our hearts are linked through the love of Christ.

June 7

Read: Galatians 5:13–16

Biblical Truth

Personal Application

Prayer Requests

Answers to Prayer

SERVING TOGETHER

Through love serve one another.
—Galatians 5:13

When Cristine Bouwkamp and Kyle Kramer got married in the spring of 2007, they did something most of us wouldn't think of doing. Instead of hosting a "sit-down dinner," they held a simple reception at the church and invited their guests to help distribute food to people in need.

They bought a truckload of food and had it delivered to the church parking lot. Then they and their wedding guests served the people of the neighborhood. Cristine and Kyle said the first thing they wished to do as a married couple was to serve others. Because God had changed their lives so radically, they wanted to "bless God for blessing us with each other." The Kramers chose a great start for their marriage—blessing God by serving others.

The apostle Paul encouraged the Christians of Galatia: "Through love serve one another" (Galatians 5:13). Some of these early Christians believed that the ceremonial practices of the Old Testament were still binding on the church. So Paul wrote that salvation is by grace through faith. It is by faith we live out our new life in Christ. He reminded them that the law was fulfilled in this: "You shall love your neighbor as yourself" (v. 14).

As followers of Jesus, we're here to serve Him out of love—to "bless God for blessing us." —AC

God blesses us so that we can be a blessing to others.

AIR WARS

A man of understanding is of a calm spirit.
—Proverbs 17:27

A spectacular air battle raged outside our window. Skilled, speedy flyers swarmed through the air, diving down from above, zooming in from left and right, climbing from underneath to knock the others out of the fight. The air was alive with sound as they attacked, eluded, hovered, and struck out at one another.

"Scrappy little things, aren't they?" my wife, Shirley, observed. Six hummingbirds filled the air with darting motion, hovering and whirring as they fought for the three positions on our red hummingbird feeder. "Why can't they just be patient?" she wondered.

Like so many disputes and quarrels that plague the church, these battles were totally unnecessary. The feeder held plenty of nectared water. We refilled it every day. Yet, for hours at a time, no hummers came near it—until they all wanted it. They seemed to prefer a good scrap.

Quarrels among believers in Jesus Christ bring dishonor to Him. They create wounds in our brothers and sisters, leaving scars. "It is honorable for a man to stop striving, since any fool can start a quarrel," says Proverbs 20:3. And "He who has knowledge spares his words" (17:27).

How much better it is when we speak gentle words of peace, not angry words of strife! —DCE

June 8

Read: Proverbs 17:14–19, 27–28

Biblical Truth

Personal Application

Prayer Requests

Answers to Prayer

Two cannot quarrel when one will not.

June 9

Read: Ephesians 1:3–10

Biblical Truth

Personal Application

Prayer Requests

Answers to Prayer

LIBERATING TRUTH

He made us accepted in the Beloved.
—Ephesians 1:6

A missionary had been disparaging herself. She was unhappy with her life in general, but she was especially displeased with what she felt was her low level of spiritual growth.

One morning she looked searchingly at herself in the mirror. Then, very slowly, she said, "God, I thank You that I am myself and can never be anybody else."

That was her moment of liberating self-acceptance. She realized that by God's design she was an absolutely unique person, a Christ-redeemed human being who could never be replaced or duplicated.

Do you condemn yourself because you aren't as spiritual as you think you ought to be? Do you see yourself as a second-rate disciple, lacking the gifts and graces possessed by fellow believers who seem to be models of prayer, witness, and service? We can rise above the mood of self-rejection and enjoy grateful self-acceptance when we put our lives into the nail-pierced hands of Jesus. "In Him we have redemption through His blood, [and] the forgiveness of sins" (Ephesians 1:7). We are accepted and chosen by Him (vv. 4–6).

If the Lord has accepted us, surely we can accept ourselves! That's the liberating truth.
—VCG

Accepting Jesus' free gift of salvation frees us to accept ourselves.

LOVING OUR GROWN-UP CHILDREN

June 10

Now abide faith, hope,
love, these three;
but the greatest of these is love.
—1 Cor. 13:13

Comedian Henny Youngman used to say, "I've got two wonderful children—and two out of five isn't bad."

When children reach adulthood, most parents have an opinion about how their offspring have "turned out." Some are proud of everything their kids have done, while other parents express misgivings or disappointment about the choices their children have made. How can we continue a positive parenting role after the birds have left our nest?

In 1 Corinthians 13, often called "the love chapter" of the Bible, Paul writes that the greatest gifts of speaking, understanding, and sacrificial service are worthless without love (vv. 1–3). Love itself is the foundation of winsome behavior, and its influence never ends. "Love suffers long and is kind; love does not envy; love does not parade itself, is not puffed up; does not behave rudely, does not seek its own, is not provoked, thinks no evil; does not rejoice in iniquity, but rejoices in the truth; bears all things, believes all things, hopes all things, endures all things. Love never fails" (vv. 4–8).

When our children no longer seek our advice, they still value our love. In every stage of parenting, it's not only what we say but what we do that counts. —DCM

Read: 1 Corinthians 13

Biblical Truth

Personal Application

Prayer Requests

Answers to Prayer

A parent's love never ends.

June 11

Read: Micah 6:6–8

Biblical Truth

Personal Application

Prayer Requests

Answers to Prayer

A CURE FOR FUTILITY

What does the Lord require of you but to do justly, to love mercy, and to walk humbly with your God?
—Micah 6:8

I once heard interviews with survivors from World War II. The soldiers recalled how they spent a particular day. One sat in a foxhole; once or twice, a German tank drove by and he shot at it. Others played cards and frittered away the time. A few got involved in furious firefights. Mostly, the day passed like any other. Later, they learned they had just participated in one of the largest, most decisive engagements of the war, the Battle of the Bulge. It didn't feel decisive at the time because none had the big picture.

Great victories are won when ordinary people execute their assigned tasks.

When followers of Ignatius (1491–1556) endured periods of futility, he always prescribed the same cure: "In times of desolation we must never make a change, but stand firm and constant in the resolutions and determination in which we were the day before the desolations." Spiritual battles must be fought with the very weapons hardest to wield at the time: prayer, meditation, self-examination, and repentance.

Perhaps you sense you're in a spiritual rut. Stay at your assigned task! Obedience to God—and only obedience—offers the way out of our futility.
—PY

If you sense your faith is unraveling, go back to where you dropped the thread of obedience.

IT'S ELEMENTARY!

Known to God from eternity are all His works.
—Acts 15:18

June 12

Read: Psalm 139:1–6

On a recent trip to London, we exited the Baker Street underground station where we were greeted by a life-size statue of legendary detective Sherlock Holmes. Created by novelist Sir Arthur Conan Doyle, Holmes was an investigative genius who could routinely assess seemingly random clues and solve the mystery.

Baffled by Holmes's uncanny brilliance, his sidekick, Dr. Watson, would ask for an explanation, to which Holmes would glibly respond, "Elementary!" and then proceed to unfold the solution.

If only life operated that way. So often we face events and circumstances that are far more baffling than a Sherlock Holmes mystery. We struggle to figure life out, but we always seem to come up short.

In times like these, it's comforting to know that we have a God who doesn't need to assess the situation—He already knows everything perfectly well. In Acts 15:18 we read, "Known to God from eternity are all His works." He never has to wonder or resort to inductive reasoning.

Despite our finiteness, our lives rest in the hands of the One who knows all the whats, whys, and whens we'll ever face. As we trust in Him, He'll guide us in the path He desires us to take—and His way is never wrong. —BC

Biblical Truth

Personal Application

Prayer Requests

Answers to Prayer

In a world of mystery, it's a comfort to know the God who knows all things.

June 13

Read: Esther 4:10–17

Biblical Truth

Personal Application

Prayer Requests

Answers to Prayer

FOR SUCH A TIME AS THIS

I will go to the king,
which is against the law;
and if I perish, I perish!
—Esther 4:16

When Sha'Ri Eggum was diagnosed with acute myeloid leukemia, doctors told her that only a bone marrow transplant from a blood relative could save her life. Complicating matters, Eggum, 32, was adopted and didn't know anything about her biological family. But a private investigator tracked down her brother, Mike Ford, who was a perfect match. Today, Eggum's leukemia is in remission. Ford was the right person for the right moment.

The book of Esther tells another story of love, sacrifice, and God's timing. Mordecai, a Jew in exile, refused to bow to Haman, second in command to King Ahasuerus. Haman became furious and plotted to destroy Mordecai and all the Jews. So Haman deceived the king and persuaded him to issue an edict condemning the Jews to death. When Mordecai told his cousin Queen Esther about the edict, he urged her to intervene. "Who knows whether you have come to the kingdom for such a time as this?" he said (Esther 4:14). Approaching the king uninvited was punishable by death. But Esther seized the moment to save her people!

When we are able to rescue others, we should do so at all costs. Ask God for His direction and act! He may have placed you here "for such a time as this."
—MW

Courage is not the absence of fear—it is the mastery of it.

FOR THOSE WHO SERVE

June 14

Let the elders who rule well be counted worthy of double honor, especially those who labor in the Word and doctrine.
—1 Timothy 5:17

When my son Steve walks into a room, he often gets immediate respect. People want to shake his hand. They smile. They congratulate him. They thank him.

It happens at church. It happens in restaurants. It happens wherever he goes—as long as he is wearing his uniform of the United States Navy.

While in uniform, Steve gets instant respect because everyone knows that he is serving. He has given up many personal freedoms and desires so that he can serve his country.

People respect service. We honor police officers who serve. We pay homage to military personnel who serve. But do we give the same honor and respect to those who are in an even greater service—service to God? Do we show respect to our pastors, missionaries, Sunday school teachers?

Scripture tells us to give honor to whom honor is due (Romans 13:7). Specifically, it tells us that double honor goes to those who direct the affairs of the church through teaching and preaching (1 Timothy 5:17).

Instead of criticizing your pastor, teacher, or spiritual leader, let others hear your words of gratitude and praise for their service. Hold them up in prayer. God's servants deserve our respect and honor. —DB

Read: Romans 13:1–7

Biblical Truth

Personal Application

Prayer Requests

Answers to Prayer

We honor God when we honor our leaders.

June 15

Read: Proverbs 20:3–7

Biblical Truth

Personal Application

Prayer Requests

Answers to Prayer

A PERFECT FATHER

The righteous man walks in his integrity; his children are blessed after him.
—Proverbs 20:7

My father once admitted to me, "When you were growing up, I was gone a lot."

I don't remember that. Besides working his full-time job, he was gone some evenings to direct choir practice at church, and he occasionally traveled for a week or two with a men's quartet. But for all the significant (and many small) moments of my life—he was there.

For instance, when I was eight, I had a tiny part in an afternoon play at school. All the mothers came, but only one dad—mine. In many little ways, he has always let my sisters and me know that we are important to him and that he loves us. And seeing him tenderly caring for my mom in the last few years of her life taught me exactly what unselfish love looks like. Dad isn't perfect, but he's always been a dad who gives me a good glimpse of my heavenly Father. And ideally, that's what a Christian dad should do.

At times earthly fathers disappoint or hurt their children. But our Father in heaven is "merciful and gracious, slow to anger, and abounding in mercy" (Psalm 103:8). When a dad who loves the Lord corrects, comforts, instructs, and provides for the needs of his children, he models for them our perfect Father in heaven. —CHK

A life lived for Christ is the best inheritance we can leave our children.

STRINGS, RINGS, TROUBLESOME THINGS

June 16

Humble yourselves in the sight of the Lord, and He will lift you up.
—James 4:10

Read: James 4:1–10

Ray Bethell is a world champion kite flyer. He can make multiple kites twist and turn in such precision that they behave as if they are one. As I watched an amazing video of Ray and his three synchronized kites, I recalled a poem I read many years ago.

In the library of Pastor Howard Sugden, I came across a well-worn book containing the works of John Newton. Inside was a poem titled "The Kite; or Pride Must Have a Fall." The kite in Newton's poem dreamed of being cut free from its string: "Were I but free, I'd take a flight, / And pierce the clouds beyond their sight, / But, ah! Like a poor pris'ner bound, / My string confines me near the ground." The kite does finally manage to tug itself free, but instead of soaring higher in the sky, it crashes into the sea.

The analogy calls me to reconsider some "strings" that make me feel constrained. Vows. Promises. Commitments. Responsibilities. Although such things make me feel tied down, God uses them to hold me up. As James teaches, it is our willingness to be humbled (or held down) that God uses to lift us up (James 4:10).

Before cutting any string, make sure it's not one that's holding you up. —JAL

Biblical Truth

Personal Application

Prayer Requests

Answers to Prayer

A Christian rises against the winds of adversity.

June 17

Read: 2 Corinthians 11:3–4, 12–15

Biblical Truth

Personal Application

Prayer Requests

Answers to Prayer

CAPTAIN THUNDERBOLT

Satan himself transforms himself into an angel of light.
—2 CORINTHIANS 11:14

When an English robber called Captain Thunderbolt escaped the law and moved to the eastern US in 1818, he began practicing medicine. He took on the name Dr. John Wilson. Often he wore three suits of clothes to escape recognition by making himself look larger and covering up a deformed leg.

Just before the man died, he asked his friends to bury him without removing his clothes. But to prepare his body for proper burial, that request could not be honored. The mortician was surprised to find scars from wounds and a withered leg. A search of "Dr. Wilson's" house revealed a stash of watches, jewelry, and diamonds. The sheriff learned that the doctor was in fact Thunderbolt, a thief in disguise. They had been fooled!

Satan and his followers have disguises too. It says in 2 Corinthians 11:15: "[Satan's] ministers also transform themselves into ministers of righteousness." But how? One way is through false doctrine. Ever since Paul's day, false teachers have taught that good deeds can earn salvation.

Paul warned us not to be deceived by the devil's craftiness (v. 3). The truth is: "By grace you have been saved through faith . . . it is the gift of God, not of works" (Ephesians 2:8–9). Don't be fooled. —AC

Satan has many tools, but deception is the handle that fits them all.

AN INVITATION TO FRIENDSHIP

No longer do I call you servants, for a servant does not know what his master is doing; but I have called you friends.
—JOHN 15:15

I grew up in a home with lots of wall plaques. One had a quotation by poet Claude Mermet that stands out in my mind: "Friends are like melons; let me tell you why: To find a good one, you must one hundred try!"

Most of us can identify with that. It's hard to find good friends.

I wonder if God ever feels that way about us? Out of all the people in the Old Testament, only one was ever called His friend. In Isaiah 41:8, God says that He chose Jacob, who was an offspring of "Abraham My friend." Pretty exclusive club! So you can imagine how shocking it was for the disciples to hear Jesus say, "No longer do I call you servants . . . but I have called you friends" (John 15:15).

Better yet, He is saying that to us as well. So, what does friendship with Jesus look like? It starts with *commitment*. As He said, "You are My friends if you do whatever I command you" (v. 14). Then He added the dynamic of *communication*. He promised to tell us all that the Father has told Him (v. 15). Are you listening? And as His friends we begin to bear fruit (v. 16), sharing a *commonality* with Him by reflecting His glory in our attitudes and actions (2 Corinthians 3:18).

Jesus welcomes you to the privilege of friendship with Him! Are you His friend? —JS

June 18

Read: John 15:9–17

Biblical Truth

Personal Application

Prayer Requests

Answers to Prayer

Welcome to the privilege of friendship with God.

June 19

Read: Romans 6:15–23

Biblical Truth

Personal Application

Prayer Requests

Answers to Prayer

JUNETEENTH

Having been set free from sin, you became slaves of righteousness.
—Romans 6:18

On June 19, 1865, over two years after President Lincoln had signed the Emancipation Proclamation, General Gordon Granger rode into Galveston, Texas, and read General Order Number 3: "The people of Texas are informed that in accordance with a Proclamation from the Executive of the United States, all slaves are free." For the first time, slaves in Texas learned that they were already free. Some were shocked; many others celebrated. June 19 soon became known as "Juneteenth."

Nearly 25 years after the "Emancipation Proclamation" of the cross of Jesus, Paul wrote to the Roman believers. Some of them still did not understand what it meant to be free from sin's bondage. They thought they could go on sinning because they were under grace (Romans 6:15). So Paul reminded them of their status in Jesus by appealing to a familiar fact: Whatever we submit to becomes our master (John 8:34). To commit sin puts us in bondage to sin.

The other option is to be a slave of righteousness. Salvation actually means a change of bondage. As we once served sin, we are now committed to lives of righteousness because of the freedom Jesus provides.

My brothers and sisters, let us become in practice what we already are in status—free!
—MW

True freedom is found in bondage to Christ.

GHOST TOWN

What does the Lord your God require of you, but . . . to serve the Lord your God with all your heart and with all your soul.
—Deuteronomy 10:12

A gold rush that began in the 1970s made Boa Vista, Brazil, a boomtown on the edge of one of the world's richest gold fields. That changed when the gold mines were shut down. Government officials say the miners were destroying the rain forest, dumping mercury into the rivers, and bringing guns and diseases that killed thousands of local residents. Today Boa Vista is a "town of lost souls and frustrated adventurers too poor to return to their bleak beginnings."

Such was the picture of God's people exiled in Babylon. All they had were memories of the days when God's favor was on them. Jerusalem was in ruins because a blessed people had been exploiting the weak, not caring for the land entrusted to them (2 Chronicles 36:19–21), and going through the motions of worshiping God. The prophet Nehemiah confessed: "We have acted very corruptly against You, and have not kept the commandments" (Nehemiah 1:7).

God loved His people too much to let them continue harming themselves and others. By letting them "do time" in Babylon, He helped them see what can happen when a blessed people get caught up in a life that leaves God out of the picture. He'll do what it takes to help us see that as well! —MD

June 20

Read: Nehemiah 1:4–11

Biblical Truth

Personal Application

Prayer Requests

Answers to Prayer

God gives blessing to us so we can give glory to Him.

Read: Psalm 104:24–35

Biblical Truth

Personal Application

Prayer Requests

Answers to Prayer

BIRD SONG

Break forth in song, rejoice, and sing praises.
—Psalm 98:4

Why do birds sing? Birds sing "because they can and because they must," says David Rothenberg, a professor at the New Jersey Institute of Technology. "Songs are used to attract mates and defend territories, but the form is much more than function. Nature is full of beauty, and of music."

Birds sing because they have a syrinx instead of a larynx. The syrinx is the bird's voice box, an organ that lies deep in a bird's chest and is uniquely fashioned for song. That, at least, is the natural explanation for their gift.

But I ask again, why do birds sing? Because their Creator put a song in their hearts. Each bird is "heaven's high and holy muse," said John Donne, created to draw our hearts up to our Creator. They are reminders that He has given us a song that we may sing His praise.

So when you hear God's little hymn-birds singing their hearts out, remember to sing your own song of salvation. Lift up your voice—harmonious, hoarse, or harsh—and join with them in praise to our Creator, Redeemer, and Lord.

The birds of the air "sing among the branches," Israel's poet observes. "[Therefore] I will sing to the Lord as long as I live; I will sing praise to my God while I have my being" (Psalm 104:12, 33).
—DHR

All creation sings God's praise.

NO GRIPPING

Do all things without complaining and disputing.
—PHILIPPIANS 2:14

During my first week of Bible college, we had several days of orientation in which we were given a rule book to study. Several days later, during a meeting to discuss those rules, one student stood up and asked, "What is 'no gripping'? And why is it against the rules?"

He was referring to a statement in the rule book he had misread. Instead of "gripping," it read "griping"—complaining or grumbling.

A rule against griping is perfectly understandable. The cancer of a complaining spirit can undermine the spiritual and emotional health of an individual and can infect an entire group. This can result in discontent, frustration, and even rebellion.

Moses heard griping among God's people a mere three days after leading them from slavery into freedom (Exodus 15:24). Centuries later, Samuel felt the weight of griping as he sought to represent God to his generation (1 Samuel 8:4–9).

A complaining spirit can destroy the effectiveness of a church too. Paul wrote to the church at Philippi: "Do all things without complaining and disputing" (Philippians 2:14).

We need to avoid a complaining spirit when serving Christ. Instead, rejoice and thank God for all He has done! No griping allowed. —BC

June 22

Read: Philippians 2:12–18

Biblical Truth

Personal Application

Prayer Requests

Answers to Prayer

When you feel like griping, start counting your blessings.

June 23

Read: Psalm 128

Biblical Truth

Personal Application

Prayer Requests

Answers to Prayer

ALL OUT OF TEENAGERS

Your children [shall be] like olive plants all around your table.
—Psalm 128:3

For eighteen years our home was blessed by the presence of teenagers. But now that our youngest is in his twenties, my wife and I are all out of teenagers.

Those years were full of challenges and demands that sometimes zapped our strength and took all of our mental and emotional reserves. Along the way, we navigated the rough seas of the sudden death of one of our four teens. We also enjoyed the thrills of success and struggled through the turmoil of rebellion. As I look back on our experiment in parenting, we learned some valuable lessons:

- Some teens follow life in a straight line, while others zigzag along life's pathway. It's best to "zig" with them in love and with courage.
- All teens need unconditional love because they live in a conditional world.
- A love of God's Word is vital to successfully transferring faith from one generation to the next.
- Teens need to develop a relationship with Christ that is based not on rules but on a deep love of Jesus.

Has God placed any young people in your life? Whatever their age, love them unconditionally. Help them learn to love God's Word. Show them how to have a deep love for Jesus. And hold on! —DB

Don't merely spend time with your children—invest it.

FIRE MOUNTAIN

June 24

Be ready, for the Son of Man is coming at an hour you do not expect.
—Matthew 24:44

Read: Matthew 24:36–44

Rising 2,900 meters (9,600 ft.) above the rainforest in Indonesia's southern Java, Mount Merapi (the Fire Mountain) is one of the world's most dangerous volcanoes.

As the Fire Mountain showed signs of renewed activity, authorities tried to evacuate local residents. Then, on May 13, 2006, Merapi spewed a gray plume of sulfurous smoke from its crater. Amazingly, villagers ignored the signs and returned to tending their livestock, apparently forgetting that in 1994 Merapi had killed 60 people. It's our human tendency to ignore signs.

When Jesus left the temple at Jerusalem for the last time, His disciples asked what would signal His return to earth (Matthew 24:3). He told them many things to watch for, but warned that people would still be unprepared.

The apostle Peter told us that in the last days scoffers would say of Jesus' return: "Where is the promise of His coming? For since the fathers fell asleep, all things continue as they were from the beginning of creation" (2 Peter 3:4).

Scoffers are with us today, just as Peter warned. Are you among them? Or are you ready for the Lord Jesus to return? Ignoring these signs is even more dangerous than living in the shadow of the Fire Mountain. —CPH

Biblical Truth

Personal Application

Prayer Requests

Answers to Prayer

To ignore the Bible is to invite disaster.

June 25

Read: Ephesians 2:11–19

Biblical Truth

Personal Application

Prayer Requests

Answers to Prayer

ANYTIME, ANYWHERE

Through Him we both have access by one Spirit to the Father.
—Ephesians 2:18

When Mike Marolt is out of town, he remotely accesses the computer and files in his Aspen, Colorado, office. On a recent overseas trip, Marolt answered e-mails and kept in touch with his clients by using his laptop through a satellite phone hookup. This time, however, he was sitting in a base camp tent at 21,000 feet on the side of Mt. Everest. These days even that doesn't surprise us because we have become used to the technology that provides access to the rest of the world anytime, anywhere.

We can easily develop a similar lack of amazement toward prayer. Talk to God? Of course. We don't have to wait in line, enter a building, or wear nice clothing. We can pour out our hearts to the Lord anytime, anywhere. It's easy to lose the wonder of that because it has become so familiar.

Paul always seemed to marvel at the door opened wide into the presence of God. "In Christ Jesus you who once were far off have been brought near by the blood of Christ," he wrote. "For through Him we both [Gentiles and Jews] have access by one Spirit to the Father" (Ephesians 2:13, 18).

The door is open for everyone. God welcomes all who come by faith. Through Christ we can enter His presence—anytime, anywhere. Amazing! —DCM

There is no place or time we cannot pray.

ONE EXCEPTION

June 26

Which of you convicts Me of sin? And if I tell the truth, why do you not believe Me? He who is of God hears God's words.
—JOHN 8:46–47

Are there any perfect people alive today? Not in the opinion of Harvard University psychiatrist Jerome Groopman. In his engrossing book *How Doctors Think*, he expresses agreement with the profound insights found in the Bible. He writes: "Everyone is flawed at some time, in thought or in deed, from Abraham to Moses to the Apostles."

But what about Jesus Christ? He challenged His listeners regarding himself: "Which of you convicts Me of sin?" (John 8:46). The disciples' verdict after they had opportunity to scrutinize His life for at least three years was that He was without sin (1 Peter 2:22; 1 John 3:5).

Was Jesus a moral miracle, the one sinless Person in the whole procession of sinful humans? Yes, He was the one spotless exception to this observation of the apostle Paul: "All have sinned and fall short of the glory of God" (Romans 3:23). And that word *all* includes both you and me!

Because all humanity has sinned, we can rejoice that Jesus was qualified—He and He alone—to be the flawless Sacrifice we need.

We give thanks for Jesus Christ, our sinless sin-bearer—the one exception! —VCG

Read: Isaiah 53:4–12

Biblical Truth

Personal Application

Prayer Requests

Answers to Prayer

Only Jesus, the perfect sacrifice, can declare guilty people perfect.

June 27

Read: 2 Corinthians 12:7–10

Biblical Truth

Personal Application

Prayer Requests

Answers to Prayer

GOD'S GREATER GOAL

I pleaded with the Lord three times that it might depart from me.
—2 CORINTHIANS 12:8

I have an unmarried friend who prays earnestly for God to lessen or even remove his sexual drive. It causes him constant temptation. As gently as I can, I tell him I doubt that God will answer his prayer the way he wants. More likely, he will learn fidelity the way anyone learns it, by relying on discipline, community, and constant pleas of dependence.

For whatever reason, God has let this broken world endure in its fallen state for a very long time. God seems to value character more than our comfort, often using the very elements that cause us the most discomfort as His tools in fashioning that character. This was true in the life of the apostle Paul, who prayed fruitlessly that his mysterious "thorn in the flesh" be removed (2 Corinthians 12:8).

In my own life, I am trying to remain open to new realities, not blaming God when my expectations go unmet but trusting Him to lead me through failures toward renewal and growth. I am seeking a trust that "the Father knows best" in how this world is run. I see that the way in which I may want God to act does not achieve the results I might expect.

When God sent His own Son—sinless, full of grace and healing—we killed Him. God himself allows what He does not prefer, to achieve some greater goal. —PY

God uses our difficulties to develop His Son's likeness in us.

June 28

AMATEUR CHRISTIANS

The love of Christ compels us.
—2 Corinthians 5:14

The word *amateur* has been redefined over the years and has lost the luster of its original meaning. The English word comes from the Latin word *amore*, which means "to love." An amateur is someone who does something simply for the love of it.

In today's way of thinking, receiving payment moves you into a "higher" category—that of a professional. The reasoning is that if someone is willing to pay for your service, you must be really good. An amateur, therefore, is considered to have less skill or talent.

As I read my Bible, however, I see a different hierarchy of values. During the time of Jesus, the religious professionals were using their position to gain power and prestige for themselves, not to serve the people. Jesus didn't choose those who were wise, mighty, or noble by human standards (1 Corinthians 1:26). He sought those willing to follow Him and be trained for loving service.

In today's world, the scene is much the same. God is still looking for "amateurs," those who will serve the Lord for the sheer love of it. Compelled by our love for Jesus, may we, like the disciples and apostles before us, proclaim the love of God for the world by following Christ's example of loving and serving others. —JAL

Read: 1 Corinthians 1:18–31

Biblical Truth

Personal Application

Prayer Requests

Answers to Prayer

One proof of our love for God is our love for our neighbor.

June 29

Read: Psalm 51:1–13

Biblical Truth

Personal Application

Prayer Requests

Answers to Prayer

TRUE CONFESSIONS

Behold, I was brought forth in iniquity, and in sin my mother conceived me.
—Psalm 51:5

I love coconut. I always have. So, after an exhausting day in second grade, I found a bag of shredded coconut in the cupboard and devoured the whole thing. When my mother went into the kitchen later to bake—you guessed it, a coconut cake—I heard, "Who ate the coconut?!"

I knew I was in trouble, but my escape plan was simple—a quick, easy lie: "Not me!"

She continued her inquiry with my sisters, but after they denied it, we all heard the familiar words: "Wait till your dad comes home!" My cover-up plan was doomed to failure, and later that evening I finally confessed.

No one had to teach me to lie. As the psalmist David admits, "I was brought forth in iniquity" (Psalm 51:5). But in his sin David knew where to go—to the God of abundant mercy who will cleanse us from our sin (vv. 1–2).

When we recognize the ongoing reality of sin in our lives, we are reminded of our ongoing need for the presence of God and the power of His Word to keep us safe and spiritually sane. He is waiting for us to confess our faults and embrace the forgiveness and cleansing that He readily offers.

Remember, a refreshing plunge into God's mercy awaits you on the other side of confessed sin!
—JS

Own up to your sin and experience the joy of confession.

LASSA FEVER

Much more then, having now been justified by His blood, we shall be saved from wrath through Him.
—ROMANS 5:9

When Lily Pinneo, a missionary nurse, was in West Africa, she contracted a deadly disease called Lassa fever. After Lily was flown to New York for medical treatment, her temperature soared to 107°F. To reduce the fever, doctors packed her in ice and fed her intravenously. The fever subsided. After nine weeks, she had lost 28 pounds and most of her hair. Yet, somehow, she survived.

In a laboratory, Dr. Casals carefully isolated and analyzed the Lassa virus. But he too fell ill from his exposure to the disease. At the time, no known treatment was effective. Fortunately, Nurse Pinneo was convalescing and had built up antibodies to the dread disease. She donated blood plasma to Dr. Casals and he recovered too. Her blood saved his life.

All of us are infected with the fatal disease of sin (Romans 6:23). There is only one cure. It resides in the cleansing power of Jesus Christ's shed blood. Paul wrote: "Much more then, having now been justified by His blood, we shall be saved from wrath through Him" (Romans 5:9). The righteous wrath of God against transgression has been fully satisfied through Jesus' death in our place. All we need do is repent, recognize Him as our Savior, and receive the spiritual cure for sin. Have you made that decision?
—DF

June 30

Read: Romans 3:19–26

Biblical Truth

Personal Application

Prayer Requests

Answers to Prayer

The price of our freedom from sin was paid by Jesus' blood.

July

July 1

Read: 1 Timothy 6:17–19

Biblical Truth

Personal Application

Prayer Requests

Answers to Prayer

JOYFUL LIVING

Command those who are rich in this present age not to be haughty, nor to trust in uncertain riches but in the living God, who gives us richly all things to enjoy.
—1 Timothy 6:17

Our search for joy takes us many different directions. Dream holidays, shopping, food, clothes, friends, cars—the list is almost endless.

My guess is that if you perked up at the mention of shopping, holidays, or cars, you might have felt a twinge of guilt. We often view the joy of temporal things as less than spiritual and show our discomfort by apologizing for nice things: "I wouldn't have bought this, but someone gave me a wonderful deal." As if real Christians never eat quiche, drive cool cars, or wear designer clothes!

God's greatest gift to us is our relationship with His Son Jesus. It's a gift beyond comparison. Jesus promised that when we abide in Him we will experience the fulfillment of His joy (John 15:11), and without that kind of deep, abiding joy the rest of life is mundane at best.

But Scripture also casts the joy of the Lord in terms of temporal things. The enjoyment of "things" can be a positive spiritual experience. When we recognize that He "gives us richly all things to enjoy" (1 Timothy 6:17) and that "every good gift . . . is from above" (James 1:17), our hearts should be full of thankfulness and praise. This, in and of itself, is an act of worship! Enjoy the Giver and the gifts. —JS

Our heavenly Father delights in bringing us delight.

BEING AN AMBASSADOR

[God] has committed to us the word of reconciliation. Now then, we are ambassadors for Christ.
—2 Corinthians 5:19–20

After visiting a homeless shelter, a group of teenagers couldn't wait to express what they had experienced. Excitedly, they wrote about their visits with men and women of all ages who were poor and destitute.

One teen wrote: "I talked with a Vietnam vet and told him that in heaven he would have a new body. I was able to reassure him in his faith."

Another said, "A guy named Michael showed me that even though he was living in a homeless shelter, having faith made all the difference."

Still another wrote: "I talked with a man who had almost stopped believing in God. I tried to [encourage him in his faith]."

While desiring to share God's message of reconciliation, these teens were surprised to find that some of the people already knew God. By cutting through the discomfort of their differences, the kids discovered people who needed the reassurance that God still cared for them. The teens' roles changed from sharing the good news to guiding their new friends toward a deeper faith.

Being "ambassadors for Christ" (2 Corinthians 5:20) opens doors of opportunity both to share the gospel and to strengthen the struggling. Seek out someone today who needs encouragement or "the word of reconciliation" (v. 19). —DB

July 2

Read: 2 Corinthians 5:14–21

Biblical Truth

Personal Application

Prayer Requests

Answers to Prayer

A word of encouragement can make the difference between giving up and going on.

July 3

Read: Numbers 13:26–33

Biblical Truth

Personal Application

Prayer Requests

Answers to Prayer

WHAT, ME WORRY?

Be anxious for nothing, but in everything by prayer and supplication, with thanksgiving, let your requests be made known to God.
—PHILIPPIANS 4:6

Whenever a preacher begins to talk about worry, I sense a pair of eyes staring at me. Without even turning my head, I know that my husband is looking at me to see if I'm paying attention.

I hate to admit it, but I'm a worrier. And precisely because there are a lot of people just like me, Jesus addressed this problem in Matthew 6:25–34 when He said: "Do not worry." Don't worry about the basic needs of life—food, clothing, shelter—and don't worry about tomorrow.

Worry may be a symptom of a bigger problem. Sometimes it's a lack of gratitude for the way God has cared for us in the past. Or perhaps it's a lack of faith that God *really* is trustworthy. Or it may be a refusal to depend on God instead of ourselves.

Some people expand the worry circle to their families, friends, and churches. They're a lot like the ten spies in Numbers 13:26–33 who spread their fear and doubt to everyone else. But those who put their trust in God alone can stand alongside Joshua and Caleb, the only ones in the group of twelve whom God allowed to enter the Promised Land.

Don't let worries hold you back from what God may be trying to teach you. He invites you to bring your anxious thoughts directly to Him (Philippians 4:6). —CHK

To be anxious about nothing, pray about everything.

THE UNPAYABLE DEBT WE OWE

July 4

Stand fast therefore in the liberty by which Christ has made us free.
—GALATIANS 5:1

Our gratitude is deepened when we remember the price others paid to help obtain freedom. In the United States, one such person was Richard Stockton.

Stockton was one of the signers of the Declaration of Independence. He was a prominent lawyer and a wealthy landowner. Because he supported the war efforts, he and his family were driven from their home, which was sacked and burned. Stockton was imprisoned for several years and subjected to harsh treatment that broke his health. He died a pauper at the age of 51. Yet few Americans remember this hero who paid such a high price for the cause of liberty. His sacrifice is largely forgotten.

Even more important, have we become so familiar with the gospel that we fail to appreciate what our salvation cost the Savior? We rejoice in the spiritual freedom we enjoy by faith in the sin-canceling death of Jesus, but do we realize at least to some small degree the price He paid?

Are we truly grateful to Jesus for all He sacrificed to set us free spiritually? If so, we are to "stand fast . . . in the liberty by which Christ has made us free" (Galatians 5:1). No matter what else may be demanding our attention, let's take time to remember the unpayable debt we owe Him.
—VCG

Read: Galatians 5:1–14

Biblical Truth

Personal Application

Prayer Requests

Answers to Prayer

Salvation is infinitely costly but absolutely free.

July 5

Read: Matthew 25:31–40

Biblical Truth

Personal Application

Prayer Requests

Answers to prayer

FINDERS KEEPERS

Inasmuch as you did it to one of the least of these My brethren, you did it to Me.
—Matthew 25:40

People who find something of value are generally eager to keep it. In such cases, the notion of "finders keepers" seems like a good thing. But what if the thing we find is a problem? In that case, we're eager to give it up.

While working for the US Justice Department, Gary Haugen discovered a big problem. *Someone needs to do something about this,* he thought. He looked around for someone who could take on the injustice and abuse of authority he had uncovered. But then he realized that God was looking at *him*. Thus, in 1997 Haugen founded International Justice Mission to rescue victims of violence, sexual exploitation, slavery, and oppression.

Just as Moses was God's answer for the slavery of His people in Egypt (Exodus 3:9–10), so too Haugen and his team are becoming God's answer for those in slavery today. As Haugen says, "God doesn't have a Plan B. His plan is you. You are the answer."

God places us in unique circumstances where our abilities match the problem He wants to fix. Jesus said that what we do for those in need, we do for Him (Matthew 25:35–40).

Have you found a problem? How might you be God's solution? God may want you to be an answer to someone's prayer.
—JAL

When God shows you a problem, He may ask you to be His solution.

WHY BOTHER WITH CHURCH?

Let us consider one another in order to stir up love and good works, not forsaking the assembling of ourselves together.
—Hebrews 10:24–25

Winston Churchill once said that he related to the church rather like a flying buttress: He supported it from the outside. (A flying buttress is an external support that reinforces the walls of old cathedrals.) I tried that strategy for a while, after coming to believe Christian doctrine sincerely and committing myself to God.

I am not alone. Fewer people attend church on Sunday than claim to follow Christ. Some feel burned by a former experience. Others simply "get nothing out of church." Why bother?

Today, I could hardly imagine life without church. Church has filled a need for me that can't be met in any other way. An early-church leader wrote: "The virtuous soul that is alone . . . is like the burning coal that is alone. It will grow colder rather than hotter."

Christianity is not a purely intellectual, internal faith. It can be lived only in community. At a deep level, I sense that church contains something I desperately need. Whenever I abandoned church for a time, I found that I was the one who suffered. My faith faded, and the crusty shell of lovelessness grew over me again. I grew colder rather than hotter.

And so my journeys away from church have always circled back to the church. —PY

July 6

Read: Ephesians 4:1–16

Biblical Truth

Personal Application

Prayer Requests

Answers to Prayer

The church is not a select circle for a few but a spiritual center open to all.

July 7

Read: Exodus 11

Biblical Truth

Personal Application

Prayer Requests

Answers to Prayer

FATAL FRAME OF MIND

Moses and Aaron did all these wonders before Pharaoh; and the Lord hardened Pharaoh's heart, and he did not let the children of Israel go.
—Exodus 11:10

When Pharaoh refused to let the people of Israel leave Egypt, thousands of innocent Egyptians died because of his stubborn will. Perhaps the knowledge of what was about to happen to Egypt's firstborn on that first Passover night caused the great anger Moses felt as he left Pharaoh (Exodus 11:8). It was going to be a night of devastation and sorrow because the ruler was in a fatal frame of mind.

It's easy for me to condemn Pharaoh's willful disobedience to God, and very difficult to face my own. But this passage forces me to ask, "Is my attitude choking the life out of someone close to me?"

Oswald Chambers said: "The right of life is insisted on all through the Bible. As long as I do not murder anyone outright the law cannot touch me, but is there someone dependent on me to whom in the tiniest way I am not giving the right to live? Someone for whom I am cherishing an unforgiving dislike? 'Whosoever hateth his brother is a murderer' (1 John 3:15)."

Our hearts become hard through repeated refusals to yield to God. But they can be softened by obedience. When we say "yes" to God, the result is relief and life-giving release for our families, colleagues, and friends.

What's my frame of mind today? —DCM

The way of obedience is the way of blessing.

THE TIME MACHINE

With the Lord one day is
as a thousand years,
and a thousand years as one day.
—2 PETER 3:8

In 1896, H. G. Wells published a book titled *The Time Machine,* an imaginative tale of a scientist who builds a machine that can transport someone through time. The time traveler is preoccupied with the future, not the past. Like many scientists, he believes "progress" will enable the human race to build a better world. Yet in Wells's book, this science-fiction story does not have a happy ending.

The protagonist travels millions of years into the future. There the world has grown cold and dark. As a bleak snow falls, he sees the last remnants of life awaiting extinction. Thoroughly sickened by the twilight of life on our planet, the scientist returns to the time of his origin to report his anguish.

The biblical view of the future is very different. It tells us that God is Lord over time itself: "With the Lord one day is as a thousand years, and a thousand years as one day" (2 Peter 3:8). We can be optimistic about the future because God will replace our world with a new one. In that new heaven and new earth we will experience blessed fellowship with our Creator for eternity (Revelation 21:1–4). Even now, Jesus is preparing a place for those who love Him (John 14:1–3), a place where "there shall be no more death, nor sorrow, nor crying" (Revelation 21:4). —DF

July 8

Read: Revelation 21:1–4

Biblical Truth

Personal Application

Prayer Requests

Answers to Prayer

Jesus is preparing a place for us and preparing us for that place.

July 9

Read: Philippians 2:1–11

Biblical Truth

Personal Application

Prayer Requests

Answers to Prayer

A CHURCH THAT CARES

Let each of you look out not only for his own interests, but also for the interests of others.
—Philippians 2:4

While traveling together, my wife and I started talking with a delightful young woman we met. The time passed quickly as we chatted about lighthearted topics.

But when she heard that I was a minister, the conversation took a heart-wrenching turn. She began to share with us that when her husband left her only a few months earlier, she had struggled with the pain of that abandonment.

Then she smiled and said, "I can't tell you how much my church has meant to me these past months." Her mood and countenance changed dramatically as she recounted the ways her church family had wrapped their loving arms around her in her season of heartache. It was refreshing to hear how that local assembly had surrounded her with the love of Christ.

Far too often, it seems, we limit the significance of church to what happens on Sunday. But the church is to be so much more. It is to be a safe haven, a rescue station, a training center for spiritual service. It is particularly to be an expression of the concerned heart of the Lord for hurting, broken people, such as our young friend.

We are to "love one another," John the disciple reminded us, "for love is of God" (1 John 4:7). —BC

Hope can be ignited by a spark of encouragement.

DON'T LET IT GROW

July 10

***Looking carefully . . .
lest any root of bitterness
springing up cause trouble, and by
this many become defiled.***
—Hebrews 12:15

In June 1966, Rubin "Hurricane" Carter, a celebrated boxer, along with an acquaintance were convicted of murder in a highly publicized and racially charged trial. The boxer maintained his innocence and became his own jailhouse lawyer. After serving 19 years, Carter was released when the verdict was overturned. As a free man, he reflected: "Wouldn't anyone under those circumstances have a right to be bitter? . . . I've learned that bitterness only consumes the vessel that contains it. And for me to permit bitterness to control or infect my life in any way whatsoever would be to allow those who imprisoned me to take even more than . . . they've already taken."

I believe that bitterness is what the writer of Hebrews had in mind when he penned his warnings. In today's text, some of the Christians may have been considering returning to Judaism because of persecution and injustice. Like a small root that grows into a great tree, bitterness could spring up in their hearts and overshadow their deepest Christian relationships (12:15).

When we hold on to disappointment, a poisonous root of bitterness begins to grow. Let's allow the Spirit to fill us so He can heal the hurt that causes bitterness. —MW

Read: Hebrews 12:14–25

Biblical Truth

Personal Application

Prayer Requests

Answers to Prayer

Bitterness is a root that ruins the garden of peace.

July 11

Read: Galatians 3:26–29

Biblical Truth

Personal Application

Prayer Requests

Answers to Prayer

SAVOR THE FLAVOR

There is neither Jew nor Greek, there is neither slave nor free, there is neither male nor female; for you are all one in Christ Jesus.
—GALATIANS 3:28

America has often been called "a melting pot." But obviously that is not the case. Politicians tend to fuel sensitivity to class and color divisions for their own gain. Gender tensions abound. Generational differences are more marked than ever. In fact, cultural observers are starting to say that the "melting pot" metaphor is outdated—that the goal should be a cultural "stew" in which the distinct taste of each ingredient is enhanced by the contribution of the other ingredients.

In a world where pride and prejudice abound, Jesus offers us the joy of unity across all the lines that so easily divide us. In His church, the unique flavors of our diverse backgrounds can complement each other, united "through faith in Christ Jesus" (Galatians 3:26) and empowered by His Spirit and our submission to His principles. In Him our diversity doesn't divide; it unites and enriches us as we recognize that we all have Jesus, His Word, and His ways in common. As we embrace Him together, our differences become secondary and our mutual love for Him drives us to love each other as He has loved us.

Jesus is the master mixer! In His kingdom, pride and prejudice are out, and love and mutual acceptance are the order of the day. —JS

Christ's love creates unity in the midst of diversity.

MARRIAGE BEFORE LOVE

July 12

Live joyfully with the wife whom you love all the days of your . . . life which He has given you under the sun.
—ECCLESIASTES 9:9

A man went to his pastor for counseling. In his hands were pages of complaints against his wife. After hours of uninterrupted listening, the pastor couldn't help but ask, "If she is that bad, why did you marry her?" Immediately the man shot back, "She wasn't like this at first!" The pastor, unable to hold back his thoughts, asked, "So, are you saying that she is like this because she's been married to *you?*"

Whether or not this story is true, it does suggest an important lesson to be learned. At times, feelings toward a spouse may grow cold. But love is much more than feelings—it's a lifelong commitment.

Although most people choose to marry because of love, in some cultures people still get married through matchmaking. In the lives of Isaac and Rebekah, recorded in the book of Genesis, love came *after* marriage. It says in chapter 24 that Isaac married Rebekah and then he loved her (v. 67).

Biblical love is about our willingness to do what is good for another. Husbands are instructed to "love their own wives as their own bodies" (Ephesians 5:28).

So, walking in obedience to the Lord, let's keep our marriage vows to love "till death do us part." —AL

Read: Genesis 24:61–67

Biblical Truth

Personal Application

Prayer Requests

Answers to Prayer

Love is more than a feeling; it's a commitment.

July 13

Read: Galatians 6:6–10

Biblical Truth

Personal Application

Prayer Requests

Answers to Prayer

THE TIME OF ANYONE'S LIFE

Let us not grow weary while doing good, for in due season we shall reap if we do not lose heart.
—Galatians 6:9

What am I getting out of life? That's a question often asked by those who focus only on themselves. But as believers we need to ask: What am I putting into the lives of others?

Years ago, Dr. Wilfred Grenfell served as a medical missionary in Labrador. On a recruiting tour, he challenged nurses at Johns Hopkins Hospital to join him for a summer in his difficult ministry. He promised them hardship and discomfort. He warned that instead of earning a salary, they would have to pay their own expenses. But he also promised them they would experience joy because "it's having the time of anyone's life to be in the service of Christ."

A nurse who accepted that challenge wrote this after her return from Labrador: "I never knew before that life was good for anything but what one could get out of it. Now I know that the real fun lies in seeing how much one can put into life for others." If we change that word *fun* to *blessing*, we have the key to Christian self-fulfillment.

Take the apostle Paul's encouragement: "[Do] not grow weary while doing good . . . Do good to all" (Galatians 6:9–10). Put yourself into the lives of others for Jesus' sake. You'll experience a fulfillment beyond compare.
—VCG

We are at our best when we serve others.

July 14

LIVING SACRIFICE

Present your bodies a living sacrifice.
—Romans 12:1

Read: Romans 12:1–8

When my son Steve left home in the summer of 2006 to join the US Navy, he knew the gravity of his decision. He understood that once he walked onto that naval base for boot camp, he was giving up everything a teenager lives for. He was leaving behind his freedom, his guitars, his music, and his girlfriend. He surrendered the right to make his own choices and to do what he wanted to do. He said, in effect, "I am making myself a living sacrifice. I no longer do things for me; I do them for the service of my country."

The sacrifice Steve and thousands of others make when they enter the military service reminds me of what the apostle Paul taught in Romans 12:1. In that passage he urged us "to present [our] bodies a living sacrifice, holy, acceptable to God, which is your reasonable service." This means we are to give up our selfish ways and surrender ourselves completely to God. We are to seek to be "holy" in all we do—to have a godly character (1 Peter 1:16), which is acceptable to God.

It wasn't easy for Steve, who cherished self-determination, to give it all up for the Navy. But he did it. And it isn't easy for us to completely surrender our will to God. How can you and I be a living sacrifice for God today? —DB

Biblical Truth

Personal Application

Prayer Requests

Answers to Prayer

A life given fully to God is at the heart of true sacrifice.

July 15

Read: Isaiah 25:1–9

Biblical Truth

Personal Application

Prayer Requests

Answers to Prayer

SILENT HELPER

I will praise Your name, for You have done wonderful things.
—Isaiah 25:1

The discovery of penicillin revolutionized health care. Prior to the 1940s, bacterial infections were often fatal. Since then, penicillin has saved countless lives by killing harmful bacteria. The men who recognized its potential and developed it for widespread use won a Nobel Prize in 1945.

Long before the discovery of penicillin, other silent killers were at work saving lives by destroying bacteria. These silent killers are white blood cells. These hard workers are God's way of protecting us from disease. No one knows how many invasions they have stopped or how many lives they have saved. They receive little recognition for all the good they do.

The Lord gets similar treatment. He often gets blamed when something goes wrong, but He seldom gets credit for all the things that go right. Every day people get up, get dressed, drive to work or school or the grocery store, and return safely to their families. No one knows how many times God has protected us from harm. But when there is a tragedy, we ask, "Where was God?"

When I consider all the wonderful things that God does silently on my behalf each day (Isaiah 25:1), I realize that my list of praises should be much longer than my list of petitions. —JAL

God keeps giving us reasons to praise Him.

THE BIBLE GUY

Having then gifts differing according to the grace that is given to us, let us use them.
—ROMANS 12:6

When the youth group in Rich's church needed Bibles for study, he went on a search for more than 70 copies. He got what they needed, but he never stopped collecting and distributing Bibles.

People and businesses donate money; others give him new and used Bibles to share. The motto on the side of the van he uses for this ministry explains his simple desire: "Need a Bible? Ask me for one." Rich is an ordinary guy, a heating and plumbing technician, who carries on this ministry in his spare time. His nickname around his church is "the Bible guy."

Do you ever wish you could have a special ministry like Rich's? The Lord has given each of us at least one spiritual gift to use for His kingdom purposes. The apostle Paul lists several in 1 Corinthians 12 and Romans 12, and some are mentioned in 1 Peter 4:9–11.

If you don't know what gifts you have, volunteer for a ministry in your church that interests you, or meet a need you learn about. Then ask yourself if you saw God work through you and if you had joy as you served. Ask fellow believers if they think you're gifted in that area. And ask the Lord to help you determine where you fit in His plans.

The Lord wants to use you too.
—AC

July 16

Read: 1 Corinthians 12:4–11

Biblical Truth

Personal Application

Prayer Requests

Answers to Prayer

Christians who bury their gifts make a grave mistake.

July 17

Read: Luke 11:1–13

Biblical Truth

Personal Application

Prayer Requests

Answers to Prayer

WHY PRAY?

When [Jesus] had sent the multitudes away, He went up on the mountain by Himself to pray.
—Matthew 14:23

As a journalist, I have spent time with famous people who make me feel very small. When I am going to meet with someone like this, I rarely sleep well the night before and have to fight a case of nerves. I wonder what I would do if seated at a banquet next to, say, Albert Einstein or Mozart. Would I chitchat? Would I make a fool of myself?

In prayer I am approaching the Creator of all that is—someone who makes me feel immeasurably small. How can I do anything but fall silent in such presence? How can I believe that whatever I say matters to God?

The Bible sometimes emphasizes the distance between humans and God—and sometimes the closeness. Without question, though, Jesus himself taught us to count on the closeness. In His own prayers He used the word *Abba* (Daddy), an informal address that Jews had not previously used in prayer. A new way of praying was born.

Jesus understood better than anyone the vast difference between God and human beings. Yet He did not question the personal concern of God, who watches over sparrows and counts the hairs on our heads. He valued prayer enough to spend many hours at the task.

If I had to answer the question "Why pray?" in one sentence, it would be, "Because Jesus did."
—PY

If Jesus needed to pray, how can we do less?

LITTLE THINGS

The tongue is a little member and boasts great things.
—JAMES 3:5

July 18

Read: James 3:1–12

A mosquito is a tiny insect, but its potential for devastation is huge. When I was in the fifth grade, I was bitten by mosquitoes on both of my knees. The bites became infected and deteriorated into a threatening case of blood poisoning. For over a month, I was pricked repeatedly with penicillin shots, and my knees had to be lanced and drained twice daily to remove the infection. It was excruciatingly painful and quite terrifying for a ten-year-old kid. To this day, I carry scars on my knees from the numerous lancings. All because of something as tiny as a mosquito.

James, the half-brother of Jesus, warns us of another little thing that can also be very destructive. He says that even though the tongue is little, it boasts great things. It's like a small spark that sets a great forest on fire (James 3:5). Although the tongue is small, there is nothing small about the damage it can do. Words carry with them the power of healing or a destructive capacity far greater than the poison of any mosquito bite.

It is essential that we use our words with great wisdom and care. Consider carefully the words you choose. Will they be seasoned with the balm of grace or with the poison of anger?
—BC

Biblical Truth

Personal Application

Prayer Requests

Answers to Prayer

It is better to bite your tongue than to let it bite someone else.

July 19

Read: Jonah 4

Biblical Truth

Personal Application

Prayer Requests

Answers to Prayer

ELEPHANTS DOWN

On the seventh day you shall rest, that your ox and your donkey may rest.
—Exodus 23:12

When rainy-season storms caused flooding in a nature preserve in Thailand, seven elephant calves became unlikely victims. As they tried to ford a river at their usual crossing point, dangerous currents swept them over a 250-foot waterfall. Wildlife advocates said the loss could have been prevented. A spokesperson for the Thailand Wildlife Fund complained that the protective barriers, which had been built at the crossing where four other young elephants had died earlier, were useless.

Long before animal rights became a global issue, the story of Jonah shows the attention our Creator gives to all His creatures. As the story ends, the Lord expresses concern not only for the citizens of Nineveh but also for their livestock (Jonah 4:11). And earlier, God gave Moses laws that extended certain protections even to animals (Exodus 23:4–5, 12).

Though humans alone are made in the image of God, the story of Jonah and other Bible texts show a link between caring for people and animals. The Creator gives us reason to provide appropriate, though different, attention to both.

The conclusion seems clear: If God cares even for livestock, how can we ignore the needs of any person for whom His Son died?
—MD

God cares for us and calls us to care for His creation.

EXPIRATION DATE

In Your book they all were written,
the days fashioned for me.
—Psalm 139:16

July 20

Read: Psalm 139:7–18

Chuck Montague was undergoing an extended series of treatments at a cancer center far from home. Then his treatments were abruptly interrupted by another medical condition. But God answered prayer and removed this problem. Later, when Chuck testified in his church back home, he told of his gratitude for the prayers of God's people and the truths from His Word that had ministered to him and his wife, Janet.

At times Chuck had wondered whether or not he would survive. That thought drove him to the Scriptures, and he carefully read Psalm 139. His attention was drawn to verse 16, which says, "In Your book they were all written, the days fashioned for me, when as yet there were none of them." Before we were created, all of our days were "fashioned" by the Lord. "It lifted my spirit to know that my life is in God's hands," Chuck said. "Every jug of milk or can of tuna has an expiration date. Well, so have I . . . God's timing is best."

As we suffer illness or grow older, we naturally think more about death. If we're believers in Christ, we can be confident that death is an open door to eternal life with Jesus. With the psalmist David, we are comforted by the truth that the God who loves us knows our "expiration date."
—DCE

Biblical Truth

Personal Application

Prayer Requests

Answers to Prayer

God's timing is perfect—even in death.

July 21

Read: Isaiah 12

Biblical Truth

Personal Application

Prayer Requests

Answers to Prayer

DON'T BE AFRAID

Behold, God is my salvation,
I will trust and not be afraid.
— Isaiah 12:2

I have an ancient leaf blower that I use to clean up our patio. It sputters, rattles, smokes, emits irritating fumes, and is considered by my wife (and probably by my neighbors) to be excessively noisy.

But our old dog is utterly indifferent to the racket. When I start up the blower, she doesn't even raise her head, and only reluctantly moves when I blow leaves or dirt in her direction. That's because she trusts me.

A young man who occasionally mows our yard uses a similar blower, but his is *not* tolerated by our dog. Years ago, when she was a puppy, he teased her with the machine and she has never forgotten. Now, when the man enters the backyard, we have to put her in the house, because she growls, barks, and snarls at him. Same set of circumstances, but the hands that use the blower make all the difference.

So it is with us. Frightening circumstances are less troublesome if we trust the hands that control them. If our world and our lives were governed by a thoughtless and indifferent force, we would have good reason to fear. But the hands that control the universe—God's hands—are wise and compassionate. We can trust them in spite of our circumstances and not be afraid. —DHR

God is in control, so we have nothing to fear.

LOVE, INC

Whatever you do in word or deed, do all in the name of the Lord Jesus.
—Colossians 3:17

When I heard about the service agency called Love, INC, I assumed that meant Love, Incorporated. But it actually means Love, In the Name of Christ. The organization's goal is to mobilize churches to reach out to a hurting and needy world in the name of Christ.

Throughout history, people have said they're acting in Jesus' name, when in reality it was for their own advantage. During World War II, the horrors of the Holocaust were sometimes rationalized by those who labeled the Jews "Christ-killers." Today racist groups dare to use "Christian" in their name or literature while using violence and hatred to intimidate people.

The Word of God is so saturated with the word *love* that it's hard to imagine how anyone could justify doing hateful acts in the name of Christ. Love is at the core of the gospel: Jesus' sacrifice on the cross was motivated by God's love. "In this the love of God was manifested toward us, that God has sent His only begotten Son into the world, that we might live through Him" (1 John 4:9).

As grateful followers of Jesus, we are told to "do all in the name of the Lord Jesus" (Colossians 3:17). When we represent Him to other people in word and deed, they should see love, in the name of Christ. —CHK

July 22

Read: Colossians 3:12–17

Biblical Truth

Personal Application

Prayer Requests

Answers to Prayer

Though I bestow all my goods to feed the poor . . . but have not love, it profits me nothing. —1 Corinthians 13:3

July 23

Read: 2 Corinthians 4:7–18

Biblical Truth

Personal Application

Prayer Requests

Answers to Prayer

BETTER WITH AGE

Even though our outward man is perishing, yet the inward man is being renewed day by day.
—2 Corinthians 4:16

Some people are obsessed with physical fitness—daily workouts, vitamins, organic food—in spite of the fact that our bodies keep ticking away in inevitable decline. In our twenties and thirties we think we're invincible. But in the decades that follow, the eyesight starts to go, then the knees, then the mind. Let's face it, trying to ensure long-lasting physical health is like trying to stem the tide with a pitchfork!

And while it is true that the older we get the more we fail and weaken physically, it doesn't have to be that way spiritually. Believe it or not, it is possible to get better with age. It's what the apostle Paul meant when he said, "Even though our outward man is perishing, yet the inward man is being renewed day by day" (2 Corinthians 4:16).

Many of us fear aging with all the trouble it brings. But when we are gradually stripped of everything that props us up—whether wealth, independence, health, dignity, beauty, or all of the above—we are left with more and more of God. So, no matter how old you are, it's not too late to dig deep in God's Word and invest more and more time in your spiritual well-being. You'll see the payoffs, now and later. The older you get, the better you can become! —JS

To get better with age, get spiritually fit.

THE POWER IN MEEKNESS

July 24

In quietness and confidence shall be your strength.
—Isaiah 30:15

Niagara Falls is one of the most spectacular sights I have ever seen. The roar of six million cubic feet of water each minute makes it the most powerful waterfall in North America. Few people, however, know that more than 50 percent of the river's water is diverted, via four huge tunnels, before it reaches those falls. This water passes through hydroelectric turbines that supply power to nearby areas in the US and Canada before returning to the river well beyond the Falls.

Some would love to have others think of their lives like Niagara Falls—wild, spectacular, and loud. But power without control dissipates into useless energy. Moses thought he could use his royal power to deliver God's people from slavery. He misused his power by killing an Egyptian, which only dissipated his power because he lost the respect of his own people (Exodus 2:11–15). God had to teach him meekness (Numbers 12:3).

The meek prosper because they are the ones who have power under control. Our Lord said, "Blessed are the meek, for they shall inherit the earth" (Matthew 5:5).

You may be trying to live in this world by your own power. Let God teach you meekness so that you can live in, and depend on, His strength. —CPH

Read: Exodus 2:11–15; 3:7–12

Biblical Truth

Personal Application

Prayer Requests

Answers to Prayer

Nothing is stronger than strength under God's control.

July 25

Read: Psalm 59

Biblical Truth

Personal Application

Prayer Requests

Answers to Prayer

WHEELCHAIR RIDE

You have been my defense and refuge in the day of my trouble.
—Psalm 59:16

Ben Carpenter has muscular dystrophy and gets around in an electric wheelchair. One day as he was crossing an intersection, the light changed and a semi-truck caught the handles of Ben's wheelchair in its grille. Unaware of what had happened, the driver started down the road, and before long Ben was being pushed along at 50 miles per hour. Soon the rubber on the wheelchair's tires began to burn off.

Passersby saw the bizarre sight and phoned 911 to inform the police. When the truck driver pulled over, he was astonished to see what was attached to his truck's grille. Ben had a big scare but escaped without injury.

Sometimes we may feel as if our lives have been hijacked by unexpected circumstances. When David was invited to King Saul's court, he soothed the king's nerves by playing on his lyre. Then, unpredictably, the jealous king threw a spear at him. David found himself caught in a dangerous drama of pursuit in which King Saul tried to take his life. Yet David looked to God for immediate protection, and he ultimately received deliverance. Because of this experience he wrote of the faithfulness of God: "You have been my defense and refuge in the day of my trouble" (Psalm 59:16).

No matter what our trouble, God is there. —DF

When troubles call on you, call on God.

BOWLING A GOOGLEY

July 26

Do not think it strange concerning the fiery trial which is to try you . . . but rejoice to the extent that you partake of Christ's sufferings.
—1 Peter 4:12–13

George Bernard Shaw once said, "England and America are two countries separated by a common language." An example from the world of sports demonstrates his point.

As a lifelong baseball fan, I'm familiar with the term *curveball.* It's a ball thrown by the pitcher in such a way that it changes direction, fooling the opponent. In cricket, the strategy is similar but the word is very different. The bowler (pitcher) tries to overcome the batsman by "bowling a googley" (pitching a curveball).

Though games and cultures differ, the concept of the curveball portrays a reality familiar in any language. Life is full of times when we are unsuspectingly "bowled a googley," and we find ourselves overwhelmed. In those moments of fear and confusion, it's comforting to know we have a God who is sufficient for any challenge.

Trials are to be expected (1 Peter 4:12), and we may well be shocked by the circumstances facing us. But God is never surprised! He permits our trials, and He can enable us to respond to them in a way that honors Him.

When we suffer, we must "commit [our] souls to Him in doing good," wrote Peter (v. 19). In God's strength, we can face life's most troublesome curveballs. —BC

Read: 1 Peter 4:12–19

Biblical Truth

Personal Application

Prayer Requests

Answers to Prayer

Nothing surprises God.

July 27

Read: Matthew 5:43–48

Biblical Truth

Personal Application

Prayer Requests

Answers to Prayer

THE REVISABLE EDITION

All Scripture is given by inspiration of God, and is profitable . . . for instruction in righteousness.
—2 TIMOTHY 3:16

Randall Peterson, a retired autoworker, thinks there could be an interest for a new kind of Bible. He sarcastically says that a publisher ought to create an electronic Bible that would allow for editing from the pew. That way individuals and churches could make the Bible say what they want it to say. He says it could be called the "LAME" Bible: "Locally Adaptive Multifaith Edition" and "could be sold to any church regardless of what it believes."

He's making a point, of course, but we might be tempted by such a product. Jesus gives us some hard teachings! As believers, our desire is to be obedient to Him in our choices and attitudes, but at times we resist the Word of God and may wish we could soften His commands.

Some of Jesus' hard teachings are found in the Sermon on the Mount. In Matthew 5, He says: "Love your enemies, bless those who curse you, do good to those who hate you, and pray for those who spitefully use you and persecute you" (v. 44). That's what He tells us to do, so we know we can't just delete it. We need to apply it to our personal situation with the Holy Spirit's enablement.

God's Word is to be obeyed by His people. We're the ones who need to be "revised"—not the Scriptures. —AC

To love God is to obey God.

DESPERATE FOR ANSWERS

When you come into the land which the Lord your God is giving you, you shall not learn to follow the abominations of those nations.
—Deuteronomy 18:9

A popular afternoon television program a few years ago was hosted by a self-proclaimed medium. He supposedly received messages from spirits of the dead to give to their family members in his studio audience. His readings prompted many people to believe in this occultic practice.

We live in a culture where people are desperate to know their future, and they'll turn to psychics and mediums for answers—a practice expressly forbidden in the Scriptures.

The ancient Israelites were desperate to know their future, and God knew that they would be tempted to consult ungodly sources for answers. So He warned them to stay away from mediums and those who contact the dead (Leviticus 19:26, 31; 20:27; Deuteronomy 18:9–14).

God knew that these practices would prevent ancient Israel from being a holy, set-apart people who would be a blessing to all nations. The future for Israel was determined by their faithfulness to God's covenant, not the words of soothsayers and psychics. Reliance on these evil practices indicated a failure to trust the Lord with their lives.

When you are desperate for information about your future, turn to the sovereign God of heaven. He is the only One who holds the answers you seek. —MW

July 28

Read: Deuteronomy 18:9–14

Biblical Truth

Personal Application

Prayer Requests

Answers to Prayer

The what of our future is determined by the Who of eternity.

July 29

Read: Philippians 1:9–18

Biblical Truth

Personal Application

Prayer Requests

Answers to Prayer

THE SIGN

Some indeed preach Christ even from envy and strife, and some also from goodwill.
—Philippians 1:15

A pastor friend told me about a sign he had seen in front of a neighborhood church. Instead of just advertising the congregation's own time of worship, the sign also listed the schedule for two other churches that met at different times in the same small town. Interestingly, my friend didn't think this was impractical or foolish. Instead, he imagined what it must do for a church to put such unselfishness at the heart of everything it did!

Whether it is a good idea to advertise the worship times of other churches is a matter of opinion. But one thing is certain—the Spirit of Christ is not found in a spirit of envy and self-serving competition. The generosity and goodwill that Paul expressed toward self-serving church leaders is a mark of the authentic Christian spirit (Philippians 1:14–18). This Christlike attitude lines up with the absence of spiritual competition that James called for in his epistle (James 3:14–17).

Churches ought to be concerned about building their congregations. But beware of setting the bar too low by worrying about numbers. The wisdom and grace of Christ are not necessarily found in conventional wisdom. Good judgment often requires that we perform counter-intuitive acts of unselfishness that reflect Jesus' life in us. —MD

Nothing is more pleasing to God than self-sacrifice that grows out of obedience.

SNAPSHOTS OF TIME

July 30

Teach us to number our days, that we may gain a heart of wisdom.
—Psalm 90:12

Read: Psalm 90:1–12

The designers of an innovative Web site call their creation a "snapshot" of our world. Every hour, computers monitor international news sources, select the most frequently occurring words and pictures, then display them as an interactive image. Over time, these hourly snapshots compose a mosaic of unfolding world events.

If a computer could track our words and actions, what would a snapshot of yesterday reveal? Over the weeks and months, what patterns would emerge? And what theme would dominate the final mosaic of our lives?

Psalm 90, a prayer of Moses the man of God, is a powerfully honest look at the brevity and significance of life. The writer compares an entire lifetime to a dream or a blade of grass, and cries out to God: "So teach us to number our days, that we may gain a heart of wisdom" (v. 12). Our days often seem so insignificant, yet they add up to so much. *The Message* renders verse 12: "Teach us to live wisely and well." It is a prayer for the snapshots of life with the final image in view.

When all the pictures of our life are complete, what story will they tell? It's worth considering as we make our choices each day.
—DCM

Biblical Truth

Personal Application

Prayer Requests

Answers to Prayer

It's not how long you live that counts, but how you live.

July 31

Read: Hebrews 4:1–7

Biblical Truth

Personal Application

Prayer Requests

Answers to Prayer

ARE YOU READY?

Today, if you will hear His voice, do not harden your hearts.
—Hebrews 4:7

It was a wild night for our family. At 11:30 p.m. I got a call from my son Steve. "Dad, I'm going to Iraq."

"Right now?" I asked in disbelief. "Yes, I'm ready to go." Earlier that day, our Navy corpsman (medic) son had told me he thought it would be several months before he would go.

We talked a little more until he had to hang up. Then family phone calls followed as we let his sisters know what was happening. They called him to wish him well and pray for him—and that was it.

A couple of restless hours later, Steve sent a text message: "We're not going. We're headed back." A helicopter ride to another state and back was the extent of Steve's trip that night, but it was still a valuable experience. It tested their readiness. The military had to know that when the call came, the corpsmen would be mentally ready to go.

When it comes to being ready for eternity, we won't get that kind of practice. No one knows when we will depart this earth through death or be called home at Jesus' return.

If you were called into eternity today, would you be prepared to meet God face-to-face? Have you opened your heart to Him (Hebrews 4:7)? Are your sins forgiven? Are you ready to go? —DB

God's call may come at any time—so be ready all the time!

August

August 1

Read: John 3:1–8

Biblical Truth

Personal Application

Prayer Requests

Answers to Prayer

THE MIDWIFE'S TALE

The wind blows where it wishes . . . So is everyone who is born of the Spirit.
—John 3:8

Historian Laurel Ulrich received a Pulitzer Prize for her book *The Midwife's Tale*. The book was based on the diary of Martha Ballard, who lived during the American Revolution. Martha was a midwife who traveled by canoe, horse, or sometimes on foot to assist women in delivering their babies. At a time when many women died in childbirth, Martha's record was extraordinary. In more than 1,000 deliveries, she never lost a mother in childbirth.

In God's kingdom there is a spiritual Helper who produces new life. But His role is to bring about "second birth" (John 3:5–8). The Holy Spirit uses a variety of ways to accomplish this. He convicts the world of sin (John 16:8), empowers the gospel (1 Thessalonians 1:5), regenerates us from within (Titus 3:5), and places believers into eternal union with Christ (1 Corinthians 12:12–13). Though He is invisible, His life-changing activity can be clearly seen.

Jesus said of the Holy Spirit: "The wind blows where it wishes, and you hear the sound of it, but cannot tell where it comes from and where it goes. So is everyone who is born of the Spirit" (John 3:8).

The Spirit desires to use us in sharing the gospel so others can experience that second birth.
—DF

The Holy Spirit is the Christian's source of power.

THEY ARE THE PROBLEM

He who glories, let him glory in the Lord.
—2 CORINTHIANS 10:17

Researchers from Virginia Tech University, along with police administrators, recently determined that distracted drivers put others in more danger than aggressive drivers. Drivers who eat, discipline children in the backseat, or talk on the phone are the most hazardous.

When residents in Grand Rapids, Michigan, were asked about the bad habits of drivers that made the highways unsafe, most felt that *others* caused more problems than they themselves. One woman said that she talked on her cell phone a little, but at least she didn't dial the phone numbers while on the road. She concluded her comments by stating that *others* "aren't following the rules of the road . . . *They* put us all at risk."

It's our nature to point a finger at others. The apostle Paul talked about fellow teachers who avoided looking at their own behavior and instead attacked him (2 Corinthians 10:12–18). He wrote, "They, measuring themselves by themselves . . . are not wise" (v. 12).

When we don't look at our own actions but instead compare ourselves with others, we often come out looking good. But, as Paul said, it's the Lord's commendation that counts, not our own approval of ourselves (v. 18).
—AC

August 2

Read: 2 Corinthians 10:12–18

Biblical Truth

Personal Application

Prayer Requests

Answers to Prayer

If you must compare yourself with someone, compare yourself with Christ.

August 3

Read: 1 Corinthians 10:1–11

Biblical Truth

Personal Application

Prayer Requests

Answers to Prayer

TELL ME THE STORY

All these things happened to them as examples, and . . . for our admonition.
—1 Corinthians 10:11

Now that I have grandkids, I'm back into the classic children's Bible stories. Wide-eyed stories like David and Goliath, Noah's ark, and Jonah and the big fish quickly capture a child's imagination!

But there's a danger here—not with the stories themselves but with our attitude toward them. If we view them simply as kids' stories, kind of like the Grimm's Fairy Tales of the Bible, we miss the point.

The stories of the Bible were never meant to be outgrown. There are profound lessons to be learned from the amazing accounts of those who faced giants, floods, and fish!

Hundreds of years after the fact, the apostle Paul explained that the things that happened to Moses and the Israelites as they wandered through the desert "happened to them as examples, and they were written for our admonition" (1 Corinthians 10:11). These stories are about us. They mirror the tensions we face daily as we too seek to apply God's will and ways to the realities of our lives. They teach us of the treachery of sin, our desperate need to trust God unflinchingly, and the importance of staying faithful and true to Him regardless of what happens.

Don't ignore the old stories. You might be surprised what God wants to teach you through them.
—JS

Stories from the past can give us pointers for the present.

A PLACE TO STAND

August 4

No other foundation can anyone lay than that which is laid, which is Jesus Christ.
—1 Corinthians 3:11

Read: 1 Corinthians 3:10–15

While taking a break during a ministry trip, we were snorkeling in the Caribbean Sea. The boat that had taken us to the deep water for better sites had gone back to shore, and I began to feel panicky about being in the open water. Finding it hard to control my breathing, I asked my son-in-law Todd and a friend, Dave Velzen, for help. They held my arms while I searched for an outcropping of coral close enough to the surface for me to stand on. Once I had a place to stand, even though surrounded by deep waters, I was okay.

Are you feeling a bit panicky about events in your life? Maybe it seems as if you are surrounded by the open waters of relationship problems, or money woes, or simply an inability to put your life in order. Perhaps you feel as if you are drowning in a sea of trials and trouble.

May I suggest two things? First, find a fellow Christian or two who can come beside you and hold you up, pray for you, talk with you, and remind you that you are not alone (see Ecclesiastes 4:10). Then rest your feet on the only solid foundation in life: Jesus Christ (1 Corinthians 3:11).

Life's troubles are too tough to take on alone. Get some help and find in Jesus a place to stand.
—DB

Biblical Truth

Personal Application

Prayer Requests

Answers to Prayer

Build your life on the solid foundation—Jesus Christ.

August 5

Read: Psalm 88

Biblical Truth

Personal Application

Prayer Requests

Answers to Prayer

SPIRITUAL THERAPY

Lord, why do You cast off my soul? Why do You hide Your face from me?
—PSALM 88:14

I once wrote a book titled *Disappointment with God.* My publishers worried that it seemed heretical to introduce a book with such a title into Christian bookstores. In the process of writing it, however, I found that the Bible includes detailed accounts of people sorely disappointed with God. Job and Moses had it out with God, as did Habakkuk, Jeremiah, and many of the unnamed psalmists.

It seems strange for sacred writings to include scenes of spiritual failure, but this reflects an important principle. A marriage therapist will warn couples, "Your relationship may get worse before it gets better." Misunderstandings must be exposed before true understanding can flourish. The psalmists do not rationalize anger or give abstract advice about pain; rather, they express emotions vividly and loudly, directing their feelings primarily at God. The anguished conclusion of Psalm 88 provides ample evidence (vv. 13–18).

The psalms present a mosaic of spiritual therapy in process. Doubt, paranoia, giddiness, delight, hatred, joy, praise, vengefulness, betrayal—you find it all in the psalms. From them I learn to bring to God whatever I feel about Him. I need not paper over my failures; far better to bring my weaknesses to Him, who alone has the power to heal. —PY

An honest talk with God is the first step in finding peace of mind.

THE APPRENTICE

August 6

As I was with Moses,
so I will be with you.
—Joshua 1:5

Read: Joshua 1:1–7

When some employers were asked what makes a good apprentice, they responded that they seek to hire "someone who wants to learn."

In the Bible, a good example of an apprentice is Joshua. We remember Joshua for marching around the wall of Jericho. He also had some important responsibilities as a spy (Numbers 13:16) and as a warrior (Exodus 17:10). But he was often in the shadow of someone else—Moses. For 40 years, Joshua served as Moses' assistant, aide, and apprentice (Exodus 24:13).

God takes His own time to prepare us for service. Sometimes that period of waiting is as valuable as learning all the needed strategies and goals. Joshua observed Moses' faith in God. He learned what it meant to be humble (Numbers 12:3), how to take instruction (Exodus 17:10), and how to be a true servant of God (Joshua 1:1; 24:29). Even a display of Moses' temper (Numbers 20:7–12) was an opportunity to watch and learn. By spending time with Moses, Joshua learned things that couldn't be learned from a book.

Joshua's own time to lead was coming. And when it came, he was able to trust God's promise to him: "As I was with Moses, so I will be with you. I will not leave you nor forsake you" (Joshua 1:5).
—CHK

Biblical Truth

Personal Application

Prayer Requests

Answers to Prayer

A person who is not willing to follow is not prepared to lead.

August 7

Read: Romans 8:12–17

Biblical Truth

Personal Application

Prayer Requests

Answers to Prayer

GOD'S TRAINING SCHOOL

[We are] heirs of God and joint heirs with Christ, if indeed we suffer with Him.
—Romans 8:17

Lew Wallace's book *Ben-Hur* tells the story of a Jewish aristocrat betrayed by his best friend and condemned to serve as a galley slave in the Roman navy. On a forced march to the ship, Judah Ben-Hur meets Jesus of Nazareth, whose compassion fills him with hope. Eventually, Ben-Hur saves the Roman commander during battle. In gratitude, the commander adopts Ben-Hur as his son, instantly elevating him from slave to heir.

That's what happens to us when God adopts us into His family. But great privilege brings great responsibility. Paul said that we become "heirs of God and joint heirs with Christ, if indeed we suffer with Him" (Romans 8:17). The gospel does not say, "Come to Jesus and live happily ever after." God's syllabus for His children's education includes training through hardships.

Ben-Hur's years of enduring hardship as a Roman slave strengthened him and increased his endurance, and he eventually defeated his "friend-turned-enemy" in a chariot race.

As endurance and training were key to Ben-Hur's victory, so are they vital to victory in the Christian's war with sin and evil. The hard times we endure are God's way to prepare us for greater service for His glory.
—CPH

We conquer by continuing.

August 8

THE GREATEST RACE

Love never fails.
—1 Corinthians 13:8

As the Olympic Games opened in Beijing in 2008, my thoughts went back to Eric Liddell, a former champion immortalized for his surprising gold medal victory in the 400 meters during the 1924 Games in Paris. A year after his triumph, Liddell went to China, where he spent the last 20 years of his life as a missionary teacher and rural pastor. There he ran the greatest race of his life against opponents we all know—difficult circumstances, war, uncertainty, and disease.

Crowded into a Japanese internment camp with 1,500 other people, Eric lived out the words he had paraphrased from 1 Corinthians 13:6–8: "Love is never glad when others go wrong. Love finds no pleasure in injustice, but rejoices in the truth. Love is always slow to expose, it knows how to be silent. Love is always eager to believe the best about a person. Love is full of hope, full of patient endurance; love never fails."

Eric served the others in camp, whether carrying water for the elderly or refereeing games for the teens. When he died of a brain tumor in February 1945, one internee described him as a man "who lived better than he preached."

In life's most difficult race, Eric Liddell crossed the finish line victorious through love. —DCM

Read: 1 Corinthians 13

Biblical Truth

Personal Application

Prayer Requests

Answers to Prayer

Love enables us to walk fearlessly, to run confidently, and to live victoriously.

August 9

Read: Ephesians 5:8–14

Biblical Truth

Personal Application

Prayer Requests

Answers to Prayer

OPEN THE SHUTTERS

Walk as children of light.
—EPHESIANS 5:8

Have you heard of the 17th-century theologian Samuel Rutherford? Perhaps it's time to resurrect his faith-inspiring memory.

Rutherford, a member of the council that wrote the Westminster Confession, was imprisoned because of his beliefs. While in prison, he wrote this soul-strengthening letter expressing the joy that sustained him through his trials: "If God had told me some time ago that He was about to make me as happy as I could be in this world, and then had told me that He should begin by crippling me in all my limbs, and removing me from all my usual sources of enjoyment, I should have thought it a very strange mode of accomplishing His purpose. And yet, how is His wisdom manifest even in this! For if you should see a man shut up in a closed room, idolizing a set of lamps and rejoicing in their light, and you wished to make him truly happy, you would begin by blowing out all his lamps; and then throw open the shutters to let in the light of heaven."

When the candles that light up our darkness are blown out, let's rejoice that God is throwing open shuttered windows and pouring in the sunshine of His love.

Like Samuel Rutherford, let's "walk as children of light" (Ephesians 5:8). —VCG

We value the light more fully after we've come through the darkness.

THE EYE OF GOD

August 10

The eyes of the Lord run to and fro throughout the whole earth, to show Himself strong on behalf of those whose heart is loyal to Him.
—2 Chronicles 16:9

The Hubble Space Telescope has taken photos of the Helix Nebula. Some astronomers describe it as "a trillion-mile-long tunnel of glowing gases." At its center is a dying star that has ejected dust and gas stretching toward its outer rim. Remarkable photos of it look like the blue iris of a human eye complete with eyelids. Because of this, some have called it the "Eye of God."

Although this nebula is not literally the eye of God, the Scriptures do talk about God's gaze on our lives. The prophet Hanani said, "The eyes of the Lord run to and fro throughout the whole earth, to show Himself strong on behalf of those whose heart is loyal to Him" (2 Chronicles 16:9).

This proclamation of God's all-seeing eye was given in response to King Asa's reliance upon another ruler for military security. Asa seemed to have forgotten that it was the Lord God, not mere soldiers, who had given him past victories over his enemies (2 Chronicles 14:11–12). This spiritual disloyalty did not escape the notice of God, who seeks to pour out blessing on acts of obedience to Him.

Although we cannot see the eyes of God, we can be assured that He sees us. His desire is to show himself strong to those who are loyal to Him with their whole heart. —DF

Read: 2 Chronicles 16:7–14

Biblical Truth

Personal Application

Prayer Requests

Answers to Prayer

To know that God sees us brings both conviction and comfort.

August 11

Read: 1 Corinthians 9:19–27

Biblical Truth

Personal Application

Prayer Requests

Answers to Prayer

TRUE TEAMWORK

They [train] to obtain a perishable crown, but we for an imperishable crown.
—1 Corinthians 9:25

Sports bring out the best and the worst in people. The news media often focus on the worst. Those who comfort players with "It's not whether you win or lose that counts; it's how you play the game" seldom make world news. But once in a while they do.

After a baseball team from Georgia defeated a team from Japan in the Little League World Series, one reporter wrote: "The boys from Warner Robins left a lasting impression of their inner character for the world to see. They proved again, it's not whether you win or lose that counts. It *is* how you play the game."

When the losing players broke down in tears, the winning team members stopped their victory celebration to console them. "I just hated to see them cry," said pitcher Kendall Scott, "and I just wanted to let them know that I care." Some referred to the moment as "sportsmanship at its best."

It was indeed heartwarming, but it points out that sports—even at its best—is an imperfect metaphor for Christianity. In sports, someone always loses. But when someone is won to Christ, the only loser is Satan.

For Christians, true teamwork is not about defeating opponents; it's about recruiting them to join our team (1 Corinthians 9:19–22). —JAL

Tact is the knack of winning a point without making an enemy.

"THIS IS IT!"

August 12

The Lord Himself will descend from heaven . . . Then we who are alive and remain shall be caught up . . . to meet the Lord in the air.
—1 Thessalonians 4:16–17

Have you ever had a time when you thought the Lord was coming back right then? Many believers in Jesus are so eager to "meet the Lord in the air," as Scripture puts it (1 Thessalonians 4:17), that they have felt "This is it!" at one time or another.

My wife, Sue, who once worked in a Christian nursing home, recalls being aboard an elevator at the facility when she had "second coming" thoughts. She had closed the door and started up to the second floor when the elevator came to a halt. Sue was stuck between floors. As she waited, there was a jolt and a quick flash of light—and then nothing again.

Sue recalled later that the power of the light and movement startled her and made her think that something unusual was happening. In that moment, her mind went toward the much-anticipated return of Jesus. It was a "This is it!" moment.

Whether we have experienced this feeling is not important. What is absolutely vital is that we know we are ready at any time for the Lord's return. If we have received Jesus as our Savior, we will find ourselves anticipating with excitement His appearing—eager to "stir up love and good works" in one another as we "see the Day approaching" (Hebrews 10:24–25). —DB

Read: 1 Thessalonians 4:13–17

Biblical Truth

Personal Application

Prayer Requests

Answers to Prayer

Christ's second coming is as certain as His first.

August 13

Read: Exodus 15:22–27

Biblical Truth

Personal Application

Prayer Requests

Answers to Prayer

THE SAME HAND

He cried out to the Lord, and the Lord showed him a tree. When he cast it into the waters, the waters were made sweet.
—Exodus 15:25

The children of Israel had not gone far from the shore of the Red Sea when the realities of their new freedom began to register. They no longer enjoyed the ample food and water supply of Egypt. Now, after traveling three days into the wilderness, the large crowd had no water. And when they finally arrived at the oasis of Marah, the water was bitter (Exodus 15:23).

Thus the children of Israel were compelled to rely on a miracle. So they cried out to Moses, and Moses cried out to the Lord. The Lord showed him a tree, which Moses cast into the water. Miraculously, the water turned sweet.

The transformation of the water was a miracle akin to the plague of blood sent to Pharaoh and the Egyptians (Exodus 7:14–25). Egypt's clean water had been sullied with blood by the hand of the Lord. The lesson of Marah was clear: the same hand that turned water into blood could turn bitter water into sweet. The same power that brought curses on Egypt could bring health to Israel.

If you have a seemingly impossible need today, remember that the hand that supplied your greatest need—forgiveness of sin—is the same hand that can adequately supply *all* your needs. Trust Him to accomplish things that seem impossible. —MW

Impossibilities compel us to rely on God.

FEED MY SHEEP

Do you love Me? . . .
Feed My sheep.
—JOHN 21:17

Just before Jesus left this earth, He instructed Simon Peter to care for the dearest object of His love—His sheep. How could anyone care for them as Jesus cares? Only out of love for Him. There is no other way.

Three times Jesus asked Peter, "Do you love Me?" Peter answered, "Yes, Lord. You know that I love You." Each time, Jesus answered, "Feed My sheep."

Was Jesus unaware of Peter's love? Of course not. His threefold question was not for himself, but for Peter. He asked His questions to underscore the essential truth that only love for Christ would sustain Peter in the work that lay ahead: the arduous, demanding work of caring for people's souls—perhaps the hardest work of all.

Jesus did not ask Peter if he loved His sheep, but if he loved *Him*. Affection for God's people in itself will not sustain us. His sheep can be unresponsive, unappreciative, and harshly critical of our efforts to love and to serve them, and in the end, we will find ourselves defeated and discouraged.

The "love of Christ"—our love for Him—is the only sufficient motivation that will enable us to stay the course, to continue to feed the flock of God. Thus Jesus asks you and me, "Do you love Me? Feed My sheep." —DHR

August 14

Read: John 21:15–17

Biblical Truth

Personal Application

Prayer Requests

Answers to Prayer

It is love for Christ that will enable us to love His children.

August 15

Read: Acts 28:1–10

Biblical Truth

Personal Application

Prayer Requests

Answers to Prayer

GATHERING STICKS

Through love serve one another.
—Galatians 5:13

A painful illness had prevented Bible teacher Billy Walker from carrying on his active schedule for several months. He told a group of men that he especially missed being able to preach, but that God was teaching him throughout his recovery.

One day during his illness, as he meditated and prayed, Billy's attention was drawn to the passage about Paul's shipwreck on Malta recorded in Acts 28. The great apostle to the Gentiles, preacher to thousands, worker of miracles, and writer of much of the New Testament, was stuck on an island as a prisoner. Did he lie back and bemoan his condition? Did he think he should be treated better than others because he was an apostle? No! The Scriptures tell us that he chose to contribute to the work and needs of his fellowmen. It was cold and rainy, so Paul "gathered a bundle of sticks" for a much-needed, warming fire (v. 3).

Perhaps you've been set aside for a while due to difficult circumstances. Maybe you've reached the time in your life when vigorous activity is no longer possible. Don't despair. Remember Paul's example, and do what you can do—even if it's simply "gathering sticks." —DCE

God never puts you in the wrong place to serve Him.

August 16

CHIP OFF THE OL' BLOCK

Be imitators of God as dear children.
—Ephesians 5:1

I'll never forget the time I was asked to bring my family to a banquet where I was to be the speaker. After dinner, my son Matt came up to me and asked to sit on my lap. "Sure," I said and picked him up.

Over the course of his young life, Matt had watched me strike up conversations with lots of strangers. As an unrepentant people-person, in restaurants I would often look at the server's name tag and start my order with, "Hey, Barbara, how are you today?" To which my kids would inevitably say, "Dad, you embarrass us!"

But now, sitting on my lap, Matt turned to the "big-shot" organizer of the banquet next to me, read his name tag, and stuck out his little hand, saying, "Hey, John, how are you?" A proud moment for me! He was acting just like his dad—a chip off the ol' block!

This is exactly what Paul had in mind when he exhorted us to "be imitators of God" (Ephesians 5:1). But life has a way of making us anything but like God. We are often uncaring, short-tempered, grumpy, and unforgiving—flat-out too much like ourselves and not enough like Him!

Remember, we are saved to bear the family resemblance, to become increasingly more like Jesus and less like ourselves.
—JS

Read: Ephesians 5:1–5

Biblical Truth

Personal Application

Prayer Requests

Answers to Prayer

Every child of God should have a growing likeness to the Father.

August 17

Read: Psalm 84

Biblical Truth

Personal Application

Prayer Requests

Answers to Prayer

IN GOD'S HOUSE

My soul longs, yes, even faints for the courts of the Lord.
—Psalm 84:2

Tobias, who recently turned three, loves to go to church. He cries when he isn't able to attend. Each week when he arrives for the children's program of Bible stories, games, singing, and dinner, he runs into the building and enthusiastically announces to the leaders and other children: "Let's get this party started!" The Lord must smile at this child's excitement about being in what he thinks is God's house.

The author of Psalm 84, one of the sons of Korah, also had a love for God's house. Some commentators have speculated that for a time he, a temple singer, was unable to go to the temple—either because of sickness or circumstances. So as he wrote this psalm, his soul was especially longing and crying out to be in "the courts of the Lord" (v. 2). He believed that one day of worship in God's house gave more satisfaction than a thousand days spent anywhere else (v. 10).

There's something special about praising God together with His people, and we should take every opportunity we can to do so. But if we can't, like the psalmist, we can still express our love for the living God and our longing to know Him (v. 2). The Lord is pleased and we'll be blessed when our heart's desire is to be with Him and His people. —AC

A good indicator of our spiritual temperature is our eagerness to worship God.

ANOTHER CHANCE

[You] have put on the new man who is renewed in knowledge according to the image of Him who created him.
—Colossians 3:10

For almost 100 years, a huge piece of flawed Carrara marble lay in the courtyard of a cathedral in Florence, Italy. Then, in 1501, a young sculptor was asked to do something with it. He measured the block and noted its imperfections. In his mind he envisioned a young shepherd boy.

For three years the sculptor chiseled and shaped the marble skillfully. Finally, when the 18-foot towering figure of David was unveiled, his student exclaimed to Michelangelo, "Master, it lacks only one thing—speech!"

Onesimus was like that flawed marble. He was an unfaithful servant when he fled from his master Philemon. But while on the run he came to know the Master Sculptor. As a changed man, he served God faithfully and was invaluable to Paul's ministry. When Paul sent him back to Philemon, he commended him as one "who once was unprofitable to you, but now is profitable to you and to me" (1:11). He asked Philemon to receive Onesimus back as a brother (v. 16).

Paul knew what it meant to be given another chance after past wrongs (Acts 9:26–28). He knew personally the transformation God can accomplish. Now he saw it in the life of Onesimus. The Lord can chisel His image on our flawed lives and make us beautiful and useful too. —AL

August 18

Read: Philemon 1:8–19

Biblical Truth

Personal Application

Prayer Requests

Answers to Prayer

Our rough edges must be chipped away to bring out the image of Christ.

August 19

Read: Joshua 24:15–24

Biblical Truth

Personal Application

Prayer Requests

Answers to Prayer

ONE SMALL CHOICE

Choose for yourselves this day whom you will serve . . . But as for me and my house, we will serve the Lord.
—Joshua 24:15

As a boy, my father often played violin in the local symphony. This budding young talent continued improving into his high school years.

Then one day he decided to join his buddies in a harmless prank. As they raced through the school hallways and out the door, my dad hurried to follow them. The door slammed just as he reached it. His left hand smashed the glass of the door, severing the tendons to three fingers. All the doctors could do was tie the tendons in knots, rendering his fingers useless and unable ever again to play the violin.

I have sometimes wondered how Dad's life might have been different had he not made that one small choice. And although "what-ifs" have dubious merit—we can always second-guess ourselves—we cannot underestimate the impact of our choices. One choice can produce lifelong consequences, for good or bad.

Joshua's counsel is a good place to start. "Choose for yourselves this day whom you will serve," he told Israel. "But as for me and my house, we will serve the Lord" (Joshua 24:15). Serving God will not always be the easy choice. But it is a choice that brings the kind of consequence we can live with.
—BC

What you will be tomorrow depends on the choices you make today.

WHOSE SIDE IS GOD ON?

August 20

The Lord searches all hearts and understands all the intent of the thoughts.
—1 Chronicles 28:9

"I do not boast that God is on my side," wrote Abraham Lincoln. "I humbly pray that I am on God's side."

Lincoln's words paraphrase the thoughts Azariah expressed to King Asa of Judah. After the Spirit of God came upon Azariah, he said, "The Lord is with you while you are with Him. If you seek Him, He will be found by you; but if you forsake Him, He will forsake you" (2 Chronicles 15:2).

Throughout history, people have done despicable deeds while boldly claiming that God was on their side. But being a Christian doesn't guarantee that God is "on our side" any more than being an ancient Israelite guaranteed that God was on theirs (Isaiah 3:14–15). God is on the side of those who are on His side—who know His heart and mind and do His will—not those who insist on convincing God and others that their way is right.

Through the prophet Isaiah, the Lord indicated that He sides with the oppressed (Isaiah 58:6–7, 10). For Christians, that means it is right to be on the side of those who are being wronged.

Instead of jumping into a situation with the presumption that God is on our side, we need to be certain that we are on His. —JAL

Read: 2 Chronicles 15:1–15

Biblical Truth

Personal Application

Prayer Requests

Answers to Prayer

It's dangerous to mistake our wishes for God's will.

August 21

Read: Psalm 8

Biblical Truth

Personal Application

Prayer Requests

Answers to Prayer

PHENOMENAL!

O Lord, our Lord, how excellent is Your name in all the earth!
—Psalm 8:1

At 3:00 one August morning, I awoke to experience a total lunar eclipse. It began at the precise moment the astronomers predicted and progressed just as they said it would. In one sense, it was a natural, recurring event, but it was also a phenomenal glimpse at the power and glory of God.

As the earth's shadow crept slowly across a bright full moon, the psalmist's words came to mind: "When I consider Your heavens, the work of Your fingers, the moon and the stars, which You have ordained, what is man that You are mindful of him, and the son of man that You visit him?" (Psalm 8:3–4).

Planet earth is not all about us, but by God's design, it involves us. The psalmist marveled at the heavens, but he was more amazed that the great Creator, whose glory is above the heavens, included us in His grand plan for the ages.

To worship any part of God's creation stops short of giving glory to the One who made it. The Bible lifts our eyes to see that all creation proclaims the glory of God, who has showered His grace and love on us through Christ. "O Lord, our Lord, how excellent is Your name in all the earth!" (Psalm 8:1). —DCM

God's glory shines through His creation.

THE FOOT-WASHING GOD

August 22

[Jesus] poured water into a basin and began to wash the disciples' feet.
—John 13:5

Questions about God's existence often troubled H. A. Hodges, a brilliant young professor of philosophy at Oxford University. One day as he strolled down the street, he passed by an art store. His attention was gripped by a simple picture in the window. It showed Jesus kneeling to wash His disciples' feet.

Hodges knew the story recorded in John 13—God incarnate washing human feet. But suddenly the sheer meaning of that scene gripped the heart of this young philosopher. God—*God!*—humbling himself to do that lowliest of tasks! He thought, *If God is like that, then that God shall be my God!* Seeing that painting was one of the circumstances that caused Hodges to surrender his life to the true God—the foot-washing God.

We Christians sometimes take God's existence for granted. We believe what the Bible tells us about the eternal Spirit who had no beginning and whose existence will never end. But we may wonder sometimes about His character. If He allows disaster, how could He also be kind and loving?

As we read John 13 thoughtfully, we see that God is the foot-washing God. His unfathomable, sacrificial love for us should cause us to surrender to Him too. —VCG

Read: John 13:1–5

Biblical Truth

Personal Application

Prayer Requests

Answers to Prayer

No life is more secure than a life surrendered to God.

August 23

Read: Philippians 4:4–13

Biblical Truth

Personal Application

Prayer Requests

Answers to Prayer

PASCAL'S PRAYER

Whatever you do,
do all to the glory of God.
—1 Corinthians 10:31

Blaise Pascal, the brilliant 17th-century intellectual, made significant contributions in the fields of science and mathematics. He established the groundwork for the development of mechanical calculators and modern hydraulic operations.

As a young man, Pascal had a profound encounter with Jesus Christ. This life-changing experience motivated him to refocus his study from science and math to theology.

Pascal wrote a remarkable prayer that can help each believer in facing the tasks of life. He prayed: "Lord, help me to do great things as though they were little, since I do them with Your power; and little things as though they were great, since I do them in Your name."

Pascal's supplication is profoundly scriptural. Paul said, "I can do all things through Christ who strengthens me" (Philippians 4:13) and admonishes us that "whatever you do, do all to the glory of God" (1 Corinthians 10:31). Pascal echoes these admonitions to depend upon God for His power and to view every act as important, since it will reflect on His glory.

The next time you face a huge task, remember that God is your strength. And when you encounter a seemingly insignificant one, determine to do it with excellence to the glory of God. —DF

Expect great things from God; attempt great things for God.
—William Carey

GOD'S RESTRAINT

Surely the wrath of man shall praise You; with the remainder of wrath You shall gird Yourself.
—Psalm 76:10

Augustine said that God "judged it better to bring good out of evil, than not to permit any evil to exist." Thus God takes the worst evil that men and women can do to us and turns it into good. Even the wrath of ungodly men brings praise to Him (Psalm 76:10).

God has not promised that your life will be easy; indeed, it may not be. But He has promised to sustain you in your struggle and uphold you with His mighty arm. If you trust Him, He will empower you to make your way bravely through extraordinary difficulty with faith, hope, and love. The trials God permits in your life will lead to His praise and glory, if only you will abide in Him.

Furthermore, there will be a restraint and a respite. The Hebrew text is somewhat obscure in Psalm 76:10. Literally it reads, "Surely the wrath of man will praise You; the remnant of wrath [God] will bind." God will use men's wrath to bring glory and praise to himself, but when that purpose is fulfilled He will then restrain it.

God will not allow you to be pressed beyond endurance. That is His sure promise. When the lesson has been learned, when the revelation of God's glory is complete and your soul has been tried and proven, then God will raise His hand and save you. He will say, "No more." —DHR

August 24

Read: Psalm 76

Biblical Truth

Personal Application

Prayer Requests

Answers to Prayer

In every desert of trial, God has an oasis of comfort.

August 25

Read: Psalm 131

Biblical Truth

Personal Application

Prayer Requests

Answers to Prayer

FOUNDATION OF THE HEART

Surely I have calmed and quieted my soul, like a weaned child with his mother.
—Psalm 131:2

The great cathedrals of Europe are not only breathtaking but intriguing in their architecture. Because their massive ceilings were too heavy for the walls to support, flying buttresses, or external extensions, were built to support the expansive roofs.

Although we are "the temple of the living God" (2 Corinthians 6:16), I wonder if we are not more like these cathedrals, with buttresses of external influences holding us up while we remain weak at the core. Pastors, friends, rules, books, and small groups are helpful to support and bolster our faith. But if we depend too heavily on them, they can actually distract us from developing a healthy heart for God.

Our heart is the place where God meets and relates to us personally. It's where He allows us to respond to His correction. Spending time in His Word and in prayer opens the door for Him to interact with us at the deepest levels of our need and gives Him opportunities to comfort and convict. As we open our hearts to Him, He fans the flame of an intimate, life-changing relationship.

Authentic Christianity is the inside-out expression of this dynamic relationship with Jesus that provides the strength to live for His glory—regardless of what is happening on the outside!
—JS

*When you open your heart to the Savior,
He opens your mind to His Word.*

THE KING'S COLORS

August 26

By this all will know that you are My disciples, if you have love for one another.
—John 13:35

In Thailand, the people greatly love and admire King Bhumibol (Rama IX), who has led them for over 60 years. To display their respect for the king, the Thai people wear bright yellow shirts every Monday because yellow is the official color of the king.

As we seek to live for our King, the Lord Jesus Christ, we should also show our colors of allegiance and appreciation for all He has done for us. But how? What are the "colors" that declare to the world that we serve the King of kings and Lord of lords?

The night before His crucifixion, King Jesus told us what our "colors" should be when He said, "By this all will know that you are My disciples, if you have love for one another" (John 13:35). His disciple John echoed this when he wrote, "Beloved, if God so loved us, we also ought to love one another" (1 John 4:11).

When we display Christ's love for our fellow believers, it is more than just kindness or care. It is one of the most tangible ways we can show our love and devotion for the Savior.

As we interact with fellow Christ-followers, let's be sure to show our colors. That will honor our King before a watching world. —BC

Read: John 13:31–35

Biblical Truth

Personal Application

Prayer Requests

Answers to Prayer

Our love for God shows in our love for others.

August 27

Read: Matthew 6:1–6

Biblical Truth

Personal Application

Prayer Requests

Answers to Prayer

AN AUDIENCE OF ONE

[Jesus] made Himself of no reputation, taking the form of a bondservant.
—PHILIPPIANS 2:7

When I worked as a young journalist for *Campus Life* magazine, my assistant kept a plaque on her desk with this two-line poem: *Only one life, 'twill soon be past / Only what's done for Christ will last.*

Reading that plaque brought me up short every time. Although I believed its truth, how could I put it into practice? How should my faith in the invisible world affect my day-to-day life in the visible world?

According to Jesus, it's what God thinks of us that matters, not what others think. Jesus instructed us to pray in a closed room, where no one could see us, rather than in a public place where we might get credit for being spiritual (Matthew 6:6). In other words, live for God and not others.

Do we clamor for attention and achievement? Jesus invites us to let go of that competitive struggle, to trust that God's opinion of us is the only one that ultimately counts.

How would our lives differ if we truly played to an audience of One? Certainly our sense of ego and rivalry would fade, because we would no longer need to worry about proving ourselves to others. We could concentrate instead on pleasing God by living in a way that would attract people to Jesus. —PY

Christ is seen most clearly when we remain in the background.

COMFORT FOOD

August 28

Whatever things were written before were written for our learning, that we through the patience and comfort of the Scriptures might have hope.
—Romans 15:4

I love the phrase "comfort food." It speaks of the things that are so good, so familiar, so right, that they can always bring a smile to your face. For me, comfort food usually includes some form of beef and potatoes. Hamburgers and French fries. Meatloaf and mashed potatoes and gravy. Also, chocolate in almost any form imaginable. These are the foods that speak to me and say that all is well with the world. (I'm not saying they're the most healthy!)

Unfortunately, all is not well with the world, and no amount of hamburgers and fries can make it right. Real comfort is not the byproduct of specific foods any more than it is the result of alcohol or drugs or money or pleasure or power. It is a much deeper need that requires a much deeper solution.

Paul told the church at Rome that the search for comfort can begin in the pages of the Bible. He wrote: "Whatever things were written before were written for our learning, that we through the patience and comfort of the Scriptures might have hope" (Romans 15:4).

God has given us His Word to draw us to himself. Through a relationship with Him, He provides the comfort we need to live in a broken world. —BC

Read: Romans 15:1–7

Biblical Truth

Personal Application

Prayer Requests

Answers to Prayer

God's Word is a life preserver that keeps the soul from sinking in a sea of trouble.

August 29

Read: 1 Timothy 6:11–16

Biblical Truth

Personal Application

Prayer Requests

Answers to Prayer

DON'T RUST OUT

But you, O man of God, flee these things and pursue righteousness, godliness, faith, love, patience, gentleness.
—1 Timothy 6:11

On June 15, 1957, a brand-new car was buried in a concrete vault under the courthouse lawn in Tulsa. In June 2007, the car was unearthed as the city celebrated Oklahoma's 100th year of statehood. Writing in the *Tulsa World,* Randy Krehbiel said: "Now we know what 50 years in a hole does to a Plymouth Belvedere." Water seeping into the vault had turned the once shiny car into a rusted monument to the past. A hot-rod expert hired to start the engine pronounced it "hopeless."

Spiritual inactivity corrodes the soul like moisture acting on metal. Paul urged Timothy, his young protégé, to "pursue righteousness, godliness, faith, love, patience, gentleness" (1 Timothy 6:11). This command had no expiration date attached to it. The spiritual disciplines require continued attention throughout our lives. If rest becomes our goal, then rust is right behind.

Oswald Chambers said: "The intellect works with the greatest intensity when it works continuously; the more you do, the more you can do. We must work hard to keep in trim for God. Clean off the rust and keep bright by use."

Our capabilities may vary with age, but pursuing the righteous life to which God has called us should never end. Don't rust out!
—DCM

Spiritual inactivity corrodes the soul.

CHANGE OF ADDRESS

He has delivered us from the power of darkness and conveyed us into the kingdom of the Son of His love.
—Colossians 1:13

If you keep in touch with family and friends through the postal service or e-mail, you probably have received or sent a change of address notice. It goes something like this: "I will no longer be receiving mail at ____________. My new address will be _______. Thank you for making a note of this change."

Paul reminded the believers in Colosse that they had "a change of address" and that they should share it with others. They had been moved from one community and "conveyed" or transplanted, by the grace of God, into a new community. They had been rescued from the kingdom of darkness and brought into the kingdom of Jesus (Colossians 1:13). Their old address was sinner@kingdomofdarkness. But when they became followers of Jesus, their new address became saved@kingdomofHisdearSon.

In Philippians 3:20, Paul declared that all believers are citizens of heaven and should live worthy of their new address. He encouraged the Christians in Colosse to walk in wisdom toward those who were outside the faith so that people could see and hear about the changes (Colossians 4:5–6).

If you have had "a change of address," tell someone about what Jesus has done in you. —MW

August 30

Read: Colossians 1:9–14

Biblical Truth

Personal Application

Prayer Requests

Answers to Prayer

When Jesus comes into a life, He changes everything.

August 31

Read: Luke 23:32–43

Biblical Truth

Personal Application

Prayer Requests

Answers to Prayer

WONDERFUL MYSTERY

As far as the east is from the west, so far has He removed our transgressions from us.
—Psalm 103:12

The headline in our *Grand Rapids Press* wasn't good news. Fifteen million gallons of partially treated waste water suddenly disappeared from a storage lagoon in a water treatment facility. Just outside the small town of Sand Lake, Michigan, a 500-by-500-foot pond disappeared into a sinkhole.

The problem was that nobody knew where the wastewater went. According to a county spokesperson, "It will depend on where it went before we can say what happened."

As I read the article, I imagined all the wrongs of my life as being like that missing filthy lagoon. In my clearest moments of faith, I can say in all honesty that I really don't know where they went, but they are gone. The last time I saw the real guilt of my envy, anger, and impatience, they were all nailed to the cross of a Man suffering for wrongs He never committed.

Where did my guilt go? The Bible gives me answers that I can't really understand: buried in the deepest sea (Micah 7:19), as far as the east is from the west (Psalm 103:12), erased from the eternal books of heaven's justice (Colossians 2:13–15).

No, all I can really understand is that I owe unending gratefulness, praise, and honor to the One who bore our sin—a mystery of inexpressibly good news.
—MD

When God forgives, He removes our sin and restores our soul.

September

September 1

Read: John 13:3–16

Biblical Truth

Personal Application

Prayer Requests

Answers to Prayer

TITLES AND RESPONSIBILITIES

If I then, your Lord and Teacher, have washed your feet, you also ought to wash one another's feet.
—John 13:14

Research conducted by a leading compensation technology firm found that among employees planning to leave their companies, a majority felt they were underpaid. Fewer than 20 percent of them, however, were receiving less than the industry standard for their duties.

Bill Coleman, of Salary.com, believes that many unhappy workers are overtitled rather than underpaid. Some companies give employees lofty titles even though their job responsibilities have not increased. In time, employees feel they deserve more money than their actual duties merit. "When it comes to salary," Coleman says, "it's what you do, not what you're called, that counts."

It's interesting how Jesus dealt with the issue of titles and responsibilities. During the Last Supper, He performed the task of a lowly servant by washing His disciples' feet, setting the stage for His astonishing statement about humility: "You call Me Teacher and Lord, and you say well, for so I am. If I then, your Lord and Teacher, have washed your feet, you also ought to wash one another's feet" (John 13:13–14).

Christ the Lord set the example for all who would follow Him, confirming that it's not what we're called, but what we do that counts. —DCM

The more we serve Christ, the less we will serve self.

PASS IT ON

Lest you forget the things your eyes have seen . . . teach them to your children and your grandchildren.
—Deuteronomy 4:9

One day as my wife was baby-sitting our granddaughter, she shared an old, familiar friend with her. With Eliana in her arms, Sue picked up a well-worn book that we had read to our daughter when she was a little girl. It's a book called *The Bible in Pictures for Little Eyes,* a staple in our efforts to share God's truth with our children.

So now it is Eliana's turn to begin to learn about God's creation, His goodness, His plan, and His salvation. It's time for her to be told about what we have seen and experienced in our walk of faith. As Deuteronomy 4:9 says, "Teach [God's statutes] to your children and your grandchildren."

Back in the days of Deuteronomy, the people were being handed a gift from God—"the statutes and the judgments" (v. 1) that would allow them to live properly in the land of God's promise. Along with those laws came an admonition for the people to share with their progeny the lessons God taught them on the way. They were told not to "forget the things your eyes have seen" (v. 9) and to teach God's words to their children and grandchildren.

We have a similar legacy to convey to the next generation. As followers of Christ, we take this as one of our greatest responsibilities. Pass it on. —DB

September 2

Read: Deuteronomy 4:5–10

Biblical Truth

Personal Application

Prayer Requests

Answers to Prayer

If children are to find their way to God, we must point the way.

September 3

Read: Haggai 1:2–7

Biblical Truth

Personal Application

Prayer Requests

Answers to Prayer

LIFE LAB

Thus says the Lord of hosts:
"Consider your ways!"
— HAGGAI 1:7

Hurricane Andrew struck the US mainland in August 1992. As residents tried to cope with the destruction, scientists turned Florida into a huge laboratory. Teams of researchers descended on the state to measure the storm's impact on everything from building materials to tropical fish. Psychologists analyzed the hurricane's influence on children. Geographers mapped sunken boats. Marine scientists cataloged the damage done to reefs, sea grass, and mangroves. Criminologists studied price-gouging and the breakdown of social order.

The prophets of the Bible did a similar evaluation after spiritual disasters. They documented the personal, social, and environmental effects of turning away from the one true God (Isaiah 1:1–9; Haggai 1:2–7).

In behalf of a loving God, Haggai urged his neighbors to give careful attention to what had happened. He noted the priority they were giving to their own comforts and wanted them to observe how dissatisfied and empty they still were.

If God didn't care, He wouldn't ask us to consider the time and effort we are spending on diminishing returns. If He didn't love us, He couldn't remind us of all that He has given us. God sees what has happened to us and knows how much we need to focus on Him today. —MD

When Christ is the center of your interests, life will be in focus.

THE SORROW OF BETRAYAL

September 4

I have sinned by betraying innocent blood.
—Matthew 27:4

When I was a boy, my dad observed my spendthrift ways and often said that money burned a hole in my pocket. I suppose it's not unlike the way those 30 pieces of silver burned a hole in Judas's heart after he had betrayed Jesus for a little cash. Imagine how Judas must have felt as he watched his friend Jesus, with hands bound, being led to trial. Judas had seen those hands calm the stormy sea and touch the blind and lame. How often those loving hands had touched his own life!

For Judas, the silver was no longer a reward but a reminder of what he had done to Jesus. With every step, the clanging coins sounded a dirge of condemnation, until in despair he admitted, "I have sinned by betraying innocent blood" (Matthew 27:4).

When we make choices that betray Jesus, eventually our lives become filled with sorrow. Even well-intentioned followers find that their desire to love and serve Him is frequently on a collision course with the lure of cash or other seductions. But the things we have gained at His expense ultimately and inevitably become clanging symbols of sorrow and regret.

The next time you have to make a choice about cash—or anything else—remember the clatter of Judas's condemning coins, and don't betray your loving Leader. —JS

Read: Matthew 27:1–10

Biblical Truth

Personal Application

Prayer Requests

Answers to Prayer

When faced with a choice, don't betray your loving Leader.

September 5

Read: Matthew 13:1–9

Biblical Truth

Personal Application

Prayer Requests

Answers to Prayer

ROOTS OR SHOOTS?

Because they had no root they withered away.
—Matthew 13:6

In the life of trees, one key to survival is having more roots than shoots. In his book *Oak: The Frame of Civilization,* author William Bryant Logan says, "If a tree puts on a lot of top growth and few roots, it is liable to be weak-wooded and short-lived . . . If a tree puts down a great deal of roots and adds shoots more slowly, however, it is liable to be long-lived and more resistant to stress and strain."

People and organizations can be like trees. The rise to prominence is exhilarating, but anything that puts up shoots faster than it puts down roots is fragile and in danger of breaking, falling, or dying.

Jesus used a similar analogy in His parable of the sower. People who hear the Word and receive it joyfully are like seed sown on stony places: they spring up quickly but endure only a short time because they have no roots (Matthew 13:6, 20–21).

Roots aren't at all glamorous, but they are the source of our strength. If our roots go deep in the knowledge of God (Jeremiah 9:24) and our lives are "hidden with Christ in God" (Colossians 3:3), we'll be strong, resistant to blight, and more likely to survive the storms of adversity.

How deep are your roots?
—JAL

The roots of stability come from being grounded in God's Word and prayer.

DO YOUR BEST AND LEAVE THE REST

September 6

He who calls you is faithful, who also will do it.
—1 Thessalonians 5:24

Have you at some time found yourself under extreme pressure? Have there been episodes in your life when you were so burdened by tasks and responsibilities that there was simply no breathing space to prepare for your service to God?

That was the experience of a pastor by the name of A. J. Gossip. During one hectic week he didn't have his customary amount of time to prepare his sermon. As he walked to his pulpit that Sunday morning, he felt guilty about the scanty sermon notes in his hand. It seemed that the Lord was asking him, "Is this the best you could do for Me this week?" And Gossip honestly replied, "Yes, Lord, it is my best." He told a friend later that Jesus took that ill-prepared piece of work and in His hands "it became a trumpet" to his congregation.

The apostle Paul encouraged the Thessalonians to give their all for God (1 Thessalonians 5:14–22). They were to exhort, warn, comfort, rejoice, pray, and express their gratitude to God—among other things. We too should always do our best in our Christian life and service. But when pressure-periods come and we just don't have the time we feel we need, we should do the best we can and then prayerfully trust God's faithfulness (v. 24).
—VCG

Read: 1 Thessalonians 5:14–24

Biblical Truth

Personal Application

Prayer Requests

Answers to Prayer

Be faithful—and leave the results to God.

September 7

Read: Deuteronomy 8:6–18

Biblical Truth

Personal Application

Prayer Requests

Answers to Prayer

THE DANGERS OF SUCCESS

Beware that you do not forget the Lord your God by not keeping His commandments, His judgments, and His statutes.
—Deuteronomy 8:11

Alexandr Solzhenitsyn said that he learned to pray in a Siberian concentration camp because he had no other hope. Before his arrest, when things were going well, he seldom gave God a thought.

Similarly, the Israelites learned the habit of depending on God in the Sinai wilderness where they had no choice; they needed His daily intervention just to eat and drink. But when they finally stood on the banks of the Jordan River, they awaited a more difficult test of faith. After they entered the land of plenty, would they soon forget God?

The Israelites knew little about the seductions of other cultures, having spent their lives in the desert. Moses was more afraid of the coming prosperity than the rigors of the desert—the alluring sensuality, the exotic religions, the glittering wealth. The Israelites might put God behind them and credit themselves for their success (Deuteronomy 8:11, 17).

Ironically, success makes it harder to depend on the Lord. The Israelites did prove less faithful after they moved into the Promised Land. Again and again they turned their hearts to other gods.

Beware of the temptation that success brings. There is grave danger in getting what we want.
—PY

There is no failure more disastrous than the success that leaves God out.

September 8

COMPLIMENTS GIVEN HERE

Each one's praise will come from God.
—1 Corinthians 4:5

Read: 1 Corinthians 4:1–8

Artist Tom Greaves knows how to give compliments. He designed a bright red-and-white-striped box for an art exhibit in Washington, DC, called "The Compliment Machine." As people walk by, the machine dishes out compliments from an internal iPod. It says things like, "Your eyes are beautiful," "You smell good," and "People are drawn to your positive energy."

Greaves won't say what his motive is for the box, other than that it's in response to a saccharine culture in which everyone is special and nobody is criticized, regardless of performance.

Everybody loves to hear a compliment now and then—if it's genuine. It makes us feel good about ourselves to have the approval or admiration of others, for a few minutes at least. The apostle Paul, though, looked at what others thought of him or even what he thought of himself as "a very small thing" (1 Corinthians 4:3). He said, "He who judges me is the Lord" (v. 4). He knew that one day our hearts will be revealed, and "then each one's praise will come from God" (v. 5).

Could there be any greater compliment than this from our heavenly Father when we meet Him: "Well done, good and faithful servant" (Matthew 25:23).
—AC

Biblical Truth

Personal Application

Prayer Requests

Answers to Prayer

Work well done for Christ will receive a "well done" from Christ.

September 9

Read: Genesis 3:1–13

Biblical Truth

Personal Application

Prayer Requests

Answers to Prayer

THE CHIMP'S BIRTHDAY CARD

The man said, "The woman whom You gave to be with me, she gave me of the tree, and I ate."
—Genesis 3:12

Not long ago my wife asked me to pick up a belated birthday card for her brother. Scanning the rack, I ran across a card with a chimpanzee on the front holding a phone receiver in his hand.

The card said: "I better not hear . . . about how upset you are that I missed your birthday. I mean, how do you know I wasn't in a serious car accident and lying in some ditch out in the middle of nowhere? . . . Well, I may have forgotten your birthday, but I didn't exactly get any phone calls to see if I was okay. All I know is you better have a good excuse why I didn't hear from you on your birthday!"

The extent to which people avoid legitimate responsibility is almost laughable, but it is nothing new. When God confronted Adam for eating the forbidden fruit, he chose to blame his wife and God: "The woman whom You gave to be with me, she gave me of the tree, and I ate" (Genesis 3:12).

When we have done something wrong, we can either accept legitimate blame for what we have done or shift the blame to others. The way that pleases God and results in spiritual growth is to accept personal responsibility for our actions. Irrationally blaming others is no laughing matter.
—DF

A good test of a person's character is his behavior when he is wrong.

September 10

HEAR THEIR CRY

You shall not afflict any widow or fatherless child. If you afflict them in any way, and they cry at all to Me, I will surely hear their cry.
—Exodus 22:22–23

CNN recently reported that there are approximately 40 million widows in India. Fifteen thousand of them live on the streets of the northern city of Vrindavan. Unfortunately, many of their families do not hear their cries. A 70-year-old widow says, "My son tells me: 'You have grown old. Now who is going to feed you? Go away.'" She cries, "What do I do? My pain has no limit."

When God gave His people instructions in the desert, He told them they had a responsibility to care for widows and fatherless children in the land (Exodus 22:22–23). They were to leave some of the harvest in the field for them, and every third year they took up a special tithe for the needy. God expected His people to hear the cries of the powerless, defend their rights, and care for them.

The Israelites were commanded to care for others as a remembrance of their experience in Egypt. When they were in trouble and cried out to God, He heard their cries and helped them. So their memory of oppression and release was intended to mold their values, attitudes, and actions toward the powerless in the land (Deuteronomy 24:18–22).

Let us imitate our Father by hearing the cries of the needy in our world. —MW

Read: Exodus 22:22–27

Biblical Truth

Personal Application

Prayer Requests

Answers to Prayer

The closer you are to God, the more you'll have a heart for others.

September 11

Read: Romans 12:3–8

Biblical Truth

Personal Application

Prayer Requests

Answers to Prayer

CALLED

Having then gifts differing according to the grace that is given to us, let us use them.
—Romans 12:6

In September 2001, Lisa Jefferson had an unexpected opportunity to be used by God. Her now well-known 15-minute conversation with a passenger on United Flight 93 forever changed the direction of her life. In her book *Called* she emphasizes that her listening skills and her ability to take charge and stay calm in a crisis were used to encourage fellow believer Todd Beamer in the last moments of his life.

She didn't ask to be used that way. But God saw a woman who was available and matched her with someone who was in need. Lisa now shares her story with whomever she can to encourage believers to always be ready to serve.

Not only has God given us natural abilities, He also equips every believer with spiritual gifts for the purpose of ministry. God doesn't use the unwilling—He won't force us to serve Him. His part is to equip us (Ephesians 4:11–13) and empower and prepare us for service. Our part is to be faithful and available and aware of opportunities to use our gifts (Romans 12:6).

When you feel impelled to help fill a need, when you are inwardly driven to serve—listen to those thoughts. You don't want to miss God's call. —CHK

God uses ordinary people to do extraordinary work.

LIFEWORK

If anyone does not provide
for his own, and especially for
those of his household,
he has denied the faith
and is worse than an unbeliever.
—1 TIMOTHY 5:8

Some of our friends have chosen to curtail or leave their ministries this year. They did so in order to care for family members—for aging parents, ill spouses, siblings, or children with special needs. All were involved in fruitful works for which they were uniquely gifted. All believed that there was much to be done.

Some have chosen to reduce the time and energy they spend on those ministries; others have left their work completely. These adjustments have been difficult because ministry has been their lifework, a work for which they spent years in preparation and had many years yet to serve.

It occurs to me, however, that they have not given up their lifework but rather have assumed another. Loving and caring for others is our life's work, and caring for those of our "own house" is the highest and holiest work of all. To deny love is to align ourselves with a cold, uncaring world.

Not everyone can leave a career or calling to care for others. Financial realities and obligations may dictate otherwise. But is not such love the mark of one who does the work of God? Did not Jesus promise that one who gives a cup of cold water to one of His children "shall by no means lose his reward"? (Matthew 10:42).
—DHR

September 12

Read: 1 Timothy 5:1–8

Biblical Truth

Personal Application

Prayer Requests

Answers to Prayer

True love is doing, not just feeling.

September 13

Read: 2 Corinthians 1:3–7

Biblical Truth

Personal Application

Prayer Requests

Answers to Prayer

A MEASURE OF HEALING

This is my comfort in my affliction, for Your Word has given me life.
—PSALM 119:50

When I asked a friend how she was doing four years after the sudden death of her husband, she said, "I feel I am healing. Tears tend to burn my eyes rather than pour down my face. To me, that is a measure of healing."

How fitting are those words to describe the changes that happen as the years pass for grievers who have endured an unexpected loss.

Scripture promises comfort in our suffering (2 Corinthians 1:3–7), but that help does not come all at once. In fact, from what I have heard, our desired healing may not arrive completely in this life. This is what others tell me who are further down the road of grief than our family is, six years after losing our teenager Melissa. In the midst of our pain, we entrust our lives to God's sovereign direction, but we also realize that gnawing sadness will always reside in our hearts.

Indeed, God has promised that He will wipe away all tears in heaven (Revelation 7:17), but until then the healing will be incomplete. Grief lessens but does not dissipate. The psalmist said that while God's Word gives life, there is still the combination of "comfort in my affliction" (Psalm 119:50). Even in life's toughest circumstances, we can, with God's help, enjoy a measure of healing. —DB

The God who washed away our sins will also wipe away our tears.

END OF CONSTRUCTION

September 14

To Him who is able to keep you from stumbling, and to present you faultless before the presence of His glory with exceeding joy.
—Jude 1:24

Years ago, Ruth Bell Graham, wife of evangelist Billy Graham, saw a sign by the road: "End of Construction—Thank you for your patience." Smiling, she remarked that she wanted those words on her gravestone.

After her death in June 2007, her desire was carried out. Her grave marker bears the Chinese character for *righteousness* (Mrs. Graham was born in China), followed by the words that made her smile.

Every follower of Christ can share the confidence that God's faithfulness will carry us through this period of spiritual building on earth. We echo Jude's words of praise: "Now to Him who is able to keep you from stumbling, and to present you faultless before the presence of His glory with exceeding joy, to God our Savior, who alone is wise, be glory and majesty, dominion and power, both now and forever" (Jude 1:24–25).

Today, we're in the construction zone. There, Jude's letter challenges us, we are to grow in faith, pray in the Spirit, and remain surrounded by God's love (vv. 20–21). But this construction is not a self-centered process. We are to show mercy to others and rescue those in danger of spiritual ruin (vv. 22–23).

One day our construction will be complete, a prospect that's worth so much more than a smile. —DCM

Read: Jude 1:20–25

Biblical Truth

Personal Application

Prayer Requests

Answers to Prayer

To build a godly life, let God be the architect and His Word the blueprint.

September 15

Read: Acts 26:9–18

Biblical Truth

Personal Application

Prayer Requests

Answers to Prayer

WHAT'S YOUR STORY?

Believe on the Lord Jesus Christ, and you will be saved.
—Acts 16:31

Every believer has a unique story of encountering Christ. Ann, a receptionist at RBC Ministries, told me that she has kept a journal for much of her life. She treasures the account she recorded about her conversion when she was 15. Here is an excerpt: "[I] went to see Billy Graham. I got saved! I'm very happy . . . When I got saved I felt warmth in my heart."

Years ago, in a personal evangelism course I taught, I asked the students to write out their story of how they came to faith in Christ. It struck me how different each journey was. Some were saved out of a life of drugs and immorality. Others were church attenders who came to Christ after years of biblical instruction.

Conversions vary. The apostle Paul had a crisis encounter with the Savior that turned him from a persecutor into a preacher of the gospel (Acts 26). In contrast, Timothy was quietly nurtured in the Scriptures from early childhood, resulting in his salvation experience (2 Timothy 3:14–15). No two faith journeys are identical. But each has the common element of turning to the Lord Jesus in faith to be saved from sin and to receive a new heart.

Can you retrace the steps that God helped you take in coming to Christ? What's your story?
—DF

We need more than a new start—we need a new heart!

RESPONDING TO CRITICISM

September 16

When they speak against you as evildoers, they may, by your good works which they observe, glorify God.
—1 Peter 2:12

Abraham Lincoln knew what it meant to face criticism. He is quoted as saying, "If I were to try to read, much less answer, all the attacks made on me, this shop might as well be closed for any other business. I do the very best I know how—the very best I can; and I mean to keep doing so until the end. If the end brings me out all right, what's said against me won't amount to anything. If the end brings me out wrong, ten angels swearing I was right would make no difference."

Lincoln, against huge opposition, went on to reunite the fractured United States, win the Civil War, and abolish slavery in the US. Had he allowed his critics to defeat him, he would not have accomplished what he did.

The apostle Peter understood the dangers of unfounded criticism. He wrote, "Having your conduct honorable among the Gentiles, that when they speak against you as evildoers, they may, by your good works which they observe, glorify God" (1 Peter 2:12).

Criticism can consume our lives to the point of emotional paralysis. Or, we can set our hearts to serve God faithfully, undeterred by that criticism, and put our God on display. When we do that, we won't need to answer our critics with words—our lives will say all that is needed. —BC

Read: 1 Peter 2:4–12

Biblical Truth

Personal Application

Prayer Requests

Answers to Prayer

The most powerful testimony is a godly life.

September 17

Read: Isaiah 45:18–25

Biblical Truth

Personal Application

Prayer Requests

Answers to Prayer

HE'S THERE ALL THE TIME

He who seeks finds.
— MATTHEW 7:8

I'll never forget my frustrating experience when I went to Chicago's Union Station early one morning to pick up an elderly relative who was arriving by train. When I got there, she wasn't where I thought she would be. With increasing anxiety I scoured the place—to no avail. Thinking she had missed her train, I was about to leave when I glanced down a hallway toward the baggage area. There she was, luggage at her feet, patiently waiting for me to arrive. She had been there all the time. And, to my chagrin, she was right where she was supposed to be.

It's that way with God. He's there, patiently waiting for us. He assures us, "I did not say . . . 'Seek Me in vain'" (Isaiah 45:19). Why, then, do we often have trouble finding Him? Probably because we are looking in all the wrong places.

You'll find Him right where He is supposed to be—in His Word, in prayer, and in the voice of the Holy Spirit who lives within you. The God who says "seek, and you will find" (Matthew 7:7) also promises that "He is a rewarder of those who diligently seek Him" (Hebrews 11:6). So, you can rejoice that God is right where He is supposed to be, and He's waiting for you right now. —JS

Have we been looking for God in all the wrong places?

SPARE BEDS

Do not forget to entertain strangers, for by so doing some have unwittingly entertained angels.
—Hebrews 13:2

In 2004, Casey Fenton co-founded a nonprofit service that helps travelers find a "friendlier alternative" to unfriendly hotels. They find homeowners who are willing to offer their spare beds and couches to others.

The group boasts almost a quarter of a million friendships that have been formed from their service. "The more we network," said Fenton, "the better chance we have of this world being a better place."

That service sounds a lot like biblical hospitality. In the final pages of his letter to the Hebrews, the writer instructed believers to practice their faith in Jesus Christ through hospitality (13:2). That was defined by the early Christ-followers as acts of generosity toward strangers.

In the first century, hospitality often included housing a guest. This was hardest to do during a time of persecution. These believers would not know whether the person was a spy or a fellow believer being pursued. But by entertaining strangers, the writer said, they could indeed be inviting a blessing into their homes.

As God's people, we are called to be hospitable to others as part of our gratitude for the salvation we have received from God.
—MW

September 18

Read: Hebrews 13:1–6

Biblical Truth

Personal Application

Prayer Requests

Answers to Prayer

People with a heart for God have a heart for people.

September 19

Read: Isaiah 50:4–6 and Luke 2:46–52

Biblical Truth

Personal Application

Prayer Requests

Answers to Prayer

A LEARNER

They found Him in the temple, sitting in the midst of the teachers, both listening to them and asking them questions.
—Luke 2:46

The poster in the church hallway pictured a young boy dressed in Middle Eastern clothing, with Bible in hand, walking up a hill to church. The caption read: "Jesus was a good Christian boy who went to Sunday school every Sunday."

As a Jewish boy, Jesus didn't go to Sunday school and church on Sunday, so the poster was inappropriate. But the picture is correct in portraying Jesus' desire to be in His Father's temple to listen to His teaching.

When Jesus was 12, He went with His parents to Jerusalem for the Feast of the Passover (Luke 2:41–42). On their way home, His parents realized He was not with them. When they returned to Jerusalem, they "found Him in the temple, sitting in the midst of the teachers, both listening to them and asking them questions" (v. 46).

Jesus had the heart of a learner-disciple. Isaiah writes of Him as Jehovah's Servant: "The Lord God . . . awakens Me morning by morning, He awakens My ear to hear as the learned. The Lord God has opened My ear" (50:4–5). In His humanity, the Son was open to learn from His Father.

Jesus' example challenges us to be listeners to God's Word. We too can become learner-disciples if we'll keep our hearts open to God's teaching. —AC

The highest goal of learning is to know God.

NOT GOOD ENOUGH

September 20

Though your sins are like scarlet, they shall be as white as snow.
—Isaiah 1:18

Read: 1 Timothy 1:12–17

A friend told me recently of a young mother who was trying to explain her father's death to her four-year-old. The girl wondered where Grandpa was. "I'm sure he's in heaven," the mother answered, "because he was very good." The girl replied sadly, "I guess I won't be in heaven." "Why not?" her mother asked in surprise. "'Cause I'm not very good."

The story saddened me, as I'm saddened when I hear of others who believe they must be very good to get into heaven, especially since we all know deep down in our hearts that we're not very good at all.

Perhaps like this little girl you're thinking about your sins and asking, "What must I do to get to heaven?" The answer has already been given: Jesus, by His death, has paid in full the price of your sins, no matter how sordid, tawdry, or shameful they may be. Your salvation is free.

God promises, "Though your sins are like scarlet, they shall be as white as snow; though they are red like crimson, they shall be as wool" (Isaiah 1:18). John Donne writes:

Or wash thee in Christ's blood,
which hath this might,
That being red, it dyes red souls
to white.

No one is good enough to get into heaven. Eternal life is a gift. Receive Jesus by faith. —DHR

Biblical Truth

Personal Application

Prayer Requests

Answers to Prayer

*No one is good enough to save himself;
no one is so bad that God cannot save him.*

September 21

Read: 2 Timothy 2:14–19

Biblical Truth

Personal Application

Prayer Requests

Answers to Prayer

RIGHTLY DIVIDING THE WORD

Be diligent . . . rightly dividing the Word of truth.
—2 TIMOTHY 2:15

In 1879, James Murray was hired as the editor of *The Oxford English Dictionary.* He had little advanced education, but he was a gifted linguist. Murray enlisted a large number of volunteers around the world to read widely and send him usages of assigned words. At Oxford, he and a small staff of scholars cataloged and edited the definitions they received.

During his lifetime, Murray was knighted and awarded an honorary doctorate from Oxford. Today, the 20-volume *Oxford English Dictionary* is still recognized as one of the most accurate and comprehensive dictionaries in the world.

Murray's legacy of precision and accuracy with words reminds me of what the apostle Paul wrote to Timothy, a young pastor of the Ephesian church: "Be diligent to present yourself approved to God, a worker who does not need to be ashamed, rightly dividing the Word of truth" (2 Timothy 2:15). The phrase "rightly dividing" is a metaphor derived from the stonemason's craft of cutting stones straight to fit into their proper place in a building.

Precision with words is essential to an accurate interpretation of God's Word. Let's be people who care deeply about what the Bible says and what it means.
—DF

Rightly dividing the Word multiplies our understanding.

ARMS OF LOVE

Let us not love in word or in tongue, but in deed and in truth.
—1 John 3:18

Many college students go on summer missions trips. But rarely does one come back with plans to rescue a baby. Mallery Thurlow, a student at Cornerstone University in Grand Rapids, went to Haiti to help distribute food. One day a mother showed up at the distribution center with a very sick infant in her arms. The woman was out of options. The baby needed surgery, but no one would perform it. Without intervention, the baby would die. Mallery took baby Rose into her arms—and into her heart.

After returning to the US, Mallery searched for someone to operate on baby Rose. Most doctors held out little hope. Finally, Rose was granted a visa to leave Haiti, and Mallery went back to get her. Detroit Children's Hospital donated the $100,000 surgery, and it was successful. A little life was saved.

It's unlikely that we will have such a dramatic impact on others. Yet challenged by this student's willingness, we can find ways to provide help. She didn't let circumstances, youth, or inconvenience stop her from saving Rose's life.

Like Mallery, we are called to love "in deed and in truth" (1 John 3:18). Who needs you to be God's arms of love today? —DB

September 22

Read: 1 John 3:16–20

Biblical Truth

Personal Application

Prayer Requests

Answers to Prayer

Compassion puts love into action.

September 23

Read: Psalm 33:8–22

Biblical Truth

Personal Application

Prayer Requests

Answers to Prayer

HE WATCHES OVER US

From the place of His dwelling
He looks on all the
inhabitants of the earth.
—Psalm 33:14

In the early 1960s, I read the novel *1984* by George Orwell, which made famous the phrase "Big Brother is watching you." In this imaginary society, all aspects of life are under surveillance.

Today, there are an estimated 4.2 million closed-circuit video cameras in the UK alone! London is saturated with them. These cameras watch lobbies and sidewalks for security reasons. They even monitor traffic.

Psalm 33 tells us that God is also watching from on high (v. 14). He sees not just images and activities but discerns thoughts and motives. As Creator God, when He speaks, it will be done (v. 9). His eternal purposes march on unhindered (vv. 10–11). Earthly obstacles are mere steppingstones to Him. Though many may depend on military strength for deliverance and safety, their hope is in vain (vv. 16–17).

Yet we who fear the Lord need not flee from this awesome God. The psalmist affirms, "The eye of the Lord is on those who fear Him, on those who hope in His mercy . . . He is our help and our shield" (vv. 18, 20).

The eye of the Lord may be fearsome, but we who trust in Him rejoice. He is not an intrusive "Big Brother" but our loving heavenly Father who watches over us. —AL

Keep your eyes on the Lord; He never takes His eyes off you.

BUILDING A CITY

They desire a better, that is, a heavenly country. Therefore God is not ashamed to be called their God.
—Hebrews 11:16

For 41 years, New York's Empire State Building enjoyed the distinction of being the world's tallest building at 1,250 feet. Since then, others have passed it, including the 1,483-foot Petronas Twin Towers in Kuala Lumpur, Malaysia, and the 1,670-foot Taipei 101 building. And the 2,717-foot Burj Khalifa in Dubai, completed in 2009, surpasses those by far.

From ancient times, man has tried to distinguish himself through monuments of all kinds. It is still the dream of many today.

The writer to the Hebrews presents a better way to achieve significance. He notes that heroes of the faith never lost sight of the fact that they "were strangers and pilgrims on the earth" (Hebrews 11:13). As a result, "God is not ashamed to be called their God, for He has prepared a city for them" (v. 16).

It is a fact of life that every monumental work will likely be surpassed. Even man's biggest "successes" are fleeting. Our best efforts can bring only temporary honor, which all too soon will be eclipsed by the new and greater achievements of others. But those who invest their efforts in living to please God have a lasting city and an everlasting honor to look forward to. God is even now preparing these for them.

Who is building your life? You or God? —CPH

September 24

Read: Hebrews 11:8–16

Biblical Truth

Personal Application

Prayer Requests

Answers to Prayer

A solid foundation gives strength to a building and a life.

September 25

Read: Jeremiah 36:1–8, 21–26

Biblical Truth

Personal Application

Prayer Requests

Answers to Prayer

READ A BANNED BOOK

Write . . . all the words that I have spoken to you . . . that everyone may turn from his evil way, that I may forgive their iniquity and their sin.
—Jeremiah 36:2–3

The American Library Association has designated the last week of September as Banned Books Week in celebration of the freedom to read and to express one's opinion "even if that opinion might be considered unorthodox or unpopular."

The Bible is the all-time bestselling book, but in some parts of the world it is banned because it's considered dangerous. The Bible is dangerous, however, only to those who fear finding out that they are wrong. It's dangerous to those who exploit the weak and the innocent, who use force to keep others enslaved in poverty and ignorance, who don't want to give up their favorite sin, who believe that salvation can be found apart from Christ.

No one wants to be told they are wrong. No one wants to hear that their behavior is putting themselves and those they love in danger, or that God's patience will eventually wear out. Yet that was the message God told Jeremiah to write (Jeremiah 36:2). When His message was read to King Jehoiakim, the king cut up the scroll and threw it into the fire (v. 23).

The only way to know we are right is to be willing to discover where we are wrong. Read the all-time bestselling banned book and let it reveal to you the truth about God—and about yourself. —JAL

The Bible shows us a picture of who we really are.

THINGS ABOVE

Seek those things which are above, where Christ is, sitting at the right hand of God.
—COLOSSIANS 3:1

Stepping outside and gazing heavenward on a star-studded evening always helps to soothe my soul after a trouble-filled day. When I peer into the night sky, I forget, at least for a moment, the cares of life on earth.

Ancient Israel's prolific songwriter wrote a poem thousands of years ago that still rings true: "When I consider Your heavens, the work of Your fingers, the moon and the stars, which You have ordained, what is man that You are mindful of him, and the son of man that You visit him?" (Psalm 8:3–4).

When we try to imagine the immensity of God's heavens, our problems indeed seem trivial. Yet God doesn't think so! With all the galaxies He has to attend to, God is mindful of us—and, He *cares* for us.

No wonder the apostle Paul advised new believers to set their minds on things above (Colossians 3:2). In doing so, we raise our thoughts above the level of earthly disputes and focus instead on our loving, heavenly Father, who wants us to know Him, to know how to live peacefully with one another, and to know that we can live eternally with Him in a place even more beautiful than the heavens.

"The heavens declare the glory of God" (Psalm 19:1). Let's join creation in praise to Him. —JAL

September 26

Read: Colossians 3:1–13

Biblical Truth

Personal Application

Prayer Requests

Answers to Prayer

Because God gives us everything, we owe Him all our praise.

September 27

Read: 2 Timothy 4:9–18

Biblical Truth

Personal Application

Prayer Requests

Answers to Prayer

FAMOUS LAST WORDS

At my first defense no one stood with me, but all forsook me. May it not be charged against them.
—2 Timothy 4:16

Just days before his death, Gandhi wrote, "All about me is darkness; I am praying for light." By contrast, evangelist D. L. Moody's last recorded words were, "This is my triumph; this my coronation day! It is glorious!" The last words of these men were significant expressions of their perspectives on life, death, and everything in between.

Aside from some personal greetings, Paul's last recorded words dealt not with what he had done in life and ministry but rather with how he viewed people. What makes it even more significant is that some of those words were about people who had disappointed him.

Regarding an individual who had harmed him by opposing his ministry, Paul trusted the Lord to deal with him. And when considering those who had abandoned him when imprisoned, he asked others to handle them graciously: "At my first defense no one stood with me, but all forsook me. May it not be charged against them" (2 Timothy 4:16). His last words were those of compassion and kindness instead of harshness and retaliation.

Will our last words show the grace of Christ or the bitterness of a wounded heart? Our answer should impact the words we use today. —BC

What words will be your legacy?

SHOWING UP

Because He has inclined His ear to me, therefore I will call upon Him as long as I live.
—PSALM 116:2

Leonardo da Vinci spent 10 years drawing ears, elbows, hands, and other parts of the body in many different aspects. Then one day he set aside these exercises and painted what he saw. Likewise, athletes and musicians never become great without regular practice.

For years I resisted a regular routine of prayer, believing that communication with God should be spontaneous and free. But I found that I needed the discipline of regularity to make possible those exceptional times of free communication with God. Eventually I learned that spontaneity often flows from discipline.

The writer Nancy Mairs says she attends church in the same spirit in which she goes to her desk every morning to write, so that if an idea comes she'll be there to receive it. I approach prayer the same way. I keep on whether it feels like I am profiting or not. I show up in hopes of getting to know God better, perhaps hearing from Him in ways accessible only through solitude.

The English word *meditate* derives from a Latin word that means "to rehearse." Often my prayers seem like a kind of rehearsal. I go over basic notes (the Lord's Prayer), practice familiar pieces (the Psalms), and try out a few new tunes. Mainly, I show up. —PY

September 28

Read: Psalm 116

Biblical Truth

Personal Application

Prayer Requests

Answers to Prayer

Prayer is an intimate conversation with our God.

September 29

Read: James 1:1–8

Biblical Truth

Personal Application

Prayer Requests

Answers to Prayer

ASK ME NOW

If any of you lacks wisdom,
let him ask of God, who gives to all
liberally and without reproach,
and it will be given to him.
—JAMES 1:5

Whether you need a weather forecast for Singapore or driving directions to a restaurant in Chicago, the answer may be just a cell-phone call away. A California-based mobile service called AskMeNow utilizes Internet content sources to send text-message replies to queries from registered users on just about any subject. In many cases, a text-message reply may be received within minutes of submitting a question.

In a sense, the invitation to ask anything, anytime, anywhere mirrors God's call to all who follow Jesus: "If any of you lacks wisdom, let him ask of God, who gives to all liberally and without reproach" (James 1:5). But this is more than a mobile information service. It is our heavenly Father's promise to provide the guidance we need, especially during trying times.

All we need is a sincere desire to follow God's direction and faith that His way is best. Because the Lord "gives generously to all men without making them feel foolish or guilty," we can ask in faith without doubting (vv. 5–6 Phillips).

The Internet is a great place to find helpful information, but there is only one source of divine wisdom to direct our steps each day. The Father invites our sincere requests anytime, anywhere.
—DCM

Be smart—ask for God's wisdom.

THAT YOU MAY KNOW

These things I have written to you who believe in the name of the Son of God, that you may know that you have eternal life.
—1 John 5:13

One day, while Wim was in the marketplace in the Netherlands, he struck up a conversation with a woman who remarked that you can get to heaven by doing good works.

His attempt to explain that it is by God's grace that we are "saved through faith" (Ephesians 2:8) brought a smile as the woman repeated confidently: "and . . . by doing good works." Then another woman volunteered, "You can hope you'll go to heaven, but you can't be sure." Wim's assertion that he did know for sure was met with a muttered, "Nobody knows for sure."

Wim then showed the woman what 1 John 5:11–13 says. He explained: "See, it doesn't say *hope* there, it says *know*." Unconvinced, she said, "Like you, my pastor says that we have to have faith, but you really never know whether you've been good enough. You may think you have, but who can be sure?"

To some, Wim's confidence may seem incredible. But he based his words on this statement: "For by grace you have been saved through faith, and that not of yourselves; it is the gift of God, not of works" (Ephesians 2:8–9).

It's true. We can't be good enough. We can never do enough good things. But we can be sure of heaven if we simply believe on the Lord (Acts 16:31). —CHK

September 30

Read: 1 John 5:6–13

Biblical Truth

Personal Application

Prayer Requests

Answers to Prayer

We are saved by God's mercy, not by our merit— by Christ's dying, not by our doing.

October

October 1

Read: Proverbs 1:8–19

Biblical Truth

Personal Application

Prayer Requests

Answers to Prayer

CARDBOARD KIDS

My son, if sinners entice you,
do not consent.
—Proverbs 1:10

When Mike Wood began to advertise his sign company, he didn't know how useful his work would become.

Some of his signs were life-size cardboard pictures of kids, which he put close to the street. Besides advertising his business, the signs had another effect. Motorists thought the cutouts were real children and began to drop their speed. Now Mike sells the cardboard kids to parents who want to slow down speeding drivers in their neighborhood. Mike said, "We truly hope that some of our standups help to control speeding in neighborhoods around the country."

Parents work at protecting their children from physical danger. But there are other dangers as well. Solomon, the writer of Proverbs 1, was concerned about the people who would pose spiritual danger to his son. He warned him about those who would entice him to do evil (vv. 10–14) and told him, "Do not walk in the way with them, keep your foot from their path; for their feet run to evil" (vv. 15–16).

We need to protect our children by teaching them God's Word and training them to avoid evil influences. Busy streets are hazardous for our children, but the enticement of taking an evil path is far more dangerous.
—AC

Tomorrow's world will be shaped by what we teach our children today.

FOR A LIMITED TIME

October 2

You do not know what will happen tomorrow. For what is your life? It is even a vapor that appears for a little time and then vanishes away.
—JAMES 4:14

On a crisp October morning, our local newspaper featured a stunning photo of sun-drenched aspen trees whose leaves had turned autumn gold. The caption read: FOR A LIMITED TIME ONLY. The irresistible invitation to take a drive through the mountains to savor the brilliant colors conveyed the urgency of doing it quickly. Autumn leaves that are golden today are often gone tomorrow.

Our opportunities to obey God's promptings are also fleeting. James warned against an arrogance that assumes endless days will be available to carry out our good intentions. "You do not know what will happen tomorrow. For what is your life? It is even a vapor that appears for a little time and then vanishes away . . . Therefore, to him who knows to do good and does not do it, to him it is sin" (4:14, 17).

Is there an act of kindness or encouragement that God has urged you to do for someone in His name? How long has it been since that first prompting? With so many demands on our time, the urgent tasks demand our attention while the important things can be postponed. But a time will come when even the important can no longer be done.

When we follow God's urging with our action now, today will be golden. —DCM

Read: James 4:13–17

Biblical Truth

Personal Application

Prayer Requests

Answers to Prayer

Doing what's right today means no regrets tomorrow.

October 3

Read: Galatians 5:16–24

Biblical Truth

Personal Application

Prayer Requests

Answers to Prayer

THE POWER OF PATIENCE

The fruit of the Spirit is . . . longsuffering.
—Galatians 5:22

We've all heard the prayer: "Lord, make me more patient—and do it now!"

Why is it that patience evaporates when we are late for a critical engagement and are caught in a traffic jam? Or we rush to the "10 items or less" line at the store, only to find someone in front of us with 16 items!

Being forced to wait ratchets up the stress and shortens our fuse. When that happens, we not only fail to be patient but we undercut the Spirit's work in our lives.

Patience is not just a virtue, it's a fruit of the Spirit (Galatians 5:22). Which means that demonstrations of impatience reveal the sour fruit of our fallen hearts rather than the sweetness of Jesus in our lives. Since God is a patient God, when we abandon patience we miss the opportunity to show our world the glory of God through our lives.

Bursts of impatience only demonstrate that we are more concerned with our own agendas than with the needs and struggles of others. So let's all take a deep breath and turn our focus away from ourselves by patiently loving others instead of ourselves in the midst of stress.

Patience gives us the privilege of sharing the refreshing fruit of God with others. —JS

Be patient. Show your world what God is really like.

October 4

CURIOSITY OR COMPASSION?

[Jesus'] disciples asked Him, saying, "Rabbi, who sinned, this man or his parents, that he was born blind?"
—John 9:2

Why is it that when we hear about someone who is suffering, we are more interested in the details of what, why, when, and where than we are about how we can help?

When the disciples passed the blind beggar (John 9:1), their curiosity about why he was suffering outweighed the possibility of reaching out to help him. "Who sinned, this man or his parents, that he was born blind?" they asked (v. 2). Their pop-quiz for Jesus revealed that lurking beneath their question was a judgmental spirit—a desire to know whom to blame—as if *that* would make anyone feel better!

Thankfully, Jesus modeled a compassionate response. Rather than speculation and condemnation, He marshaled His resources to help, which in this case meant complete healing. He made it clear that the man's blindness was intended to provide a moment for God to be magnified through Jesus' compassionate touch.

Feeling curious about somebody's problem? Shift into Jesus' mode and move past the point of curiosity to his or her point of need. Reach out and touch someone's pain. Show the compassionate love of Jesus in action. —JS

Read: John 9:1–12

Biblical Truth

Personal Application

Prayer Requests

Answers to Prayer

Do you want to be like Jesus? Replace curiosity with compassion.

October 5

Read: Ephesians 3:1–7

Biblical Truth

Personal Application

Prayer Requests

Answers to Prayer

ROSETTA STONE

The mystery of Christ, which in other ages was not made known to the sons of men . . . has now been revealed by the Spirit.
—Ephesians 3:4–5

For centuries, the hieroglyphic word pictures painted on Egyptian ruins were a mystery. Then in 1799 a French archaeological expedition at the Egyptian harbor of Rosetta discovered an ancient stone. It weighed 1,676 pounds and reflected beautiful dark gray, blue, and pink hues. But that is not what made it valuable.

The stone was inscribed with an identical message in different ancient scripts. Among them were hieroglyphics and classical Greek. Using Greek to translate, scholars soon understood the meaning of the hieroglyphics. They were no longer a mystery.

The Bible has also contained an ancient mystery. For centuries, it seemed as if God's purposes were limited to the Jews. Yet with the appearance of Jesus of Nazareth, the promise to Abraham to bless the whole world came to light (Genesis 12:1–3). Paul wrote: "The mystery of Christ, which in other ages was not made known . . . has now been revealed by the Spirit" (Ephesians 3:4–5). The meaning behind the mystery? God provides salvation to all people who repent and believe in His Son (Galatians 3:8–9, 28).

The revelation of the New Testament describes a glorious future when people from every ethnic group, nation, and language will share in the inheritance of the children of God (Revelation 5:9).
—DF

The Christian's inheritance is guaranteed forever!

NOT MUCH IN BETWEEN

October 6

That you may be filled with all the fullness of God.
—Ephesians 3:19

Read: Ephesians 3:14–21

In the western panhandle of Texas is a small town named Texline. It had an ostentatious beginning in the late 1800s as a thriving center along a new railroad line. Within a few years, though, most of the shops had closed and the town's population shriveled to about 400. In 2000, the population was still just over 500. One online description of Texline says that it has "a city limits sign at one end, another at the other end, and not much in between."

What a waste if the same description could be given of our spiritual journey! The journey of the Christian life on earth begins at the moment of faith in Jesus and ends when the believer goes to be with the Lord. This raises an important question: What happens in between?

A rich and full life is available to all who believe in and serve Jesus. The apostle Paul prayed that believers would "be filled with all the fullness of God" (Ephesians 3:19). He wanted them to know life "abundantly" (John 10:10). But how many of us experience even a small part of the abundant life Christ promised to those who are faithful to Him?

God desires to give us a marvelous beginning with salvation and a great ending in Glory—with much in between. —DCE

Biblical Truth

Personal Application

Prayer Requests

Answers to Prayer

A life given fully to God becomes a God-filled life.

October 7

Read: 1 Corinthians 12:14–27

Biblical Truth

Personal Application

Prayer Requests

Answers to Prayer

UNUSED MUSCLES

The manifestation of the Spirit is given to each one for the profit of all.
—1 Corinthians 12:7

My wife recently visited a physiotherapist to seek relief for her neck and shoulder pain. When the problem did not go away after several visits, she asked why. She was told that her pain was because of some "lazy neck muscles."

Apparently, the neck muscles that were supposed to hold her head upright were not doing their job. As a result, her shoulder muscles had to take over the function of holding up her head. This caused unnaturally stiffened shoulder muscles. The solution? Exercises were prescribed to train her neck muscles to do what they were designed to do.

In a way, her problem depicts what happens in the body of Christ. God has given each believer gifts that are to be exercised for the common good of the church (1 Corinthians 12:7). But when some don't pull their weight, others far less gifted in those areas must pitch in. Although the body of Christ continues to function, it is not functioning at its best. There are some overworked Christians around!

God wants us to use our spiritual gifts to benefit others in the church. When we work together, we keep the body strong. What has God gifted you to do so that you can help relieve the strain the church is suffering? —CPH

Teamwork divides the effort and multiplies the effect.

EREV YOM KIPPUR

October 8

First be reconciled to your brother, and then come and offer your gift.
—MATTHEW 5:24

In Judaism, the holiest day of the year is Yom Kippur, the Day of Atonement. On that day, the nation seeks God's forgiveness for sins both personal and national.

What is interesting, however, is the day before Yom Kippur, known as Erev Yom Kippur. It represents a person's last opportunity to seek forgiveness from other people before Yom Kippur begins. This is important because, in Jewish thought, you must seek forgiveness from other people before you can seek the forgiveness of God.

Today, we are called to do the same. Jesus pointed out that in order to worship Him with all our heart, we first need to resolve matters with others. He said, "If you bring your gift to the altar, and there remember that your brother has something against you, leave your gift there before the altar, and go your way. First be reconciled to your brother, and then come and offer your gift" (Matthew 5:23–24).

Even in a matter as basic as our giving, the ability to truly worship God is hindered by the reality of relationships broken by our wrong actions, attitudes, and words.

So that our worship can be pleasing and acceptable to God, let us make every effort to be reconciled to one another—today.
—BC

Read: Matthew 5:21–26

Biblical Truth

Personal Application

Prayer Requests

Answers to Prayer

An offense against your neighbor is a fence between you and God.

October 9

Read: Matthew 6:9–15

Biblical Truth

Personal Application

Prayer Requests

Answers to Prayer

THE CHAIN OF UNGRACE

Forgive us our debts, as we forgive our debtors.
—MATTHEW 6:12

When I feel wronged, I can contrive a hundred reasons against forgiveness. "He needs to learn a lesson." "I'll let her stew for a while; it'll do her good." "It's not up to *me* to make the first move." When I finally soften to the point of granting forgiveness, it seems a leap from hard logic to mushy sentiment.

One factor that motivates me to forgive is that as a Christian I am commanded to, as the child of a Father who forgives. Jesus said, "If you have anything against anyone, forgive him, that your Father in heaven may also forgive you your trespasses" (Mark 11:25).

But beyond that, I can identify three pragmatic reasons. First, forgiveness halts the cycle of blame and pain, breaking the chain of ungrace. Without it we remain bound to the people we can't forgive, held in their vise grip.

Second, forgiveness loosens the stranglehold of guilt in the perpetrator. It allows the possibility of transformation in the guilty party, even if a just punishment is still required.

And third, forgiveness creates a remarkable linkage, placing the forgiver on the same side as the party who did the wrong. We are not as different from the wrongdoer as we would like to think, for we too must ask our heavenly Father, "Forgive us our debts" (Matthew 6:12). —PY

He who cannot forgive others burns the bridge over which he himself must pass. —HERBERT

A HANDFUL OF THORNS

October 10

Give thanks to the Lord for His goodness, and for His wonderful works to the children of men!
—Psalm 107:21

Jeremy Taylor was a 17th-century English cleric who was severely persecuted for his faith. But though his house was plundered, his family left destitute, and his property confiscated, he continued to count the blessings he could not lose.

He wrote: "They have not taken away my merry countenance, my cheerful spirit, and a good conscience; they have still left me with the providence of God, and all His promises . . . my hopes of Heaven, and my charity to them, too, and still I sleep and digest, I eat and drink, I read and meditate. And he that hath so many causes of joy, and so great should never choose to sit down upon his little handful of thorns."

Although we may not be afflicted with the grievous difficulties that Jeremy Taylor endured, all of us face trials and troubles. Are we grumbling? Or do we refuse to let our "little handful of thorns," our troubles, obscure the overwhelming abundance of our blessings?

When we feel like complaining, let's remember God's faithfulness and "give thanks to the Lord! Call upon His name; make known His deeds among the peoples! . . . Remember His marvelous works which He has done!" (Psalm 105:1, 5). —VCG

Read: Psalm 105:1–6

Biblical Truth

Personal Application

Prayer Requests

Answers to Prayer

Spend your time counting your blessings, not airing your complaints.

October 11

Read: Matthew 4:18–25

Biblical Truth

Personal Application

Prayer Requests

Answers to Prayer

THE ART OF COMMON PEOPLE

I have not come to call the righteous, but sinners, to repentance.
—Luke 5:32

The 16th-century Italian painter Caravaggio received scathing criticism in his day for depicting people of the Bible as common. His critics reflected a time when only members of royalty and aristocracy were considered appropriate subjects for the "immortality" of art. His commissioned canvas of *St. Matthew and the Angel* so offended church leaders that it had to be redone. They could not accept seeing Matthew with the physical features of an everyday laborer.

According to one biographer, what the church fathers did not understand was that "Caravaggio, in elevating this humble figure, was copying Christ, who had himself raised Matthew from the street."

Caravaggio was right about the people of the Bible. Jesus himself grew up in the home of a laborer. When His time came to go public, He was announced by a weather-worn man of the wilderness known as John the Baptizer. His disciples were fishermen and common people.

Jesus lived, loved, and died for wealthy people too. But by befriending those who had been demon-possessed, lepers, fishermen, and even despised tax collectors, the teacher from Nazareth showed that no one is too poor, too sinful, or too insignificant to be His friend. —MD

Jesus wants you for a friend.

LIFE ACCORDING TO PLUMB

October 12

Your Word I have hidden in my heart, that I might not sin against You.
—PSALM 119:11

Read: Psalm 119:9–16

Biblical Truth

Personal Application

Prayer Requests

Answers to Prayer

Charlie Riggs has been called "the man behind Billy Graham." For nearly 40 years, Riggs was the director of counseling and follow-up for Mr. Graham's evangelistic meetings. In his counselor training classes, Charlie taught thousands of people the basic principles of how to live for Christ and share their faith with others.

At Charlie's 90th birthday celebration, many tributes mentioned his lifelong practice of memorizing Scripture. His goal was not merely to know the Bible, but to know Christ and live by His Word.

Charlie followed Psalm 119:9–11: "How can a young man cleanse his way? By taking heed according to Your Word . . . Your Word I have hidden in my heart, that I might not sin against You." He likened the Scriptures to "plumb bobs" for his heart. Like the weight that holds a builder's plumb line straight and true, these divine principles never change, no matter what the circumstances. He sought to measure his own thoughts, feelings, and behavior by God's Word, not the other way around.

Charlie Riggs's life was quiet and steady behind the scenes. His example challenges us today to hide God's Word in our hearts and let it guide our lives. Charlie demonstrated what it means to live according to plumb. —DCM

The Bible: Know it in your head, stow it in your heart, show it in your life, sow it in the world.

October 13

Read: Psalm 119:17–24

Biblical Truth

Personal Application

Prayer Requests

Answers to Prayer

ERASMUS

Your Word was to me the joy and rejoicing of my heart.
—JEREMIAH 15:16

For centuries, many Christians were not permitted to read God's Word in their own language. Instead, they were encouraged to attend Latin services that few could understand.

Then, in 1516, the Dutch scholar Erasmus compiled and published the first New Testament in the original Greek language. This landmark work was the basis for the later publication of Luther's German Bible, Tyndale's English Bible, and the King James Version. These translations made the Scriptures understandable to millions of people around the world.

Erasmus could not have known the influence his Greek New Testament would have, but he did have a passion for getting its message to laypeople from all walks of life. In the preface he wrote: "I would have [the Gospels and the Epistles] translated into all languages . . . I long for the plowboy to sing them to himself as he follows the plow [and] the weaver to hum them to the tune of his shuttle."

The prophet Jeremiah reflected this same passion for the Word: "Your words were found, and I ate them, and Your Word was to me the joy and rejoicing of my heart" (15:16).

Having God's Word in our own language allows us to experience the joy of meditating on it each day. —DF

The treasures of truth in God's Word are best mined with the spade of meditation.

THE USHPIZZIN

October 14

Pure and undefiled religion before God and the Father is this: to visit orphans and widows in their trouble, and to keep oneself unspotted from the world.
—James 1:27

In Jewish legend, the *ushpizzin* are guests who visit the pious at Sukkot, the Feast of Tabernacles. They are supposedly the great Old Testament heroes who come offering comfort and encouragement to the faithful. According to Jewish lore, these unseen guests only visit the sukkah (shelter) where the poor are welcome—a reminder of each person's responsibility to care for others. It also reminds them that unseen watchers may be observing their conduct.

The story of the *ushpizzin* isn't true, of course. But the lore and legend can serve as a reminder to us that we as Christ-followers are living observed lives. Others are watching us. And our concern for others, particularly the least among us, is an expression of the compassion Christ displayed to the hurting and outcast of His generation.

James, the half-brother of Jesus, challenged believers to put the love of Christ into practice. He wrote, "Pure and undefiled religion before God and the Father is this: to visit orphans and widows in their trouble, and to keep oneself unspotted from the world" (James 1:27).

The example of Christ and the words of Scripture inspire us to care for our hurting world.

Who's watching us? Our world is watching. And so is our Lord!
—BC

Read: James 1:19–27

Biblical Truth

Personal Application

Prayer Requests

Answers to Prayer

When people observe your life, do they see the love of Christ?

October 15

Read: Deuteronomy 31:9–13

Biblical Truth

Personal Application

Prayer Requests

Answers to Prayer

JOY TO THE WORLD

The Word became flesh and dwelt among us, and we beheld His glory, the glory as of the only begotten of the Father, full of grace and truth.
—John 1:14

When Christmas displays go up before Halloween displays come down, I long for the days when people didn't think about Christmas until after Thanksgiving. However, there may be a legitimate reason to celebrate Christmas in October.

No one knows the exact day when Jesus was born, but December 25 is unlikely. His birth may have been in autumn, when the weather was still warm enough for shepherds to be outdoors with their flocks. We know that Jesus was crucified on Passover, and that the Holy Spirit came on Pentecost. So some scholars have reasoned that Jesus' birth may have occurred on another Jewish holiday, the Feast of Tabernacles, or Sukkot, usually celebrated about mid-September to mid-October.

Sukkot was a time when observant Jews lived in temporary dwellings and listened to the Word of the Lord being read (Deuteronomy 31:10–13). Although we cannot know for sure, we do know that it would be in keeping with God's way of working to send His Son—the Word made flesh who "dwelt" ("tabernacled") among us (John 1:14)—on the Feast of Tabernacles.

For Jews, Sukkot is "the time of our rejoicing." For all of us, our time of rejoicing is the birth of Christ, who brings the joy of salvation to all the world. —JAL

The date of Christ's birth may be debatable, but the fact of His life is indisputable.

A SPECIAL SEAT

[Martha] had a sister called Mary, who also sat at Jesus' feet and heard His word.
—Luke 10:39

I've never sat in the first-class section of an airplane. But I still hold out the hope that someday I'll get on the plane and the flight attendant will stop me and say, "Come with me. I have a special seat for you."

That's why I was pretty excited when a friend gave my sister some tickets for an event and we realized that they were for box seats. Instead of sitting shoulder to shoulder with strangers all around us, we sat in a private compartment where we could see and hear everything perfectly. That evening, we felt privileged and special.

Remember Jesus' friends, Mary and Martha? Although Martha had the opportunity to enjoy having Jesus as her guest, she soon became frustrated with her sister Mary and overwhelmed with the busyness of her preparations. Certainly understandable to a lot of us! Jesus made it clear to her, however, that sometimes it's necessary to step away from the unending pressures of life and spend undistracted time with Him.

God has given us the opportunity to have personal moments with Him. By taking the time just to be with the Lord, we are fed, refreshed, and renewed.

Jesus commended Mary for taking time to sit and learn at her Savior's feet (Luke 10:42). As it turned out, she had the best seat in the house! —CHK

October 16

Read: Luke 10:38–42

Biblical Truth

Personal Application

Prayer Requests

Answers to Prayer

Jesus longs for our fellowship even more than we long for His.

October 17

Read: John 8:42–47

Biblical Truth

Personal Application

Prayer Requests

Answers to Prayer

BREAKING THE SPIN CYCLE

[Satan] was a murderer from the beginning, and does not stand in the truth, because there is no truth in him . . . He is a liar and the father of it.
—John 8:44

Politicians are adept at "spinning" the details of a story to advance their own agenda. During a political campaign, spin doctors massage stories to ensure that their candidate is cast in a positive light, often at the expense of the truth. This leaves us with serious questions about what the real truth is.

According to Jesus, Satan is the "spin doctor" of hell—the master deceiver who "speaks from his own resources, for he is a liar" (John 8:44). He casts himself as the one who wants to give us unfettered freedom and pleasure, carefully masking his plan to steal, kill, and destroy us (John 10:10). He even spins the loving laws of God by claiming that God's boundaries are restrictive, simply intended to take all the fun out of living. When we buy into Satan's damaging lies, we will eventually find ourselves empty and broken—sidelined in our journey with God.

Thankfully, Jesus warns us. He says that Satan is the father of lies. And we know Satan is lying when what he tells us contradicts God's Word. Jesus, on the other hand, is the truth (John 14:6). So, when it comes to sorting out the spin, our only defense against the spin doctor of hell is to listen constantly for the voice of Jesus as we pray and study His Word. And that's the truth! —JS

God's truth stops the spin of Satan's lies.

A HILL TOO HIGH

October 18

Do not worry about tomorrow,
for tomorrow will
worry about its own things.
—MATTHEW 6:34

My wife and I like to rollerblade. Near the end of one of our favorite routes is a long hill. When we first started taking this route, I tried to encourage Sue by saying, "Are you ready for the hill?" just before pushing our way to the top. But one day she said, "Could you please not say that? You make it sound like a huge mountain, and that discourages me."

It was better for Sue to face the hill thinking only about one "step," or one rollerblade push, at a time instead of an entire steep hill to conquer.

Life can be like that. If we peer too far ahead of today, the challenges may feel like a Mt. Everest climb. They can appear impossible to handle if we think we have to be "ready for the hill."

The Bible reminds us that today is all we need to tackle. We don't need to worry about tomorrow's tasks (Matthew 6:34). Imagine Moses thinking, "I've got to feed all these people for who knows how long. How can I get that much food?" God took care of that mountain with manna—but only enough for one day at a time (Exodus 16:4).

Every hill in life is too high if we think we must climb it all at once. But no hill is insurmountable if we take it one step forward at a time—with God's help.
—DB

Read: Exodus 16:1–5

Biblical Truth

Personal Application

Prayer Requests

Answers to Prayer

God is there to give us strength for every hill we have to climb.

October 19

Read: Matthew 15:1–11

Biblical Truth

Personal Application

Prayer Requests

Answers to Prayer

LOOKS CAN BE DECEIVING

These people draw near to Me with their mouth, and honor Me with their lips, but their heart is far from Me.
—MATTHEW 15:8

On June 22, 2002, a 33-year-old pitching star for the St. Louis Cardinals was found dead in his Chicago hotel room. He was young, physically active, and appeared to be in good health. However, the autopsy revealed that he had a 90-percent blockage in two of three coronary arteries, an enlarged heart, and a blood clot in one of the arteries. His appearance misled many to think that he was physically healthy.

Jesus said that appearances can deceive people into thinking that they are *spiritually* healthy. After the Pharisees accused Him and His followers of breaking religious traditions by not washing their hands before they ate, Jesus said that the Pharisees had laid aside commands of God for man-made, religious traditions. He reminded them that kingdom righteousness was not an outside-in job but an inside-out, transforming work of God. Jesus said that they looked impressive spiritually, but their hearts were diseased and distant: "[They] honor Me with their lips, but their heart is far from Me" (Matthew 15:8). Their talk never matched their walk, thus producing the illegitimate child of hypocrisy.

Spiritual health is not determined by how we look, but by how we live. Let's ask God to search us, know our hearts, test us, and lead us in His way (Psalm 139:23–24). —MW

As we talk the talk, let's make sure we walk the walk.

DO SOMETHING WITH NOTHING

October 20

Walk circumspectly, not as fools but as wise, redeeming the time, because the days are evil.
—Ephesians 5:15–16

Read: Ephesians 5:15–21

A newspaper ad showed three people waiting for a city bus. Two of them were bored and listless, while the third was happily playing a game on a small electronic device. "Do something with your nothing," the ad said. "That nothing time. The time in between everything else you have to do." The idea was to sell the portable player so people could use all those segments of wasted "waiting" time.

I suspect that many of us already constructively use those small increments of waiting time to read a book, memorize a verse, or pray for a friend. It's our longer waiting periods filled with uncertainty and indecision that may leave us anxious and frustrated.

Paul challenged the Christians in Ephesus to "walk circumspectly, not as fools but as wise, redeeming the time, because the days are evil" (Ephesians 5:15–16). The Greek scholar Kenneth Wuest suggests that this refers to time in its "strategic, opportune seasons" and means "making a wise and sacred use of every opportunity for doing good."

During those seasons when we wonder, "How did I get here and when can I leave?" it's best to look for our God-given opportunities instead of focusing on the obstacles. That's the way to do something with our nothing. —DCM

Biblical Truth

Personal Application

Prayer Requests

Answers to Prayer

When you find time on your hands, put them together in prayer.

October 21

Read: Hosea 11

Biblical Truth

Personal Application

Prayer Requests

Answers to Prayer

GOD'S LOVE STORY

How can I give you up, Ephraim? How can I hand you over, Israel? . . . My heart churns within Me; My sympathy is stirred.
—HOSEA 11:8

Is there any human feeling more powerful than that of betrayal? Ask a high school girl whose boyfriend has dumped her for a pretty cheerleader. Or tune your radio to a country-western station and listen to the lyrics of infidelity. Or check out the murders reported in the daily newspaper, an amazing number of which trace back to a quarrel with an estranged lover.

In the Old Testament, God through Hosea's marriage demonstrates in living color exactly what it is like to love someone desperately and get nothing in return. Not even God, with all His power, will force a human being to love Him.

Many people think of God as an impersonal force, something akin to the law of gravity. The book of Hosea portrays almost the opposite: a God of passion and fury and tears and love. A God in mourning over Israel's rejection of Him (11:8).

God the lover does not desire to share His bride with anyone else. Yet, amazingly, when Israel turned her back on God, He stuck with her. He was willing to suffer, in hope that someday she would return to Him.

Hosea, and later Jesus, prove that God longs not to punish but to love. In fact, He loved us so much that He sent His Son to die for us! —PY

God loved us so much, He sent His only Son.

ON HIS SHOULDERS

October 22

He shall dwell between His shoulders.
—Deuteronomy 33:12

Read: Luke 15:3–7

Our family likes to hike, and we've had some grand adventures together. But when our boys were small, our enthusiasm caused us to walk too fast and too far, and their legs often grew weary. They couldn't keep up the pace, despite their determined efforts and our assurance that the end of the trail was just over the next hill.

"Dad," would come the plaintive request, accompanied by upraised arms, "will you carry me?" "Of course," I would reply, and hoist the child on my shoulders. He was not a burden, for he was little and light.

How often, like my children, I've grown weary, and the end of my efforts is not even in sight. I can no longer keep up or accomplish the task. But I am learning that I can turn with arms upraised to my heavenly Father, who walks beside me, and I can ask Him to carry me.

I know He will lay me on His shoulder as a shepherd carries the lamb that was lost (Luke 15:5). There He will joyfully carry me all day long, for I am little and light—no burden to Him. There I find rest, for "the beloved of the Lord shall dwell in safety by Him, who shelters him all the day long; and he shall dwell between His shoulders" (Deuteronomy 33:12).
—DHR

Biblical Truth

Personal Application

Prayer Requests

Answers to Prayer

The God who holds the universe is the God who is holding you.

October 23

Read: Lamentations 1:12–16; 3:19–23

Biblical Truth

Personal Application

Prayer Requests

Answers to Prayer

SILHOUETTE

Through the Lord's mercies
we are not consumed,
because His compassions fail not.
—Lamentations 3:22

In the 18th century, silhouettes (shadow profiles traced and cut from black paper) were a popular alternative to costly portraits. The word took its name from the French controller general of finance, Étienne de Silhouette. During the Seven Years War against England, he tried to raise revenues by heavily taxing the wealthy. Victims of his high taxes complained and used the word *silhouette* to refer to their wealth being reduced to a mere shadow of what it once was.

With the destruction of Jerusalem, Jeremiah lamented over the shadow of what once was a great city and center of worship now devastated by war. "Is it nothing to you, all you who pass by? Behold and see if there is any sorrow like my sorrow" (Lamentations 1:12).

But Jeremiah did not remain in despair. He recognized God's sovereignty in suffering. Later in this book of sorrow, the prophet reflected: "I have hope. Through the Lord's mercies we are not consumed, because His compassions fail not. They are new every morning" (3:21–23).

Has sorrow or suffering made your life feel like a dark silhouette of what it once was? Remember, God's mercies are new every morning. He is compassionately working in your life for His glory and your blessing. —DF

To see beyond earth's shadows, look to Christ the Light.

SATISFACTION

October 24

The world is passing away,
and the lust of it; but he who does
the will of God abides forever.
—1 JOHN 2:17

Read: 1 John 2:12–17

Pornography, once a secretive backdoor industry, is now out in the open. The easy access and anonymity of the Internet have turned it into a multibillion-dollar-a-year "business." But it leaves a trail of broken families, ineffective Christian leaders, and men who have lost the respect of their loved ones.

The apostle John was known for his great love for Christ and His church. In 1 John 2:12–17 he warned fathers and young men against these three lusts:

- The lust of the flesh—the insatiable appetite to indulge in pleasures that inflame the flesh but never satisfy.
- The lust of the eyes—wandering eyes that continually want more riches and possessions but always remain covetous.
- The pride of life—the vain mind that thirsts for man's applause. But the glory evaporates quickly.

Pornography damages users and victims alike. It feeds lustful desires in ways that can never satisfy. True satisfaction is found only when we give our affections to eternal things—to a right relationship with our heavenly Father and with those He has created in His image.

"The world is passing away, and the lust of it; but he who does the will of God abides forever" (v. 17).
—AL

Biblical Truth

Personal Application

Prayer Requests

Answers to Prayer

Inner peace springs out of inner purity.

October 25

Read: Hebrews 12:1–11

Biblical Truth

Personal Application

Prayer Requests

Answers to Prayer

SHARK TONIC

Let us lay aside every weight, and the sin which so easily ensnares us, and let us run with endurance the race that is set before us.
—Hebrews 12:1

Have you ever heard of shark "tonic"? It isn't a serum that prevents shark attacks or a medicine given to sharks. The actual term is "tonic immobility," described as "a natural state of paralysis that animals enter . . . Sharks can be placed in a tonic immobility state by turning them upside down. The shark remains in this state of paralysis for an average of 15 minutes before it recovers."

In other words, a dangerous shark can be made vulnerable simply by turning it upside down. The state of tonic immobility makes the shark incapable of movement.

Sin is like that. Our ability to honor our Lord, for which we are created in Christ, can be put into "tonic immobility" by the power and consequences of sin. To that end, the writer of Hebrews wants us to be proactive. He wrote, "Therefore we also, since we are surrounded by so great a cloud of witnesses, let us lay aside every weight, and the sin which so easily ensnares us, and let us run with endurance the race that is set before us" (Hebrews 12:1).

If we are to run the race of the Christian life effectively, we must deal with sin before it immobilizes us. We need to lay aside the sin that hinders us from pleasing Him—starting today. —BC

We must face up to our sins before we can put them behind us.

THE RIPENING SELF

October 26

May the God of all grace . . .
after you have suffered a while,
perfect, establish,
strengthen, and settle you.
—1 Peter 5:10

In his early years of ministry, the English preacher Charles Simeon (1759–1836) was a harsh and self-assertive man. One day he was visiting a friend and fellow pastor in a nearby village. When he left to go home, his friend's daughters complained to their father about Simeon's manner. So the father took the girls to the backyard and said, "Pick me one of those peaches." It was early summer, and the peaches were green. The girls asked why he wanted green, unripe fruit. He replied, "Well, my dears, it is green now, and we must wait; but a little more sun, and a few more showers, and the peach will be ripe and sweet. So it is with Mr. Simeon."

Simeon, in due time, did change. The warmth of God's love and the "showers" of misunderstanding and disappointment were the means by which he became a gentle, humble man.

The God of all grace works in all His children, humbling the proud and exalting the humble, to make them ripe and sweet. Our task is to take hold of God's grace to endure our afflictions with patience, without growing weary.

In time, He will "perfect, establish, strengthen, and settle" us (1 Peter 5:10). We must "wait on the Lord" and "be of good courage" (Psalm 27:14). —DHR

Read: 1 Peter 5:5–11

Biblical Truth

Personal Application

Prayer Requests

Answers to Prayer

Salvation is the miracle of a moment; growth is the labor of a lifetime.

October 27

Read: Psalm 32:1–5

Biblical Truth

Personal Application

Prayer Requests

Answers to Prayer

MAKE A U-TURN

All we like sheep have gone astray; we have turned, every one, to his own way; and the Lord has laid on Him the iniquity of us all.
—Isaiah 53:6

When we went on a weekend road trip with some friends, we had our first experience using a Global Positioning System. The GPS has a female voice, so our friends John and Mary call their device Gladys. We programmed our destination into the GPS, and Gladys did her job and plotted our course. Then we sat back. Having put our faith in this little navigator, we let her direct us.

"Turn right in .2 miles," Gladys said confidently. She was right—Gladys is always right. In fact, when we made an unexpected detour to get gas, she got a bit insistent: "Please make a U-turn . . . Please make a U-turn at your earliest convenience!"

Gladys had calculated a route for us, but we had gone a different way. That was our choice, naturally. But if we had continued going our own way, we would have become lost.

Isaiah 53:6 reminds us that just like sheep, we have a tendency to go astray. That's why we need a Shepherd to guide us and a Savior to pay the penalty for our sin.

No matter how far you've traveled in the wrong direction, it's not too late to turn around. God is ready to forgive and restore (Psalm 32:5). If you're headed down the wrong road, please make a U-turn. —CHK

No matter how far you've run from God, He's only a prayer away.

IN YOUR HEAD

I marvel that you are turning away so soon from Him who called you in the grace of Christ, to a different gospel.
—GALATIANS 1:6

I love the prayer that begins, "God be in my head, and in my understanding." When I first heard it, admittedly I thought it sounded a little weird. But then I got to thinking how unfortunate it is if in our efforts to get closer to Jesus we focus on our emotional experience of Him and check our brains at the door. Without His truth ringing in our heads, we're bound to get off track.

Just look at the early Christians. False teachers filled their heads with misinformation, saying that salvation and spiritual growth could be attained only through keeping the requirements of the law. When Paul heard of it, he was astonished at how quickly they had gotten off track: "I marvel that you are turning away so soon from Him who called you in the grace of Christ" (Galatians 1:6).

It's not just false teachers who lead us astray. Our world is full of twisted thinking like, "If it feels good, do it," or, "The one with the most toys wins."

Let's face it, you and I can't afford to check our brains at the door. In fact, intimacy with Jesus begins with getting to know Him, and it's the facts about Him that make us want to get close to Him. So, strange as it may sound, if you want to stay on track with Jesus, start each day by asking Him to be in your head! —JS

October 28

Read: Galatians 1:6–9

Biblical Truth

Personal Application

Prayer Requests

Answers to Prayer

To stay on track, let God guide your thinking.

October 29

Read: Isaiah 40:12–13, 25–31

Biblical Truth

Personal Application

Prayer Requests

Answers to Prayer

PERSPECTIVE

He . . . sits above the circle of the earth, and its inhabitants are like grasshoppers.
—Isaiah 40:22

Question: When is a bird bigger than a mountain? Answer: When the bird is closer than the mountain.

In reality, the bird is not bigger than the mountain, but it sure looks that way when the feathery fellow is perched on my window ledge and the mountain is far away in the distance.

Sometimes we perceive God this way in relationship to our problems. The troubles facing us seem huge because they are so close—like a big black bird with beady eyes and a sharp beak waiting for a smaller animal's weariness to turn into helplessness so it can devour it. At such times, God seems as far away as a distant mountain, and we perceive Him as being small and unreachable.

The prophet Isaiah changes our perspective by asking these rhetorical questions: "Who has measured the waters in the hollow of His hand, measured heaven with a span and calculated the dust of the earth in a measure? Weighed the mountains in scales and the hills in a balance?" (40:12). The Lord "gives power to the weak, and to those who have no might He increases strength" (v. 29).

Just as a bird is never bigger than a mountain, no problem is ever bigger than God. It's all a matter of changing our perspective. —JAL

We worship a God who is greater than our greatest problem.

GOD-OGRAPHY

October 30

Without faith it is impossible to please Him, for he who comes to God must believe that He is, and that He is a rewarder of those who diligently seek Him.
—HEBREWS 11:6

A *National Geographic News* survey in 2006 reported that many young Americans are geographically illiterate. According to the survey, 63 percent of Americans aged 18–24 failed to correctly locate Iraq on a map of the Middle East. The results for US geography are even more dismal. Half could not find New York State on the map, a third could not find Louisiana, and 48 percent could not locate the state of Mississippi.

Understanding geography is helpful in daily life, but "God-ography" (finding God) is infinitely more crucial—for now and for eternity.

In Hebrews 11:6 we are told that to find God and please Him, we first have to believe that He exists. How can we prove that God exists? Finding God is a matter of faith—confidence in Him and commitment to Him. This confidence and commitment should remain strong even though the objects of our faith are unseen. The writer of Hebrews and the apostle John agree that ultimately the way to find the Lord and please Him is by believing in His Son Jesus (Hebrews 11:6; John 14:6).

Finding God is solely a work of God. Those who seek Him will find Him because God will give them a heart to recognize Him as Lord (Jeremiah 29:13–14). —MW

Read: Hebrews 11:1–6

Biblical Truth

Personal Application

Prayer Requests

Answers to Prayer

To find God, we must be willing to seek Him.

October 31

Read: Deuteronomy 6:1–6

Biblical Truth

Personal Application

Prayer Requests

Answers to Prayer

WHO IS YOUR GOD?

You shall love the Lord your God with all your heart, with all your soul, and with all your strength.
—Deuteronomy 6:5

At a funeral, I overheard someone say of the deceased, "He was close to *his* god. He's safe now."

At times like that, I wish it were true that everyone could have their own god, live in whatever way they want, and also be assured of eternal life in heaven. Then we wouldn't have to think too seriously about death. We wouldn't have to be concerned about where our unbelieving loved ones go when they die.

But the Scriptures say that there is only one true God. "The Lord our God, the Lord is one!" (Deuteronomy 6:4). And He is holy (Leviticus 19:2). He says that we don't measure up to His standard for a relationship with Him. "All have sinned and fall short of the glory of God" (Romans 3:23). Our sin has alienated us from Him.

In love, the heavenly Father provided the way to himself through His perfect Son Jesus who died to pay the penalty for our sin. "For God so loved the world that He gave His only begotten Son, that whoever believes in Him should not perish but have everlasting life" (John 3:16). But we need to humble our hearts and receive His gift of forgiveness.

There is only one true God. He is holy and has provided the only way of eternal life through Jesus. Is He the God you are trusting in? Think about it—seriously. —AC

To get into heaven, it's who you know that counts.

November

November 1

Read: James 3:13–18

Biblical Truth

Personal Application

Prayer Requests

Answers to Prayer

"GIMME IT!"

My thoughts are not your thoughts, nor are your ways My ways.
—Isaiah 55:8

I heard the screams long before I could see him, but as I wheeled my grocery cart around to the next aisle of the store, there he was!

With angry tears streaming out of squinty eyes, the little boy was shouting, "Gimme it!" His mom glanced at me for a moment. I won't debate the merits of her actions, but, embarrassed and worn down, she grabbed the cheap trinket and tossed it into her cart.

I think I recognized that kid. He looked a lot like me. Yes, I've often been the willful child. And sometimes I've even pleaded with God, "Why not? Why can't I have it?" On occasion, God's given me what I wanted, but not because I wore Him down. No, I think He wanted me to see what happens when I put myself in charge.

What we think is best is not necessarily the best that God desires for us. In Isaiah 55:8, the Lord said, "My thoughts are not your thoughts, nor are your ways My ways."

In his book *Days of Grace,* tennis champion Arthur Ashe paraphrased James 1:5 when he wrote this advice to his young daughter: "Ask God for the wisdom to know what is right, what God wants done, and the will to do it."

That's just the kind of sincere prayer that God wants to hear from His children. —CHK

If God doesn't give us what we ask for, we can be sure that He has something far better.

CLASS PARTICIPATION

The entrance of Your words gives light.
—Psalm 119:130

As a high school teacher and college professor, I have observed that learning is a cooperative effort between the student and the instructor. That's why educators try to get the student involved in class participation. The teacher does some work; the student does some work. Together progress is made. Education happens.

In Psalm 119, the writer suggests a similar pattern in verses 129–136. God is the teacher; we are the students.

Let's look at God's role in our education. He shows us mercy (v. 132). He guides our steps (v. 133). And He redeems us from outside trouble (v. 134).

But first we must be eager students, ready to accept God's teaching, guidance, and help. We should enter His classroom with anticipation: "The entrance of Your words gives light; it gives understanding to the simple . . . I longed for Your commandments" (vv. 130–131). In our role as students of God's Word, we should fulfill three requirements: (1) examine God's words for what they are teaching, (2) gain understanding from those words, and (3) obey His statutes.

It's time to enter God's classroom and listen and learn from Him. When we do, we'll look at God with renewed love and at the world with renewed concern (v. 136). —DB

November 2

Read: Psalm 119:129–136

Biblical Truth

Personal Application

Prayer Requests

Answers to Prayer

Careful meditation on the Scriptures makes for a closer walk with the Savior.

November 3

Read: John 17:20–26

Biblical Truth

Personal Application

Prayer Requests

Answers to Prayer

GOD'S CATALOG

By this all will know that you are My disciples, if you have love for one another.
—John 13:35

'Tis the season to receive catalogs in the mail. Every trip to the mailbox ends with an armload of slick holiday catalogs. Each one claims to offer me something I need—immediately. "Don't wait!" "Limited offer!" "Order now!"

The lure works. I open the pages to discover what I didn't know I needed. Sure enough, I see things that suddenly seem essential, even though a few minutes earlier I didn't know they existed. Manufacturers use catalog illustrations to create desire for their products.

In a way, Christians are God's catalogs. We are His illustration to the world of what He has to offer. His work in our lives makes us a picture of qualities that people may not know they need or want until they see them at work in us.

Jesus prayed that His followers would be unified so the world would know that God sent Him and loved them as God loved Him (John 17:23). When Christ is alive in us, we become examples of God's love. We can't manufacture love. God is the manufacturer, and we are His workmanship.

As you browse holiday catalogs, consider what the "catalog" of your life says about God. Do people see qualities in you that make them long for God? —JAL

As a Christian, you are "God's advertisement." Do people want what they see in you?

BETTER YET

For to me, to live is Christ,
and to die is gain.
—PHILIPPIANS 1:21

Sir Francis Bacon said, "I do not believe that any man fears to be dead, but only the stroke of death." Woody Allen said, "I'm not afraid to die. I just don't want to be there when it happens."

It's not death that's so frightening. It's the dying that scares us. As Paul faced imprisonment and the prospect of dying in a jail cell, he shared his view about life and death: "To live is Christ, and to die is gain" (Philippians 1:21). What a perspective!

Death is our enemy (1 Corinthians 15:25–28), but it does not possess the finality that so many dread. There is something waiting for believers beyond this life—something better.

Someone has said, "What the caterpillar thinks is the end of life, the butterfly thinks is just the beginning." George MacDonald wrote, "How strange this fear of death is! We are never frightened at a sunset."

I love this paraphrase of Philippians 1:21: "To me, living means opportunities for Christ, and dying—well, that's better yet!" (TLB). During our physical life, we have opportunities to serve Jesus. But one day we will actually be in His presence. Our fear will melt away when we see Him face to face.

That's the "better yet" the apostle Paul is talking about! —CHK

November 4

Read: Philippians 1:19–26

Biblical Truth

Personal Application

Prayer Requests

Answers to Prayer

For the Christian, the fear of death will give way to the fullness of life.

November 5

Read: Hebrews 4:11–16

Biblical Truth

Personal Application

Prayer Requests

Answers to Prayer

EXPLORATORY PROCEDURE

The Word of God is living and powerful . . . a discerner of the thoughts and intents of the heart.
—Hebrews 4:12

I have a friend who recently underwent a laryngoscopy. I winced as he explained how his doctor took a camera with a light on the end and stuck it down his throat to try to find the cause of his pain.

It reminded me, however, of the exploratory nature of God's Word. It invades the unseen areas of our lives, exposing the diseased and damaged spiritual tissue that troubles us. If you're wincing at the thought of how uncomfortable this divine procedure might be, consider Jesus' words: "Everyone practicing evil hates the light and does not come to the light, lest his deeds should be exposed" (John 3:20). Internal intrusions may be uncomfortable, but do you really want the disease?

Welcoming God's Word to penetrate the deep, dark places of our hearts is the only way to find true healing and the spiritual health we long for. Believe me, the procedure will be thorough. As the writer of Hebrews assures, God's Word is "sharper than any two-edged sword" (4:12)—piercing all the way through the external stuff of our lives, all the way down to our thoughts, intentions, and motives.

So what are you waiting for? With God's Word you don't need an appointment. The divine Surgeon is ready when you are! —JS

Let God's Word explore your inner being.

November 6

SERVE OR DIE

The Son of Man did not come to be served, but to serve.
—MARK 10:45

Read: Mark 10:35–45

Dr. Paul Brand told me of a memorable Frenchman named Pierre, who had served in Parliament until he became disillusioned with the slow pace of political change. During a harsh winter, many Parisian beggars froze to death. In desperation, Pierre became a friar to work among them and organize the beggars themselves.

He divided them into teams to scour the city for bottles. Next, he led them to build a warehouse out of discarded bricks and start a business processing the bottles. Finally, he gave each beggar responsibility to help another poorer than himself. The project caught on. In a few years he founded the charitable organization Emmaus.

Eventually, there were few beggars to be found in Paris. So Pierre went to India. "If I don't find people worse off than my beggars," he said, "this movement could turn inward. They'll become a powerful, rich organization, and the whole spiritual impact will be lost. They'll have no one to serve."

At a leprosy colony in India, Pierre met patients worse off than his former beggars. Returning to France, he mobilized the beggars to build a leprosy ward at a hospital in India.

"It is you who have saved us," he told the grateful patients. "We must serve or we die." —PY

Biblical Truth

Personal Application

Prayer Requests

Answers to Prayer

If you want a field of service, look around you.

November 7

Read: Psalm 70

Biblical Truth

Personal Application

Prayer Requests

Answers to Prayer

WAITING

Make haste to help me, O Lord!
—Psalm 70:1

"Make haste to help me, O Lord!" the psalmist David prayed (Psalm 70:1). Like him, we don't like to wait. We dislike the long lines at supermarket checkout counters, and the traffic jams downtown and around shopping malls. We hate to wait at the bank or at a restaurant.

And then there are the more difficult times of waiting: a childless couple waiting for a child; a single person waiting for marriage; an addict waiting for deliverance; a spouse waiting for a kind and gentle word; a worried patient waiting for a diagnosis from a doctor.

What we wait for, however, is far less important than what God is doing while we wait. In such times He works in us to develop those hard-to-achieve spiritual virtues of meekness, kindness, and patience with others. But more important, we learn to lean on God alone and to "rejoice and be glad" in Him (Psalm 70:4).

F. B. Meyer said, "What a chapter might be written of God's delays! It is the mystery of the art of educating human spirits to the finest temper of which they are capable. What searchings of heart, what analyzings of motives, what testings of the Word of God, what upliftings of soul . . . All these are associated with those weary days of waiting, which are, nevertheless, big with spiritual destiny." —DHR

God stretches our patience to enlarge our soul.

November 8

FLAWED AND FRAIL

God has chosen
the foolish things of the world
to put to shame the wise.
—1 CORINTHIANS 1:27

One of my boyhood heroes was Davy Crockett, the "King of the Wild Frontier." I looked up to him, admiring his courage and exploits. Years later, my brother gave me a book that traced the experiences of the real-life David Crockett, and I was surprised by his humanness. The real Davy Crockett made mistakes and had serious personal problems. The book depicted him as both flawed and frail.

This was both disappointing and reassuring to me. It was disappointing because he was less than I had come to believe, but reassuring because that reality made Crockett more accessible to me—and even more of a hero.

In the Bible we see that God consistently used people who were far from perfect. That shouldn't surprise us. God is glorified by showing himself strong through our weaknesses. It shows us that He desires to work through our lives not because we are perfect but because *He* is. And since He uses weak and foolish things (1 Corinthians 1:27), it means you and I are prime candidates for His work.

The Lord isn't looking for superheroes. He uses those of us who are flawed and frail so that He can show His strength and grace. He wants those with a willing and available heart. —BC

Read: 1 Corinthians 1:18–31

Biblical Truth

Personal Application

Prayer Requests

Answers to Prayer

In God's service, our greatest ability is our availability.

November 9

Read: Psalm 103:6–14

Biblical Truth

Personal Application

Prayer Requests

Answers to Prayer

THEY NEVER MEET

You have cast all my sins behind Your back.
—Isaiah 38:17

Did you know that the farthest point east and the farthest point west in the United States are both in Alaska? It's a geographical trick, actually. Pochnoi Point in the Aleutians is as far west as you can go and still be in the US. But if you travel a few miles farther west, you'll end up at Alaska's Amatignak Island. Because that spot is *west* of the 180th meridian separating the Eastern and Western Hemispheres, it is technically *east* of the rest of the US.

But you'll never find a spot where east and west are actually next to each other. In going west, you never "find" east. East goes on forever. West goes on forever. They never meet. You can't get farther from something than that.

What difference does this make? Just this: When you read in Scripture that your forgiven sins are separated from you "as far as the east is from the west" (Psalm 103:12), you are assured that they are an immeasurable distance away—gone forever. If that's not enough, try this: God says, "I, even I, am He who blots out your transgressions for My own sake; and I will not remember your sins" (Isaiah 43:25).

Concerned about your sins? Through Jesus' death on the cross, God is able to say, "What sins?" But He will do that only if you put your faith in His Son. —DB

We invite defeat when we remember what we should forget.

GOSSIP-FREE ZONE

A man who bears false witness against his neighbor is like a club, a sword, and a sharp arrow.
—PROVERBS 25:18

In some offices you can get fired for gossiping. According to a 2002 survey, the average employee gossips 65 hours a year. One Chicago firm decided to become a "gossip-free zone." They require that employees never talk badly about co-workers behind their backs. If you're caught, you lose your job.

A ministry for people in the entertainment industry takes a refreshing alternative to gossip. They combat it with prayer. Instead of putting down famous people who get in trouble with bad choices, they encourage people to pray for them.

Among God's commands to His people is "You shall not bear false witness against your neighbor" (Exodus 20:16). While this may be talking primarily about lying at judicial proceedings, gossip could also be included in the command because it violates the law of love toward our neighbor. Proverbs uses strong language to describe this use of our words. It's like "a club, a sword, and a sharp arrow" against others (25:18).

Gossip feeds into our natural desires to feel superior to others and to belong or fit in, so combating it in our personal lives can be a challenge. But if we choose to love through prayer, our lives can be a gossip-free zone. —AC

November 10

Read: Proverbs 25:8–18

Biblical Truth

Personal Application

Prayer Requests

Answers to Prayer

You can never justify gossip.

November 11

Read: John 15:9–17

Biblical Truth

Personal Application

Prayer Requests

Answers to Prayer

NO GREATER LOVE

Greater love has no one than this, than to lay down one's life for his friends.
—John 15:13

Melbourne, Australia, is home to the Shrine of Remembrance, a war memorial honoring those who died for their country. Built following World War I, it has since been expanded to honor those who served in subsequent conflicts. It's a beautiful place, with reminders of courage and devotion, but the highlight of the shrine is a hall containing a carved stone that simply reads, "Greater Love Hath No Man." Every year on the 11th day of the 11th month at 11:00 a.m., a mirror reflects the sun's light onto the stone to spotlight the word *love*. It is a poignant tribute to those who gave their lives.

We honor the memory of those who paid the ultimate price for freedom. Yet the words on that stone carry a far greater meaning. Jesus spoke them the night before He died on the cross for the sins of a needy world (John 15:13). His death was not for freedom from political tyranny but freedom from the penalty of sin. His death was not just to give us a better life, but to give us eternal life.

It is important to remember those who have given their lives for their country—but may we never forget to praise and honor the Christ who died for a dying world. Truly, there is no greater love than this. —BC

The cross of Jesus is the supreme evidence of the love of God.

OUT OF OBSCURITY

I have found the Book of the Law in the house of the Lord.
—2 Kings 22:8

In an old house close to a Civil War battleground in Virginia, workers are painstakingly restoring graffiti. Unsightly scribbling similar to what we scrub from public view is considered a clue to knowledge of the past. Workers are ecstatic when a new letter or word emerges from obscurity to provide information that has remained hidden for over 145 years.

This story brings to mind a scene in ancient Israel when Hilkiah the priest found the long lost book of the law in the temple of the Lord. The very words of God, entrusted to the nation of Israel, had been ignored, forgotten, and eventually lost. But King Josiah was determined to follow the Lord, so he instructed the priest to restore worship in the temple. In the process, the Law of Moses was discovered.

But an even greater discovery was yet to be made. Many years later, after meeting Jesus, Philip reported to his friend Nathanael: "We have found the one Moses wrote about in the Law" (John 1:45 NIV).

People today get excited about discovering the scribbles of Civil War soldiers. How much more exciting it is to discover the words of Almighty God expressed in the Word made flesh, Jesus the Messiah. —JAL

November 12

Read: 2 Kings 22:3–11

Biblical Truth

Personal Application

Prayer Requests

Answers to Prayer

The Bible is old, but its truths are always new.

November 13

Read: Philippians 3:1–11

Biblical Truth

Personal Application

Prayer Requests

Answers to Prayer

WHOM WILL YOU TRUST?

By grace you have been saved through faith, and that not of yourselves; it is the gift of God.
—Ephesians 2:8

Ayn Rand, an American philosopher who died in 1982, gathered a sizable following who read her books and attended her lectures. An avid individualist, she had this to say: "Now I see the free face of god and I raise this god over all the earth, this god who men have sought since men came into being, the god who will grant them joy and peace and pride. This god, this one word, *I*." When asked if she believed in God, she answered, "This god is myself, *I*." Egotism—faith in oneself—that's what this philosopher believed in.

The apostle Paul bore witness to a trust that is exactly the opposite of that misplaced self-confidence. He declared: "[We] worship God in the Spirit, rejoice in Christ Jesus, and have no confidence in the flesh" (Philippians 3:3). He put his trust solely in Jesus Christ, who is God incarnate, the true God of love and mercy.

We read in the book of Ephesians, "By grace you have been saved through faith, and that not of yourselves; it is the gift of God" (2:8).

Are we embracing the philosophy of egotism, which is really a confidence that will prove eternally self-destructive? Or have we, like Paul, embraced the self-sacrificing grace of Jesus Christ?
—VCG

We are saved not by what we do but by trusting what Christ has done.

November 14

THE PERSON MAKES THE PLACE

God Himself will be with them and be their God. And God will wipe away every tear from their eyes.
—Revelation 21:3–4

Engaged couples often spend hours poring over travel brochures and vacation Web sites looking for just the right honeymoon spot. They can hardly wait for their romantic getaway. But it's not so much about the place; it's about being with the person they love.

We get used to places no matter how glorious they are. But being with a person who loves us never gets old!

In Revelation, John paints a beautiful picture of what heaven will be like. But it's not really about the place—it's about the Person we'll be with. The day is coming when Jesus will come to take us to be with Him in the place He has prepared for us. And the wonderful news is that He says: "Behold, I am coming quickly!" (22:7).

If you're thinking, He may come back for others, but surely not for me, don't miss verse 17: "The Spirit and the bride say, 'Come!' And let him who hears say, 'Come!' And let him who thirsts come. Whoever desires, let him take the water of life freely." Anyone is welcome to join the wedding feast. All we have to do is believe in the One who died for us, Jesus Christ, the Lover of our souls.

Make no mistake, the place—heaven—will be incredible beyond our dreams. But our greatest joy will be the experience of being with Jesus forever! —JS

Read: Revelation 22:6–17

Biblical Truth

Personal Application

Prayer Requests

Answers to Prayer

The greatest aspect of heaven will be spending eternity with Jesus.

November 15

Read: Exodus 12:13–17, 25–27

Biblical Truth

Personal Application

Prayer Requests

Answers to Prayer

YOUR CHILDREN WILL ASK

When your children say to you, "What do you mean by this service?" . . . you shall say, "It is the Passover sacrifice of the Lord."
—Exodus 12:26–27

One of the most important events in Jewish history is the exodus, when God freed His people from the bondage of Egypt. Prior to leaving Egypt, the Israelites were commanded to eat a special meal called the Passover. As an act of judgment upon the Egyptians, God said that He would strike down every firstborn son, but He would pass over the houses that had the blood of a lamb on the top and sides of the door frame (Exodus 12).

To commemorate this act of judgment and grace, God's people would share in the Passover meal. God said that one day their children would ask: "What do you mean by this?" They were then responsible to retell the story of the exodus and God's salvation. God did not want the story of His great salvation to get lost in one generation.

When our children ask us about our values, lifestyle, prayer in decision-making, Bible-reading, church attendance, and worship, we have a responsibility to answer them. We are followers of Jesus. We must retell the story of how He became our Passover Lamb. His blood is the marker over our lives. We are no longer slaves to sin but are free to serve the Eternal One of heaven.

What are you teaching the children in your life? —MW

A parent's life is a child's guidebook.

"I DID NOT KNOW IT"

Jacob awoke from his sleep and said, "Surely the Lord is in this place, and I did not know it."
—Genesis 28:16

As Jacob did in Genesis 28, I like to remind myself each morning when I awaken that God is here, "in this place," present with me (v. 16). As I spend time with Him each morning, reading His Word and responding in prayer, it reinforces my sense of His presence—that He is near.

Although we do not see Him, Peter reminds us that we can love Him and rejoice in His love for us with "inexpressible," glorious joy (1 Peter 1:8). We take the Lord's presence with us all through the day, blending work and play with prayer. He is our teacher, our philosopher, our companion—our gentle, kind, and very best friend.

God is with us wherever we go. He is in the commonplace, whether we know it or not. "Surely the Lord is in this place," Jacob said of a most unlikely spot, "and I did not know it" (Genesis 28:16). We may not realize He is close by. We may feel lonely and sad. Our day may seem bleak and dreary without a visible ray of hope—yet He is present.

Amid all the clamor and din of this visible and audible world, listen carefully for God's quiet voice. Listen to Him in the Bible. Talk to Him frequently in prayer. Look for Him in your circumstances. Seek Him. He is with you wherever you go! —DHR

November 16

Read: Genesis 28:10–16

Biblical Truth

Personal Application

Prayer Requests

Answers to Prayer

Our greatest privilege is to enjoy God's presence.

November 17

Read: Acts 5:1–11

Biblical Truth

Personal Application

Prayer Requests

Answers to Prayer

CLOSING THE GAPS

Why have you conceived this thing in your heart? You have not lied to men but to God.
—Acts 5:4

After the final episode of the 2002 TV program *Survivor: Africa*, a wrap-up special focused on the final contestants. The show's host Jeff Probst said that the victor won "mostly by sticking with his principles." The champion later explained that he wanted to win while retaining "dignity and self-respect." He elaborated that you don't have to lie, cheat, or do underhanded things to win. You can be competitive, yet still be truthful and nice. In short, he permitted no discrepancy between image and reality.

In the book of Acts we read about Ananias and Sapphira, who did have a gap between what they wanted to be known for and who they really were (5:1–11). Satan filled their hearts with a deceptive plan. They sold a piece of property and brought just a portion of the money to the apostles, while pretending they were giving all the proceeds. They wanted to be recognized as a generous couple, but they were not what they appeared to be. This gap caused them to lie to the Holy Spirit and to the faith community. They paid a terrible price—death. And their example stands as a stark warning to us all.

What discrepancies have we permitted in our lives? We must confess them and close the gaps.
—MW

Integrity means never having to look over your shoulder.

COOLER HEADS

A man of understanding is of a calm spirit.
—Proverbs 17:27

A Christian I know was angry with someone at his workplace over a perceived injustice. A colleague listened to his grievance and, sensing that his temper still ran high, gave him this wise advice to consider before confronting those involved: "Cooler heads prevail."

As we interact with others, disagreements are inevitable. The discerning believer understands his own heart and takes steps to deal with conflict diplomatically.

Proverbs 17:27 tells us: "He who has knowledge spares his words." This means keeping in check a multitude of opinions that could ignite further anger in others. Someone who displays wisdom will think before speaking, and then will share only insights likely to be helpful.

The Proverbs also give us wise counsel on the emotional side of controlling our frustrations. "A man of understanding is of a calm spirit." A mature person exhibits understanding by keeping cool in conflict. Problem-solving is enhanced by an even-tempered approach.

The next time you become angry, stop and prayerfully reflect for a moment. Ask God for a calm spirit and the right words to say. Remember, cooler heads prevail.
—DF

November 18

Read: Proverbs 17:22–28

Biblical Truth

Personal Application

Prayer Requests

Answers to Prayer

The best time to stop an argument is before it starts.

November 19

Read: 2 Kings 5:1–3, 9–15

Biblical Truth

Personal Application

Prayer Requests

Answers to Prayer

OUT OF OPTIONS?

Now I know that there is no God in all the earth, except in Israel.
—2 Kings 5:15

As ancient Syria's mightiest military commander, General Naaman had all the benefits the empire could offer: influence, affluence, and power. All, that is, except for health! Naaman was a leper (2 Kings 5:1–3).

In contrast, the servant girl in the general's household had no options or power at all. As a captive from an army raid, she had been forced into a lifetime of slavery (v. 2). But she did not permit herself to be overcome by despair and bitterness. Rather, she rose above her no-option estate to serve wholeheartedly the best interests of her master.

This servant girl didn't see her master's leprosy as God's punishment but as an opportunity to point Naaman to God's prophet in Samaria (v. 3). Her recommendation led to Naaman's complete healing. He declared, "Now I know that there is no God in all the earth, except in Israel" (v. 15).

Today, many people have abundant options. Others, however, have their choices curtailed by poverty, poor health, or other adverse circumstances. When a crisis comes, even their limited options evaporate.

Yet one choice always remains. Like Naaman's servant girl, we can still choose to serve God and point others to Him—regardless of our limited circumstances.
—AL

Facing an impossibility gives us the opportunity to trust God.

LIFE'S SURPRISES

The Lord does not see as man sees; for man looks at the outward appearance, but the Lord looks at the heart.
—1 Samuel 16:7

No one watching *Britain's Got Talent* (a popular televised talent show) expected much when mobile phone salesman Paul Potts took the stage. The judges looked skeptically at one another when the nervous, unassuming, ordinary-looking chap announced he would sing opera—until Potts opened his mouth.

He began to sing Puccini's "Nessun Dorma"—and it was magical! The crowd roared and stood in amazement while the judges sat stunned in tearful silence. It was one of the greatest surprises any such television program has ever had, in large part because it came wrapped in such an ordinary package.

In the Old Testament, the rescuer of Israel arrived at the battlefield in a most unlikely form—a young shepherd boy (1 Samuel 17). King Saul and his entire army were surprised when David defeated Goliath and won the day. They were surprised because they were judging from appearances. But, as God said to the prophet Samuel, "The Lord does not see as man sees; for man looks at the outward appearance, but the Lord looks at the heart" (16:7).

If we judge others only by their outer appearance, we might miss the wonderful surprise of what's in their heart. —BC

November 20

Read: 1 Samuel 16:1–7

Biblical Truth

Personal Application

Prayer Requests

Answers to Prayer

It's what's in the heart that counts.

November 21

Read: 2 Samuel 12:1–13

Biblical Truth

Personal Application

Prayer Requests

Answers to Prayer

OFF TRACK

Why have you despised the commandment of the Lord, to do evil in His sight?
—2 SAMUEL 12:9

When I sat in my car at the start of the automatic car wash, I didn't know that my left front tire was not properly lined up with the track. The car wash started but my car wasn't moving, so I accelerated. That caused my tire to jump the track.

Now I was stuck—I couldn't move forward or backward. The car wash continued through its cycle without my car. Meanwhile, cars began lining up and waiting for me. I was glad when two workers at the station helped me get my car back on the track.

Sometimes in our Christian lives we get off track too. King David did in a big way. He committed adultery with Bathsheba and later ordered that her husband be put "in the forefront of the hottest battle" and left there to be killed (2 Samuel 11:3–4, 15–17). David's actions were way out of line with how God wanted him to behave as His chosen king.

David needed help to get back on track. The Bible says that "the Lord sent Nathan to David" (12:1). He confronted David about stealing another man's wife, and David wisely repented (v. 13), even though his sin still had dire consequences.

Does someone you know need your help to get back on track?
—AC

True love dares to confront.

HOW WILL THEY KNOW?

November 22

He who loves God must love his brother also.
—1 John 4:21

Did you ever notice that some Christians act decidedly unchristian while trying to prove how godly they are?

One example is a man who angrily shuts his hymnbook and pouts through the rest of the service if the song leader does not sing every verse of a song.

Another example is church members who argue against adding a new service geared toward youth because they dislike the music.

Then there is the church in which the middle aisle is a demarcation line between two social classes of people who refuse to mix.

As Christians, we must stand for truth as spelled out in the Bible. Though truth was not violated in any of the above situations, these professing followers of Christ acted in decidedly unloving ways. They chose to protect personal preferences rather than demonstrate the love of Jesus to a watching world.

As we read 1 John 4:7–21, we see that God's love seeks to transform our behavior. In His love, we don't react disdainfully toward others simply because we don't agree.

Jesus said, "By this all will know that you are My disciples, if you have love for one another" (John 13:35). Do others see the love of Jesus in you? —DB

Read: 1 John 4:7–21

Biblical Truth

Personal Application

Prayer Requests

Answers to Prayer

A church with one heart and one mind will make for a won world.

November 23

Read: Job 38:31–41; 42:5–6

Biblical Truth

Personal Application

Prayer Requests

Answers to Prayer

HOW GREAT IS OUR GOD!

Can you bind the cluster of the Pleiades, or loose the belt of Orion?
—JOB 38:31

A team of astronomers from the University of Minnesota say they have found a giant hole in the universe. The void they've discovered is in a region of sky southwest of Orion. The mysterious empty place has no galaxies, stars, or even dark matter. One of the astronomers said that the hole in the heavens is a billion light-years across.

When I try to capture the meaning of such immensity, something happens to me. The fight goes out of me. I don't know what to do with my thoughts. Who can relate to the magnitude of such emptiness?

Then I remember what the Lord did with Job. He drew His suffering servant's attention to the same part of the night sky. Using the region of the constellation Orion along with the wonders of the weather and the natural world, the Lord brought Job to the end of his reasonings and arguments (Job 38:31; 42:5–6).

In the presence of such wonder, I want to join Job in collapsing before the Lord in surrender to His inexpressible power and wisdom. I want to let go of my anxiety, my anger, and my resistance to the mysterious leading of God. I want to claim my only confidence as being in the immeasurable greatness of our God. —MD

The wonders of the universe compel us to worship our wonderful God.

IMPOSSIBLE ITOKAWA

With God all things are possible.
—MATTHEW 19:26

In 2005, Japan's unmanned Haya-busa spacecraft visited an "impossible" asteroid. Images and data indicate that the asteroid, named Itokawa, is twice as porous as loose sand. This has astonished scientists, who believe that asteroids make repeated impacts with other space rocks and hence should be very dense. As they make additional discoveries, scientists may learn why Itokawa is different. But for now, we have an asteroid that challenges scientific understanding.

Two thousand years ago, a young ruler asked Jesus an "impossible" question: "What good thing shall I do that I may have eternal life?" (Matthew 19:16). After an intriguing exchange, the man "went away sorrowful" (v. 22) when he realized he would have to give up his wealth—the very thing he valued more than a relationship with Jesus.

This upright man had kept the letter of the law, yet had fallen short. "Who then can be saved?" asked the astonished disciples (v. 25). Jesus answered, "With men this is impossible, but with God all things are possible" (v. 26).

The One who created this universe out of nothing has a history of accomplishing the impossible. When we forsake what this life has to offer and follow Him, He does the impossible once again—He gives us eternal life! —CPH

November 24

Read: Matthew 19:16–26

Biblical Truth

Personal Application

Prayer Requests

Answers to Prayer

Our limited ability accents God's limitless power.

November 25

Read: Psalm 73

Biblical Truth

Personal Application

Prayer Requests

Answers to Prayer

HOLDING YOUR HAND

Nevertheless I am continually with You; You hold me by my right hand.
—Psalm 73:23

One of the joys of being with kids is holding their hands. We do it to keep them safe while crossing the street, or to keep them from getting lost in a crowd. And whenever they stumble and lose their footing, we grab their little hands tighter to keep them from falling.

That's what God does for us. Inevitably there are stones and cracks that trip us up on the sidewalks of life. That's why it's easy to identify with the psalmist, who said, "My steps had nearly slipped" (Psalm 73:2).

We all face a variety of issues that threaten to make us stumble. For the psalmist Asaph, seeing the prosperity of the wicked caused him to question the goodness of God. But God squeezed his hand and reassured him that, given the judgment of God, the wicked do not really prosper. True prosperity, the psalmist discovered, was found in the fact that God was always with him: "You hold me by my right hand" (v. 23). And just for good measure, God reminded him that He would also guide him through life and ultimately welcome him home to heaven (v. 24). How good is that!

So, next time you stumble, remember that the powerful hand of God is holding your hand and walking you through life—all the way home! —JS

Let God do the holding and you do the trusting.

CATCH AND RELEASE

Jesus answered them,
"Most assuredly, I say to you, whoever commits sin is a slave of sin."
—JOHN 8:34

I'm a "catch and release" fisherman, which means I don't kill the trout I catch, but net and handle them gently and set them free. It's a technique that ensures "sustainability," as conservation officers like to say, and keeps trout and other target species from disappearing in heavily fished waters.

I rarely release a trout without recalling Paul's words about those who have been "taken captive" by Satan to do his will (2 Timothy 2:26), for I know that our adversary the devil does not catch and release but captures to consume and destroy.

We may think we can deliberately sin in a limited way for a short period of time and then get ourselves free. But as Jesus teaches us, "Whoever commits sin is a slave of sin" (John 8:34). Even "little" sins lead to greater and greater unrighteousness. Sin becomes the consequence of sin. We find ourselves entrapped and enslaved, and like a luckless trout, we cannot wriggle free.

Sin enslaves us. But when we yield ourselves in obedience to Christ and call upon Him for the strength to do His will, we are "released." The result is increasing righteousness (Romans 6:16).

Jesus assures us, "If the Son makes you free, you shall be free indeed" (John 8:36). —DHR

November 26

Read: Romans 6:15–23

Biblical Truth

Personal Application

Prayer Requests

Answers to Prayer

Christ releases us from sin's slavery into salvation's liberty.

November 27

Read: Psalm 100

Biblical Truth

Personal Application

Prayer Requests

Answers to Prayer

GLADLY!

Make a joyful shout to the Lord, all you lands!
—Psalm 100:1

Psalm 100 is one of the great songs of thanksgiving in the Bible. It calls us to realize that we belong to God our Maker and to praise Him for His goodness, mercy, and truth (vv. 3–5).

During a recent reading, however, I was struck by a phrase that speaks of expressing thanks in a tangible, willing way: "Serve the Lord with gladness" (v. 2). Many times my service to God is more grudging than glad. I do what I consider my duty, but I'm not happy about it.

Oswald Chambers put his finger on my unthankful attitude when he said: "The will of God is the gladdest, brightest, most bountiful thing possible to conceive, and yet some of us talk of the will of God with a terrific sigh—'Oh well, I suppose it is the will of God,' as if His will were the most calamitous thing that could befall us . . . We become spiritual whiners and talk pathetically about 'suffering the will of the Lord.' Where is the majestic vitality and might of the Son of God about that!"

True thankfulness is more than being grateful for what we possess. It's an attitude that permeates our relationship with the Lord so that we may serve Him with gladness and joy. —DCM

For the Christian, thanksgiving is not just a day but a way of life.

SIN CROUCHES AT THE DOOR

November 28

Sin lies at the door.
And its desire is for you, but you should rule over it.
—GENESIS 4:7

The award-winning author John Steinbeck often used biblical themes in his novels. In his book *East of Eden*, he describes characters who illustrate the conflict of jealousy and revenge reflected in the story of Cain and Abel. Steinbeck shows how an angry heart burning with revenge doesn't have to act a certain way. There's always a choice.

When Abel's animal sacrifice received divine favor and Cain's offering of fruit was rejected, Cain burned with anger (Genesis 4:1–6). But the Lord admonished him: "Sin lies at the door. And its desire is for you, but you should rule over it" (4:7). The original Hebrew words paint the picture of an animal crouching, ready to devour its prey. Cain's anger and jealousy, if not brought under control, would "eat him up" and spill out in destructive behavior. Tragically, Cain gave in to his evil desires, which resulted in the first homicide and his departure from the presence of the Lord (4:8–16).

Do you have feelings of jealousy or anger toward someone? If so, you have a choice. If you ignore the internal struggle, it will only get worse and control you. But if you bring your anger to the Lord and ask for His help, in His strength you will have victory. —DF

Read: Genesis 4:1–16

Biblical Truth

Personal Application

Prayer Requests

Answers to Prayer

Control your anger, or it will control you.

November 29

Read: Matthew 16:24–28

Biblical Truth

Personal Application

Prayer Requests

Answers to Prayer

A CONVENIENT CHRISTIANITY

Whoever loses his life for My sake will find it.
—MATTHEW 16:25

So many television programs, so little time to watch them. Apparently that's what our culture thinks, because now technology allows us to see an hour-long program in just six minutes or less! The Minisode Network has pruned episodes of popular series into shorter, more convenient packages for interested viewers. "The shows you love—only shorter" is how it's advertised. All to make our life more convenient.

Some have tried to make the Christian life more convenient. They choose to practice Christianity on Sunday only. They attend a religious service at whatever church makes them most comfortable. They give a small offering and are nice to fellow churchgoers—nothing that requires much effort on their part. That way they can have the rest of the week to themselves, to live as they please.

That would be a convenient Christianity. But we know that following Jesus is a lifestyle and not a Sunday-only convenience. Being a "disciple" calls for giving up our lives for Him (Matthew 16:25). It's about living as Jesus calls us to live, daily giving up our plans and purposes for His. A relationship with Him causes us to be concerned with our thoughts, decisions, attitudes, and actions—all to make our life joy-filled for us and pleasing to God. —AC

Faith in Christ is not just a single step but a life of walking with Him.

LEND A HAND

Rejoice with those who rejoice, and weep with those who weep.
—Romans 12:15

The next month will be very difficult for many people who are still reeling from a loss this past year. The crippling hurt caused by the absence of a loved one can cloud holiday gatherings and even dim the desire to celebrate the birth of Jesus. Poet Ann Weems has written:

Some of us walk into Advent
tethered to our unresolved
yesterdays,
the pain still stabbing,
the hurt still throbbing.
It's not that we don't know better;
it's just that we can't stand up
anymore by ourselves.
On the way to Bethlehem,
will you give us a hand?

In Romans 12:9–21, Paul gives ways to express practical Christianity in our relationships. One seems especially needed at this time of year: "Rejoice with those who rejoice, and weep with those who weep" (v. 15). We can "give a hand" to grieving friends and family by understanding their sorrow and not expecting them to "get over it" in time to celebrate the holidays. We can freely mention the name of the person whose death has brought such desolation and then share a fond memory. We can be quiet, listen, and pray for God's help.

Only God can heal the deep wounds of the heart, but we can lend a hand. —DCM

November 30

Read: Romans 12:9–21

Biblical Truth

Personal Application

Prayer Requests

Answers to Prayer

No one is strong enough to bear his burdens alone.

December

December 1

Read: 2 Corinthians 4:8–18

Biblical Truth

Personal Application

Prayer Requests

Answers to Prayer

WAITING FOR JOY

Weeping may endure for a night, but joy comes in the morning.
—Psalm 30:5

A large part of life centers around anticipation. How much we would lose if we were to wake up one day to the unexpected announcement: "Christmas begins in 10 minutes!" The enjoyment in many of life's events is built on the fact that we have time to anticipate them.

Christmas, vacations, mission trips, sporting events. All grow in value because of the hours we spend looking forward to them—eagerly running through our minds the fun, challenges, and excitement they'll bring.

I think about the value of anticipation and the thrill it can bring to the human heart when I read Psalm 30:5: "Weeping may endure for a night, but joy comes in the morning." The psalmist is declaring the comforting idea that our earthly sorrow lasts but a short time when compared with the anticipated joy that will begin in heaven and last forever. Paul pens a similar idea in 2 Corinthians 4:17, where we discover that our "light affliction" leads to a glory of eternal value.

For now, those of us who weep can dwell on hope instead of hopelessness and anticipation instead of sorrow. It may be nighttime in our hearts, but just ahead lies the dawn of eternity. And with it, God promises the endless joy of heavenly morning. —DB

We can endure this life's trials because of the next life's joys.

A PASSION FOR PEOPLE

He died for all, that those who live should live no longer for themselves, but for Him who died for them and rose again.
—2 Corinthians 5:15

December 2

Read: 2 Corinthians 5:9–21

Mark Twain said, "Twenty years from now you will be more disappointed by the things that you didn't do than by the ones you did do. So throw off the bowlines. Sail away from the safe harbor. Catch the trade winds in your sails. Explore. Dream. Discover."

This quote appears on a Web site intended to help people discover what they are passionate about so they can live with greater significance.

The apostle Paul's passion in life was largely driven by concern for the eternal destiny of others. In 2 Corinthians 5 he names three things that fueled his passion. First, he recognized that he was accountable to Christ for his service and wanted to give a good accounting at the judgment seat of Christ (vv. 9–10). Second, Paul was driven by Christ's love and a desire that others would know the love that he had experienced. "For the love of Christ compels us," he wrote (v. 14). Finally, he understood that a lost and dying world needs the Savior (v. 20).

What are you passionate about? Paul's passion for people was fueled by the love of Christ—and ours should be as well. Let's apply Twain's words of challenge to our efforts in outreach: "Sail away from the safe harbor." Share the love of Christ with someone today. —BC

Biblical Truth

Personal Application

Prayer Requests

Answers to Prayer

Talking to Christ about others helps us to talk to others about Christ.

December 3

Read: Philippians 1:12–21

Biblical Truth

Personal Application

Prayer Requests

Answers to Prayer

EXPECTATIONS

My earnest expectation and hope [is] that . . . Christ will be magnified in my body, whether by life or by death.
—PHILIPPIANS 1:20

Expectations! We all have them. We expect that people will be nice to us, that we'll have good health, great marriages, faithful friends, successful careers. But what do we do when life doesn't live up to our expectations? In Philippians 1, Paul shows us the way. He faced broken expectations of place, people, and the future, yet he remained surprisingly upbeat.

Paul was stuck in prison—not a great *place* to be! When we get stuck in a tough marriage, an unrewarding job, or a challenging neighborhood, it's easy to get discouraged. But Paul was wonderfully positive. He said that his suffering helped to advance the gospel (Philippians 1:12).

Maybe *people* haven't lived up to our expectations. Paul likely expected other believers to encourage him. Instead, some were actually glad he was in jail and were preaching out of "envy and strife" (v. 15). Paul's response? "Christ is preached; and in this I rejoice" (v. 18).

Maybe it's an uncertain *future*—the loss of a spouse, a job transfer, or a health crisis. Paul knew that at any moment Nero might give the order for his execution, yet he declared, "For to me, to live is Christ, and to die is gain" (v. 21).

Adopt Paul's only expectation—for Christ to be honored no matter what! —JS

You can expect to enjoy God's presence when you honor Him with your life.

GONE WITH THE WIND

All is vanity and grasping for the wind.
—ECCLESIASTES 1:14

The epic film based on Margaret Mitchell's novel *Gone with the Wind* opens with these lines: "There was a land of Cavaliers and Cotton Fields called the Old South. Here in this pretty world, Gallantry took its last bow . . . Look for it only in books, for it is no more than a dream remembered, a Civilization *gone with the wind.*"

Not only does a way of life disappear but also the dreams that drive the main characters. Throughout the Civil War, Scarlett O'Hara is preoccupied with her love for Ashley Wilkes. But by story's end, she is disillusioned in every way.

Solomon saw the futility of seeking satisfaction in people and things. Despite amassing wealth and knowledge, completing great projects, and marrying many wives, he said, "All is vanity and grasping for the wind" (Ecclesiastes 1:14).

Why does chasing transitory things leave us unfulfilled? The biblical answer is that we were created to find our ultimate fulfillment in God. Jesus promised, "I have come that they may have life, and that they may have it more abundantly" (John 10:10).

People and things come and go. But the spiritual satisfaction Christ offers sustains us in this world and will endure into eternity. —DF

December 4

Read: Ecclesiastes 1:2–9, 14

Biblical Truth

Personal Application

Prayer Requests

Answers to Prayer

Invest your life in what pays eternal dividends.

December 5

Read: Isaiah 53:1–6

Biblical Truth

Personal Application

Prayer Requests

Answers to Prayer

SEEING JESUS

He has no form or comeliness; and when we see Him, there is no beauty that we should desire Him.
—Isaiah 53:2

When I was young, I thought I knew exactly what Jesus looked like. After all, I saw Him every day whenever I looked at some pictures in my bedroom. One showed Jesus knocking at a door and the other depicted Him as a Shepherd with His sheep.

What I didn't know was that a mere decade before I was born, those pictures of Jesus didn't exist. Warner Sallman painted the well-known "Head of Christ" and other portraits of Jesus in the 1940s. Those images were just one man's idea of what Jesus might have looked like.

The Bible never gives a physical description of Jesus. Even the men who saw Him every day didn't tell us what He looked like. In fact, the only clue we have is a passage in Isaiah that says: "There is no beauty that we should desire Him" (53:2). It seems that Jesus' human form was deliberately de-emphasized. He looked like an ordinary man. People weren't drawn to Him because of a regal appearance but because of what He said and did and because of the message of love He came to give (John 3:16).

But the next time Jesus comes to earth, it will be different. When our Savior returns, we will recognize Him as the sovereign King of kings and Lord of lords! (1 Timothy 6:14–15). —CHK

To see Jesus will be heaven's greatest joy.

A COMMITMENT TO WALK

December 6

Enoch walked with God;
and he was not, for God took him.
—Genesis 5:24

One thing that impresses me about my wife is her commitment to walk two to four times a week for at least an hour. Come rain, snow, sleet, or shine, my wife layers up or down (depending on the weather), puts on her headphones, and off she goes walking through our community.

My wife's commitment to walking reminds me of a man named Enoch. Genesis 5:18–24 is a short paragraph about his life, and it shines like a diamond amid the earthly record of deaths. In a storyline where the funeral bells tolled out their mournful drone ("and he died" is repeated eight times in the chapter), there is a ray of hope—Enoch walked with God.

What did it mean for Enoch to walk with God? It describes Enoch's close communion with God—as if literally walking by His side. Also, it refers to Enoch's unswerving obedience to God in a corrupt culture. God rewarded Enoch's faithfulness by taking him to heaven while he was still alive. Death would not have the final word in God's creation.

Enoch's walk with God reminds us that it is possible for all of us to enjoy intimate communion with the Lord. Let's commit ourselves to walking faithfully with Him every day.
—MW

Read: Genesis 5:18–24

Biblical Truth

Personal Application

Prayer Requests

Answers to Prayer

You're headed in the right direction when you walk with God.

December 7

Read: Matthew 26:20–30

Biblical Truth

Personal Application

Prayer Requests

Answers to Prayer

EAT THIS BREAD

Bethlehem Ephrathah, though you are little among the thousands of Judah, yet out of you shall come forth to Me the One to be Ruler in Israel.
—MICAH 5:2

Christmas isn't the time of year when our thoughts naturally turn to the Last Supper, or what the Jews called Passover. But that particular Passover is critical to Christmas. After breaking bread and giving it to His disciples, Jesus said, "Take, eat; this is My body" (Matthew 26:26). Breaking bread was a traditional part of Passover, but adding "this is my body" was a striking departure from the familiar liturgy. The disciples must have been bewildered.

Later the meaning became clear. Jesus was born in Bethlehem, which means "house of Bread." He was laid in a manger, a feeding trough. He once said, "I am the living bread which came down from heaven. If anyone eats of this bread, he will live forever; and the bread that I shall give is My flesh" (John 6:51).

The prophet Micah indicated that One born in Bethlehem would rule over Israel (5:2). But not until Jesus came did anyone realize the uniqueness of this Kingdom. Christ's rule would not be imposed upon anyone; it would be imparted to those who accepted this new citizenship.

As we sing of Bethlehem's manger, let's remember that the heaven-sent infant King came so that we might "eat this bread" and partake of His divine nature.
—JAL

Only Christ the Living Bread can satisfy our spiritual hunger.

HERE COMES THE BOSS!

December 8

If we confess our sins,
He is faithful and just to forgive us
our sins and to cleanse us from
all unrighteousness.
—1 JOHN 1:9

A number of computer games come with a special feature called the "Boss Key." If you're playing a game when you're supposed to be working, and someone (like the boss) walks into your office, you quickly strike the Boss Key. Your computer screen changes immediately, hiding what you've been doing.

Trying to hide from others when we've done something wrong comes naturally. We may feel guilty, but our desire to avoid admitting our responsibility is often stronger than our guilt.

Achan tried to hide his sin. He had stolen silver and gold and hidden it in his tent (Joshua 7:20–21). But when the Israelites were defeated in battle, the Lord told their leader Joshua that the loss was due to sin in the camp (vv. 11–12). The Lord identified Achan as the one who had sinned. And even though Achan confessed, he and his family were executed (v. 25).

We may not understand why God dealt so harshly with Achan's sin, but we do know He was instructing His people in His holiness and their need for obedience to His commands (Exodus 20:17).

If you've been disobedient, it's time to come out of hiding. God is lovingly calling you and offering His cleansing, forgiveness, and restoration. —AC

Read: Joshua 7:16–22

Biblical Truth

Personal Application

Prayer Requests

Answers to Prayer

Confession is the key that opens the door to forgiveness.

December 9

Read: Romans 5:15–21

Biblical Truth

Personal Application

Prayer Requests

Answers to Prayer

LESSONS OF THE COKE BOTTLE

Where sin abounded, grace abounded much more.
—Romans 5:20

Pastor Louie was preaching on the pervasiveness of sin. "It's everywhere!" he stated emphatically. He told about waiting for a traffic light when he saw the man in the car in front of him finish his Coke, open the door, set the glass bottle on the street, and drive away.

"That was wrong!" Louie said. "It was a selfish sin! He could have caused someone to have a flat tire or even an accident." We don't typically think of littering as sin, but it is clear evidence of our inherent selfishness.

Later, as Louie was greeting people by the door, a man who was a Bible professor at a local Christian university said quietly as he walked by, "Sin puts the bottle on the street, but grace picks it up."

Now, many years later, Louie has not forgotten the lesson of that scriptural principle. It comes right out of Romans 5, one of the most uplifting texts in the Bible describing the grace of God. Adam's transgression brought sin into the world (v. 12), and its consequences spread to all people. But God responded with grace, offering forgiveness through His Son to all who choose to believe. The human race sinned, and God answered with abounding grace (v. 20).

God does much more than just "pick up the bottle." He cleanses the heart of the transgressor!
—DCE

Confession of sin is the soil in which forgiveness flourishes.

December 10

MARRED

She will bring forth a Son, and you shall call His name Jesus, for He will save His people from their sins.
—Matthew 1:21

During an all-night festival in Paris, five young people, apparently drunk, broke into the Orsay Museum and left a four-inch gash in a priceless painting by Claude Monet. Culture Minister Christine Albanel said the painting could be restored, but she was deeply disturbed at the damage done by "a purely criminal act."

One news headline read: "Monet Masterpiece Marred." To *mar* is to injure or damage; to spoil, disfigure, or impair. It's an apt description of sin's effect on us. We know well the results of our own choices made in ignorance or defiance of God.

As we approach Christmas, it's good to remember why Jesus was born. The Son of God did not come to establish a nostalgic, family-oriented, commercially successful holiday. The angel told Joseph: "[Mary] will bring forth a Son, and you shall call His name Jesus, for He will save His people from their sins" (Matthew 1:21).

Christmas began with a present from God to His sin-damaged world: "For the wages of sin is death, but the gift of God is eternal life in Christ Jesus our Lord" (Romans 6:23).

The masterpiece of God's human creation, marred by turning away from Him, can be restored when we give our hearts to Christ. —DCM

Read: Matthew 1:18–25

Biblical Truth

Personal Application

Prayer Requests

Answers to Prayer

Jesus came to earth to repair our sin-damaged lives.

December 11

Read: Exodus 4:10–17

Biblical Truth

Personal Application

Prayer Requests

Answers to Prayer

ABSOLUTELY NOBODY

Surely I am more stupid than any man, and do not have the understanding of a man.
—Proverbs 30:2

He wanted to be a nobody. In 1992, a Seattle man running for the office of Washington State's lieutenant governor legally changed his name to "Absolutely Nobody." As he entered the race, he said he wanted to greet the voters, saying, "Hi, I'm Absolutely Nobody. Vote for me." He later admitted that the purpose of his campaign was to abolish the office of lieutenant governor.

This man used a name as a gimmick, but the Bible has a lot to say to those of us who present ourselves to others as a nobody. The right kind of humility is healthy. The songwriters of Israel knew how important it is to see our foolishness apart from God (Psalm 73:22; Proverbs 30:2). Jesus himself showed us that without God we won't accomplish anything of lasting value (John 5:30; 15:5).

But there's a downside to insisting that we are "nobody" if it is to avoid doing what God commands, as we are warned in the story of Moses (Exodus 4:1–17). When we do that, our motives make us into somebody who resists the loving purposes of God.

We may treat ourselves and others as having no worth. But remember, God doesn't make nobodies. Like Moses, if we surrender to God, we can do anything God wants us to do—in His strength. —MD

Without Christ we can do nothing.
With Him we can do everything He wants us to do.

EBENEZER

Samuel took a stone . . . and called its name Ebenezer, saying, "Thus far the Lord has helped us."
—1 Samuel 7:12

In *A Christmas Carol* by Charles Dickens, the central character is Ebenezer Scrooge. As a boy, I enjoyed watching the old black-and-white movie version of that story with Alastair Sim portraying Scrooge. Sim did a phenomenal job presenting the heartless, miserly, self-centered Scrooge. I still check the television schedule each Christmas to learn when I can watch that particular rendition of Dickens's tale.

Years of watching the travails of Scrooge have spoiled something for me though—the name "Ebenezer." I have associated it with Scrooge, but its original meaning was very different from that. In 1 Samuel, following a decisive battle with the Philistines, the Israelites erected a stone as a reminder of the Lord's help in the battle. They named that stone Ebenezer, which means "Stone of Help," to remind people of how God rescued them from their enemies (7:12).

What a contrast! A name that I had come to associate with man's selfishness can actually serve as a reminder of the readily available help of God. As we move through life, may we focus on the faithfulness of the Lord and not the selfishness of humanity. Let's look to Him as our true Ebenezer—our help in the challenges of life. —BC

December 12

Read: Psalm 42:1–5

Biblical Truth

Personal Application

Prayer Requests

Answers to Prayer

Our only hope here below is help from God above.

December 13

Read: Genesis 1:1, 20–27

Biblical Truth

Personal Application

Prayer Requests

Answers to Prayer

WHODUNIT?

God said, "Let Us make man in Our image, according to Our likeness."
—Genesis 1:26

The word *whodunit* is actually in the dictionary. It means "detective story." The most important whodunit of all time is the question of creation.

Some people wish the Bible said, "In the beginning, God wasn't needed." To them, it's unacceptable to say, "In the beginning God created the heavens and the earth" (Genesis 1:1), or "Let Us make man in Our image" (v. 26). Instead, they believe that after an explosion of energy and matter, somehow an atmosphere conducive to life was formed. Then, single-celled organisms morphed into the exceedingly complex life forms we have today.

No need for God, they say, for it all happened naturally. On an earth and in an atmosphere not of anyone's making, forces with a blueprint designed by no one joined together to place the earth *perfectly* for life to thrive.

What we do with "In the beginning God" is at the center of it all. We must either believe His Word—and everything His Word claims—or we must believe that our meaningless lives resulted from an accidental, mindless chain reaction. What a stark contrast to "Let Us make man in Our image"!

In the beginning. Was it God? Or was it chance? Our answer to this whodunit reveals whether or not we truly worship the awesome God of creation. —DB

Only God could create the cosmos out of nothing.

THE GLORY OF HUMILITY

December 14

The glory of the Lord shall be revealed, and all flesh shall see it together.
—Isaiah 40:5

I remember sitting one Christmas season in London listening to Handel's *Messiah*, with a full chorus singing about the day when "the glory of the Lord shall be revealed." I had spent the morning viewing remnants of England's glory—the crown jewels, the Lord Mayor's gilded carriage—and it occurred to me that just such images of wealth and power must have filled the minds of Isaiah's contemporaries who first heard that promise.

The Messiah who showed up, however, wore a different kind of glory—the glory of humility. The God who roared, who if He so desired could order armies and empires about like pawns, this God emerged in Bethlehem as a baby who could not speak or eat solid food. This God who created all things became dependent on a teenager for shelter, food, and love.

Rulers stride through the world with bodyguards, fanfare, and flashing jewelry. In contrast, God's visit to earth took place in a shelter for animals, with no attendants present and nowhere to lay the newborn King but a feed trough. Indeed, the event that divided history into two parts may have had more animal than human witnesses.

In most religions, fear is the primary emotion when approaching God. In Jesus, God made a way of relating to us that did not involve fear. —PY

Read: Isaiah 40:1–5

Biblical Truth

Personal Application

Prayer Requests

Answers to Prayer

In Christ, God veiled His deity to serve and to save humanity.

December 15

Read: 1 Kings 8:54–61

Biblical Truth

Personal Application

Prayer Requests

Answers to Prayer

NEVER DISAPPOINTED

There has not failed one word of all His good promise.
—1 Kings 8:56

As an avid baseball fan, my favorite team is the Chicago Cubs. The interesting thing about being a Cubs fan is that the team has a way of letting us down. They have not won a World Series since 1908. And while they often have great promise at the beginning of the season, they usually disappoint their loyal fans in the end. One die-hard fan had it right when he said, "If they didn't disappoint us, they wouldn't be our Cubs!"

Thankfully, God is not like the Cubs! You can count on Him. He will not disappoint you in the end. He always keeps His promises, and His Word provides comfort, hope, and wise advice that never fail.

When King Solomon dedicated the temple, he attested to the fact that God had not let His people down: "Blessed be the Lord, who has given rest to His people Israel, according to all that He promised. There has not failed one word of all His good promise" (1 Kings 8:56).

Thousands of years later, those words still ring true. And better yet, we are heirs of the greatest fulfilled promise of all time—Jesus! The longer you know Him, the more compelling He becomes.

So if you are looking for someone who won't disappoint you, look no further. Jesus never fails!
—JS

Looking for someone who won't disappoint you? Look to Jesus.

THE TASK REMAINS

He will not be afraid of evil tidings; his heart is steadfast, trusting in the Lord.
—Psalm 112:7

Our life had always been rather simple. When my wife and I were first married, we were not looking for riches or fame—just a way to glorify God with whatever He gave us to do. In all arenas of our life, that purpose stayed clear. As our children grew and I began working at RBC Ministries, our goal continued to center around glorifying God.

But then, in 2002, came bad news of the worst kind. Our third child, 17-year-old Melissa, was unexpectedly ushered into heaven. Suddenly, we were forced to rethink things. Could we, in our new identity as bereaved parents, still find a way to glorify God? Or did this unbearable circumstance alter our perspective and goal?

We've spent a lot of time pondering that question. When the One you've entrusted with your children allows one of them to be taken, it would be easy to stop trusting, serving, and pointing others to God. But the psalmist's words showed us the way. He said that the person who fears God "will never be shaken . . . His heart is steadfast" (Psalm 112:6–7). And so we—and you, no matter what you are facing—can continue to be "steadfast, trusting in the Lord."

Even in the face of "evil tidings," the task remains: Glorify God. —DB

December 16

Read: Psalm 112

Biblical Truth

Personal Application

Prayer Requests

Answers to Prayer

Trust through sorrow brings triumph over sadness.

December 17

Read: 1 Corinthians 2:6–16

Biblical Truth

Personal Application

Prayer Requests

Answers to Prayer

DISCOVERY

God has revealed them to us through His Spirit.
—1 CORINTHIANS 2:10

Imagine Christmas morning without wrapping paper! The joy would be short-lived, for much of the excitement is the anticipation of finding out what's in the package.

Apparently God created us with a "normal" setting that causes us to enjoy the process of discovery, because finding something is often more exciting than having it. That is, after all, why we wrap presents.

Many passages in Scripture allude to this concept. In Proverbs we read of wisdom: "Those who seek me diligently will find me" (8:17). And the prophet Jeremiah wrote of the Lord: "You will seek Me and find Me, when you search for Me with all your heart" (29:13).

God could have revealed all truth to all people at the very beginning of time, but He chose to reveal himself gradually (1 Corinthians 2:7–8). Perhaps that's because we value things more when we have to search and wait for them.

God is not playing a cruel game of hide-and-seek. He is allowing us to enjoy the process of discovering who He is and what He is up to in the universe. So don't be discouraged over what you don't know about God. Be excited about unwrapping all there is yet to discover. —JAL

God's gift of himself to us is a present we will always be unwrapping.

DESERT PETE

The word which they heard did not profit them, not being mixed with faith.
—HEBREWS 4:2

In the 1960s, the Kingston Trio released a song called "Desert Pete." The ballad tells of a thirsty cowboy who is crossing the desert and finds a hand pump. Next to it, Desert Pete has left a note urging the reader not to drink from the jar hidden there but to use its contents to prime the pump.

The cowboy resists the temptation to drink from the jar immediately and uses the water as the note instructs. In reward for his obedience, once he has primed the pump he receives an abundance of cold, satisfying water. Had he not acted in faith, he would have had only a single jar of unsatisfying, warm water to drink.

This reminds me of Israel's journey through the wilderness. When their thirst became overwhelming, Moses sought the Lord and was told to strike the rock of Horeb with his staff (Exodus 17:1–7). Moses believed and obeyed, and water gushed from the stone.

Sometimes life can seem like an arid desert. But God can quench our spiritual thirst in the most unlikely circumstances. When by faith we believe the promises of God's Word, we can experience rivers of living water and grace for our daily needs.
—DF

December 18

Read: Exodus 17:1–7

Biblical Truth

Personal Application

Prayer Requests

Answers to Prayer

Only Jesus, the Living Water, can satisfy our thirst for God.

December 19

Read: Ephesians 1:15–23

Biblical Truth

Personal Application

Prayer Requests

Answers to Prayer

NO BATTERIES?

That you may know what is the hope of His calling . . . and what is the exceeding greatness of His power toward us who believe.
—Ephesians 1:18–19

My two-year-old grandson was fascinated by the bubbling mud pool, the result of geothermal activity in Rotorua, New Zealand. On moving to another spot and seeing no bubbles there, he remarked, "No batteries?" He was so accustomed to his electronic toys that he attributed even natural phenomena to battery power!

Christians can make a similar mistake—they look to their own puny power to live righteous lives. But the high moral and ethical standards of a holy God prove impossible to live up to. The result is joyless Christians, hopelessly burdened and defeated.

Paul's prayer for the believers in Ephesus was that "the eyes of your understanding [be] enlightened; that you may know what is the hope of His calling . . . and what is the exceeding greatness of His power toward us who believe" (Ephesians 1:18–19). He wanted them to see that the power available to help them live God-honoring lives is the same power that "raised [Christ] from the dead and seated Him at His right hand in the heavenly places" (v. 20).

The power to live according to God's standards comes only when we plug into His inexhaustible power. How do we do that? By daily seeking His face and asking Him to fill us with His Holy Spirit. —CPH

The Light of the World knows no power failure.

HALLELUJAH!

I know that my Redeemer lives.
—Job 19:25

Composer George Frideric Handel was bankrupt when n 1741 a group of Dublin charities offered him a commission to vrite a musical work. It was for benefit performance to raise unds to free men from a debtors' rison. He accepted that commission and gave himself tirelessly to vork on it.

In just 24 days Handel comosed the well-known masteriece *Messiah*, which contains The Hallelujah Chorus." During hat time he never left his home nd often went without eating. At ne point, a servant found him veeping over his evolving score. Recounting his experience, Handel wrote, "Whether I was in my ody or out of my body as I wrote t I know not. God knows." Aftervard he also said, "I did think I lid see all heaven before me and he great God himself."

"The Hallelujah Chorus" stirs ny soul whenever I hear it, as 'm sure it does yours. But let's e sure we do more than resoate to that magnificent music. et's open our hearts in faith and doration for the Messiah promsed in the book of Isaiah (Isaiah):1–7). He has come to us in the erson of Jesus Christ to be our avior. "Unto us a Child is born, nto us a Son is given; and the overnment will be upon His houlder" (v. 6). —VCG

December 20

Read: Isaiah 9:1–7

Biblical Truth

Personal Application

Prayer Requests

Answers to Prayer

God's highest Gift awakens our deepest gratitude.

December 21

Read: Luke 2:25–35

Biblical Truth

Personal Application

Prayer Requests

Answers to Prayer

WHAT CHILD IS THIS?

This Child is destined for the fall and rising of many in Israel . . . that the thoughts of many hearts may be revealed.
—LUKE 2:34–35

One of our most beloved Christmas carols was written in 1865 by William Dix, an Englishman who managed a maritime insurance company and loved to write hymns. Sung to the English melody "Greensleeves," some versions use the latter half of the first verse as a chorus for the other verses

This, this is Christ the King,
Whom shepherds guard and
angels sing;
Haste, haste to bring Him laud—
The Babe, the Son of Mary.

But in other versions, each stanza is unique. The second verse, rarely sung today, looks beyond the manger to the cross:

Why lies He in such mean estate,
Where ox and ass are feeding?
Good Christian, fear, for sinners here
The silent Word is pleading.
Nails, spear shall pierce Him through
The cross be borne for me, for you
Hail, hail the Word made flesh,
The Babe, the Son of Mary.

Simeon said to Mary, "This Child is destined for the fall and rising of many in Israel, and for a sign which will be spoken against (yes, a sword will pierce through your own soul also), that the thoughts of many hearts may be revealed" (Luke 2:34–35).

The Child of Christmas came to be our Savior. "Joy, joy for Christ is born, the Babe, the Son of Mary." —DCM

The birth of Christ brought God to man; the cross of Christ brings man to God.

DECEMBER DESIRE

December 22

They need no lamp nor light of the sun, for the Lord God gives them light.
—Revelation 22:5

Read: Revelation 22:1–5

December is a month when people celebrate miracles. The Jewish tradition of Hanukkah—the Holiday of Lights—commemorates the time when a small amount of oil lasted eight days and kept the light in the temple from going out. And Christmas celebrates the coming of the "Light of the World," God in human form—Jesus.

A miracle is generally thought of as something that contradicts nature. But a true miracle is the introduction of God's supernatural power into our world in a way that suspends the laws of physics as we understand them.

In December, it seems that more of us are willing to suspend disbelief and entertain the possibility that "nature" is not the final authority. Even the non-religious yearn for miracles. Deep down, everyone wants to believe that darkness, disease, and death can be overcome.

Perhaps the most wondrous thing about miracles is that it is God's nature to do the supernatural. The closing chapters of Scripture assure us that this "December desire" for all to be well will become a reality: "There shall be no more death, nor sorrow, nor crying. There shall be no more pain" (Revelation 21:4). God will one day bring to an end the unnatural rule of Satan and begin His righteous reign as the rightful Ruler of the universe. —JAL

Biblical Truth

Personal Application

Prayer Requests

Answers to Prayer

A miracle needs no explanation to those who believe in God; to those who don't, no explanation is enough.

December 23

Read: John 14:5–20

Biblical Truth

Personal Application

Prayer Requests

Answers to Prayer

INVISIBLE MAN

Looking unto Jesus, the author and finisher of our faith, who for the joy that was set before Him endured the cross.
—Hebrews 12:2

As a boy, I was fascinated by the book *The Invisible Man*. The main character played an elaborate game of hide-and-seek, staying just out of reach of mere mortals "cursed" with a visible nature. To have a physical presence, he wore clothes and wrapped his face in bandages. When it was time to escape, he simply removed everything and disappeared.

I wonder if we have similar thoughts about our unseen God. We may feel He is beyond our reach, as expressed in these lines from one of my favorite hymns: "Immortal, invisible, God only wise, / In light inaccessible hid from our eyes."

We may perceive that God is distant, far off, inaccessible, and hidden, yet we need a God who is accessible, and we wonder how to have a meaningful relationship with Him.

We will never fully comprehend what God is like. Yet He himself is accessible to us. In part, that is why Jesus came—to "show us the Father" (John 14:8–11) and to bring us close to Him, because "He is the image of the invisible God, the firstborn over all creation" (Colossians 1:15).

Our God is an invisible God, beyond our limited comprehension. Thankfully, Jesus came to show us how near to us He really is. —BC

God's presence with us is His greatest present to us.

CHRISTMAS IN TOKYO

The One whom you worship without knowing, Him I proclaim to you.
—ACTS 17:23

On Christmas Eve 2003, noted painter Makoto Fujimura gathered with other artists for a party at Sato Museum in Tokyo. Many had donated their works for a benefit exhibit to raise money for children in Afghanistan. After the meal, Mr. Fujimura, an ardent Christian who lives in New York, shared some words about the true meaning of Christmas and their opportunity as artists to create works that help bring hope into the world.

Reflecting on that event, Fujimura wrote: "I was convinced, that evening in Tokyo, that Jesus invited himself to be among artists who may not even know His name. Some of these artists, I suspect, have already sensed His presence in their studios as they labored to create peace via their paintings. All gifts of creativity, like the Magi's [star], point straight to a stable in Bethlehem."

Paul said that God is at work among people of all nations "so that they should seek the Lord, in the hope that they might grope for Him and find Him, though He is not far from each one of us; for in Him we live and move and have our being" (Acts 17:27–28).

We should be alert for the Lord's presence where we least expect to see Him. Jesus may invite himself to any Christmas party. After all, it's His birthday.
—DCM

December 24

Read: Acts 17:22–34

Biblical Truth

Personal Application

Prayer Requests

Answers to Prayer

This Christmas, be alert for the work and presence of Jesus.

December 25

Read: Micah 5:2–6

Biblical Truth

Personal Application

Prayer Requests

Answers to Prayer

A GIFT MOST LAVISH

Though He was rich,
yet for your sakes He became poor,
that you through His poverty
might become rich.
—2 CORINTHIANS 8:9

I have a piece of old plaster on my desk that comes from the ancient site of the Herodium in the land of Israel. It reminds me of the humility of our Lord Jesus.

Herodium was a lavish residence that served as King Herod's summer palace, a sumptuous villa with opulent apartments furnished for the royal family and their guests. It boasted a Roman bath with hot and cold pools, surrounded by colonnaded gardens.

It's said that Herod built this palace to commemorate a victory in battle; but knowing Herod's selfish ambition, it's possible he had another purpose in mind. Some have conjectured that Herod, despite inquiring of the scribes (Matthew 2:4–6), knew about Micah's prediction that Israel's Messiah would be born in Bethlehem. He may have wanted Israel's King to be born in his palace.

The Father's plan, however, was for our Lord to be born not in a castle but in a cave. It was in a lowly manger that the little Lord Jesus was born.

This is the grace of our Lord Jesus Christ, "Though He was rich, yet for your sakes He became poor, that you through His poverty might become rich" (2 Corinthians 8:9). This is the gift of lavish salvation—of all gifts, the greatest gift that you and I will ever receive. —DHR

The goodness and love of God became incarnate at Bethlehem.

December 26

HE CAN LEAD YOU OUT OF IT

After the earthquake a fire, but the Lord was not in the fire; and after the fire a still small voice.
—1 Kings 19:12

Almost everyone will at some time in their life be affected by depression, either their own or someone else's. Some common signs and symptoms of depression include feelings of hopelessness, pessimism, worthlessness, and helplessness. Although we cannot say for certain that characters in the Bible experienced depression, we can say that some did exhibit a deep sense of despondency, discouragement, and sadness that is linked to personal powerlessness and loss of meaning and enthusiasm for life.

Elijah is one biblical character who fits this description. After defeating the prophets of Baal, he received a death threat from Jezebel. His hope was shattered, and despondency set in. He wanted to die!

God helped Elijah deal with his despondency in several ways. The Lord did not rebuke him for his feelings but sent an angel to provide for his physical needs. Then, the Lord revealed himself and reminded Elijah that He was quietly working among His people. Next, He renewed Elijah's mission by giving him new orders. Finally, God reminded Elijah that he wasn't alone.

In our times of discouragement, let us remember that God loves us and desires to lead us to a place of a renewed vision of himself! —MW

Read: 1 Kings 19:1–12

Biblical Truth

Personal Application

Prayer Requests

Answers to Prayer

The weak, the helpless, and the discouraged are in the Shepherd's special care.

December 27

Read: Psalm 62

Biblical Truth

Personal Application

Prayer Requests

Answers to Prayer

FEELINGS-DEFICIENT

I sought the Lord,
and He heard me.
—Psalm 34:4

Mallory doesn't feel loved by God. She received Jesus as her Savior several years ago and is confident that she is forgiven and will spend eternity with Him. She believes what God says in His Word. But she would also like to *feel* loved.

Her friends give her what she thinks is a pat answer: "It's not about feelings! Just believe and the feelings will come later." She says, "Okay, but when is *later*?" She believes she's "feelings-deficient."

God created us in His image to have emotions, so the longing to feel loved is legitimate and good. One way that many of us sense we're loved is when someone talks with us and listens to us.

God provides those needs in our relationship with Him too. He speaks through His Word to our heart (Hebrews 4:12), and He wants us to pour out our heart to Him about everything (Psalm 62:8)—even our longing to feel His love. Besides a relationship with Him, He daily gives us our breath, clothing, food, and shelter. Like the psalmist, we can find Him to be our "rock" and "refuge" as we trust Him (vv. 2, 7).

God loves us. Now, we walk by faith. One day, when we're in His very presence, we'll never again be feelings-deficient. —AC

Knowing that God loves us comes by faith;
feeling His love for us comes by relationship.

December 28

SOUL FOOD

Your words were found, and I ate them, and Your word was to me the joy and rejoicing of my heart.
—Jeremiah 15:16

Grocery shopping with my wife, Martie, is like taking a seminar in nutrition. I'll often pick up a box of something that looks good, and she'll say: "Look at the label. Are there trans-fats? What's the calorie count? How about the cholesterol rating?" I have to confess that if she weren't the nutrition cop in my life, I'd look like Shamu the whale!

More important than making good choices in the grocery store is thinking carefully about the food we digest for our souls. I love the verse that says: "Your words were found, and I ate them" (Jeremiah 15:16).

When we read God's Word, we have to be doing more than checking it off our to-do list. We have to read it to digest it. Slow, thoughtful absorption of the Word of God with quiet reflection on its implications is high in nutrition. His Word provides all the ingredients we need to thrive spiritually:

- a direct connection to the sustainer of our soul
- brain food that makes us wise and discerning
- a daily check-up revealing the condition of our hearts
- preventive medicine keeping us from sin
- a spiritual shower of peace, hope, and comfort

Eat God's Word. It's a spiritual feast! —JS

Read: Psalm 19:7–14

Biblical Truth

Personal Application

Prayer Requests

Answers to Prayer

The Bible contains all the nutrients for a healthy soul.

December 29

Read: Psalm 85:1–7

Biblical Truth

Personal Application

Prayer Requests

Answers to Prayer

HEARTS AND BANJOS

Will You not revive us again, that Your people may rejoice in You?
—Psalm 85:6

While working my way through graduate school, I taught five-string banjo in a music store. The job provided me with the opportunity to buy a brand-new, professional-quality instrument for nearly half-price.

That was over 30 years ago, and that banjo has accompanied me on ministry efforts around the world. But despite its excellent craftsmanship, eventually it needed to be refurbished. A master repairman pointed out how imperfections had worn into the banjo. He was confident that his repairs would result in the instrument sounding better than new.

I wasn't disappointed. The action on the strings and the clarity of the sound are astonishingly superior to its original condition when I purchased the instrument.

In a way, our lives are like musical instruments intended for "the praise of the glory of [God's] grace" (Ephesians 1:6). But over time, life wears us down. Our hearts cry out for renewal. The psalmist prayed: "Will You not revive us again?" (Psalm 85:6). The Hebrew word for *revive* means not only "to restore and refresh" but also "to repair."

It's vital that we submit our souls to the Master's restorative touch. Why not set aside some time for spiritual retreat and ask the Lord to repair your heart?
—DF

Time in Christ's service requires time out for renewal.

NO FEAR IN THE NEW YEAR

December 30

Fear not, for I have redeemed you; I have called you by your name; you are Mine.
—Isaiah 43:1

Hours before 2007 began, some friends of ours in the UK were aboard their boat, anticipating the arrival of the new year, when a violent storm struck. But they were able to send us this reassuring note: "John and Linda are sitting on board the good ship *Norna*, and happy to say that we are secure . . . The wind is storm force ten [48–55 knots]. Hope that all of you have a happy and prosperous new year."

Jesus' disciples also encountered a stormy experience. They were on the Sea of Galilee when a windstorm whipped up (Mark 6:48). The storm was so violent that, despite being experienced fishermen who knew the lake well, they feared for their lives. But Jesus walked out to them and saved them.

No one can predict with certainty how stormy the new year will be. We do know, though, that everyone will face storms. But we who have Jesus have our future securely moored to Him. Jesus, who did not fail us in the past, will not fail us in the future.

How will you fare in the storms of the new year? If you're anchored in Jesus, you have nothing to fear. —CPH

Read: Mark 6:45–52

Biblical Truth

Personal Application

Prayer Requests

Answers to Prayer

Faith in Christ will keep us steady in the stormy sea of change.

December 31

Read: Ecclesiastes 3:1–8

Biblical Truth

Personal Application

Prayer Requests

Answers to Prayer

TIMES AND SEASONS

To everything there is a season,
a time for every
purpose under heaven.
—Ecclesiastes 3:1

The Rev. Gardner Taylor has been called "the dean of American preaching." Born in Louisiana in 1918, the grandson of slaves, he overcame the segregation of his youth to become the pastor of a large New York congregation and a leader in the struggle for racial equality. For six decades he traveled the world as a much sought-after preacher.

But at age 89, Rev. Taylor's health gave way and he could no longer accept speaking engagements. He told Rachel Zoll of the Associated Press: "I at first felt rather crestfallen." But then he spoke of his belief that "there are seasons and eras, and we have to see what they are as best as we can, and to find what is positive in them."

In an effort to face the challenges of life, we often turn to Solomon's words: "To everything there is a season, a time for every purpose under heaven" (Ecclesiastes 3:1). We readily admit that we would rather laugh than weep, dance than mourn, and gain than lose (vv. 4, 6). Yet we know that as we embrace the lessons and opportunities of every season that comes to us, we find that "God is our refuge and strength" (Psalm 46:1).

Whatever season we're in, it's always the season to trust in Him. —DCM

Whatever the season of life, attitude makes all the difference.

THE *OUR DAILY BREAD* WRITERS

DAVE BRANON (DB), for eighteen years the managing editor of *Sports Spectrum* magazine, now is an editor for Discovery House Publishers and RBC Ministries. He has written over two thousand devotional articles and fourteen books. His most recent book, *Beyond the Valley,* is available from Discovery House Publishers. Dave and his wife, Sue, love rollerblading and spending time with their children and grandchildren. Dave also enjoys traveling overseas with students on ministry trips.

ANNE CETAS (AC) the managing editor of *Our Daily Bread* (ODB), has been on the editorial staff of *Our Daily Bread* for over thirty years and began writing for ODB in September 2004. Anne and her husband, Carl, enjoy long walks and bicycling together, and they work as mentors in an inner-city ministry. Anne also teaches Sunday school and disciples new believers.

BILL CROWDER (BC), who spent over twenty years in pastoral ministry, is an associate Bible Teacher for RBC Ministries. Bill spends much of his RBC time in a Bible-teaching ministry for Christian leaders around the world. He is also the author of five books, all available from Discovery House Publishers. Bill and his wife, Marlene, have five children and several grandchildren.

HENRY G. BOSCH (HGB) served as the first editor of the daily devotional booklet that became *Our Daily Bread* and contributed many of the earliest articles. He was also one of the singers on the Radio Bible Class live broadcast.

MART DEHAAN (MD) is the grandson of RBC founder, Dr. M. R. DeHaan, and the son of former president, Richard W. DeHaan. Mart is the president of RBC Ministries and is heard regularly on the *Discover the Word* radio program and is seen on *Day of Discovery* television. Mart's book *Been Thinking About* is available from Discovery House Publishers. Mart and his wife, Diane, have two children.

DR. M. R. DEHAAN (MRD) was the founder of Radio Bible Class and one of the founders of *Our Daily Bread.* A physician who later in life became a pastor, he was well known for his gravelly voice and impassioned Bible teaching. His commitment to ministry was to lead people of all nations to personal faith and maturity in Christ. RBC Ministries continues to build upon the spiritual foundation of Dr. DeHaan's vision and work. A biography of Dr. DeHaan, *M. R. DeHaan: The Life Behind the Voice* by James R. Adair, is available from Discovery House Publishers.

RICHARD DEHAAN (RDH) was President of RBC Ministries and teacher on RBC programs for twenty years. He was the son of RBC founder, Dr. M. R. DeHaan, and wrote a number of full-length books and study booklets for RBC. Often called "the encourager," Richard was committed to faithfulness to God's Word and to integrity as a ministry. Richard went to be with the Lord in 2002.

DAVID C. EGNER (DCE) is retired from RBC Ministries. During his years at RBC, Dave was editor of *Discovery Digest* and *Campus Journal* (now called *Our Daily Journey*). Dave still teaches English and writing at Cornerstone University and has enjoyed occasional guest-professor stints at Bible colleges in Russia. He and his wife, Shirley, live in Grand Rapids, Michigan.

DENNIS FISHER (DF) was a professor of evangelism and discipleship at Moody Bible Institute for eight years. In 1998 he joined RBC Ministries, where he currently serves as managing editor of ChristianCourses.com. Dennis has two adult children and one grandson. He and his wife, Janet, live in DeWitt, Michigan.

VERNON C. GROUNDS (VCG), went to be with the Lord on September 12, 2010, at the age of 96. He wrote over five hundred articles for ODB from 1993-2009. Former president of Denver Seminary and then chancellor, Dr. Grounds also had an extensive preaching, teaching, and counseling ministry. He will be deeply missed by many for his godly wisdom and example.

TIM GUSTAFSON (TG) has worked with RBC Ministries for more than fifteen years and currently serves as Associate Director of Publications for RBC. Tim and his wife, Leisa, have one daughter and seven sons.

C. P. HIA (CPH) and his wife, Lin Choo, reside in the island nation of Singapore. C. P. has been a teaching leader for a men's Bible study for the past eighteen years. A retired businessman, he serves in the RBC Ministries Singapore office as Assistant International Director.

CINDY HESS KASPER (CHK) has served for more than thirty years at RBC, where she is now associate editor for *Our Daily Journey*. She is a daughter of longtime RBC senior editor Clair Hess, from whom she learned a love for singing and working with words. Cindy and her husband, Tom, have three grown children and seven grandchildren, in whom they take great delight.

ALBERT LEE (AL) is Director of International Ministries for RBC and has the passion, vision, and energy to help expand the work of RBC Ministries. Albert grew up in Singapore, attended Singapore Bible College, and served with Singapore Youth for Christ from 1971 to 1999. Albert and his wife, Catherine, have two children and live in Singapore.

JULIE ACKERMAN LINK (JAL) is a founding partner of Blue Water Ink, a company that provides writing, editing, designing, and typesetting services. She has edited hundreds of books, including many for Discovery House Publishers. She has been writing for ODB since 2000 and is the author of *Above All Love* and *A Heart for God*. Julie and her husband, Jay, are both involved in ministry at their church in Grand Rapids, Michigan.

DAVID C. MCCASLAND (DCM) researches and helps develop biographical documentaries for *Day of Discovery* television. His books include the award-winning biography *Oswald Chambers: Abandoned to God* and *Eric Liddell: Pure Gold*, available from Discovery House Publishers. David and his wife, Luann, have four grown children and live in Colorado Springs, Colorado.

DAVID H. ROPER (DHR) was a pastor for more than thirty years and now directs Idaho Mountain Ministries, a retreat dedicated to the encouragement of pastoral couples. David is the author of thirteen books, including *Psalm 23: The Song of a Passionate Heart,* all available from Discovery House Publishers. David enjoys fishing, hiking, and being streamside with his wife, Carolyn.

JOE STOWELL (JS), former president of Moody Bible Institute, currently serves as president of Cornerstone University in Grand Rapids, Michigan. An internationally recognized speaker, Joe has also written numerous books, including *Radical Reliance, Eternity,* and *The Upside of Down,* available from Discovery House Publishers. He and his wife, Martie, have three children and ten grandchildren.

HERB VANDER LUGT (HVL) remained a vital contributor to *Our Daily Bread* up to the time he went to be with His Lord and Savior on December 2, 2006. Herb served as Senior Research Editor for RBC Ministries and had been with the ministry since 1966. Herb pastored six churches and, after retiring from the pastorate in 1989, held three interim ministerial positions.

MARVIN WILLIAMS (MW) has been writing for *Our Daily Bread* since 2007 and also writes for *Our Daily Journey*. Marvin is Senior Teaching Pastor at Trinity Church in Lansing, Michigan. He has also been associate pastor of youth at New Hope Baptist Church and assistant pastor at Calvary Church in Grand Rapids. Marvin and his wife, Tonia, have three children.

PHILIP YANCEY (PY) is the well-known and award-winning author of twenty books. His books include classics such as *Where Is God When It Hurts?*, *The Jesus I Never Knew*, and *What's So Amazing About Grace?* Philip also serves as editor-at-large for *Christianity Today* magazine. Philip and his wife, Janet, live in Colorado, where they enjoy hiking, wildlife, and the other delights of the Rocky Mountains.

JOANIE YODER (JY), a favorite among ODB readers, went home to be with her Savior in 2004. She and her husband established a Christian rehabilitation center for drug addicts in England many years ago. Widowed in 1982, Joanie learned to rely on the Lord's help and strength. She wrote with hope about true dependence on God and His life-changing power. A collection of over one hundred of her devotionals, *God Alone*, is available from Discovery House Publishers.

ACKNOWLEDGMENTS

"Quiet Time with God" by David C. McCasland is from *Our Daily Bread*, January 2010, © 2010 by RBC Ministries. All rights reserved.

February 5, "The Atrocious Mathematics of the Gospel," is excerpted and adapted from *What's So Amazing About Grace?* by Philip D. Yancey, © 1997 by Zondervan. Published by permission of Zondervan.

March 4, "The Miracle of Restraint," is excerpted and adapted from *The Jesus I Never Knew*, by Philip D. Yancey, © 1995 Zondervan. Published by permission of Zondervan.

March 11, "Agents of Grace," is excerpted and adapted from *What's So Amazing About Grace?* by Philip D. Yancey, © 1997 Zondervan. Published by permission of Zondervan.

April 10, "The Challenge of Forgiveness," is excerpted and adapted from *What's So Amazing About Grace?* by Philip D. Yancey, © 1997 Zondervan. Published by permission of Zondervan.

April 28, "The Greatest Gift," is excerpted and adapted from *Where Is God When It Hurts?* by Philip D. Yancey, © 1977 Zondervan. Published by permission of Zondervan.

May 27, "Can We Really Hear from God?" is excerpted and adapted from *The Bible Jesus Read*, by Philip D. Yancey, © 1999 Zondervan. Published by permission of Zondervan.

June 11, "A Cure for Futility," and June 27, "God's Greater Goal," are excerpted and adapted from *Reaching for the Invisible God*, by Philip D. Yancey, © 2000 Zondervan. Published by permission of Zondervan.

July 6, "Why Bother with Church?" is excerpted and adapted from *Church: Why Bother?* by Philip D. Yancey, © 1998 Zondervan. Published by permission of Zondervan.

July 17, "Why Pray?" is excerpted and adapted from *Prayer: Does It Make Any Difference?* by Philip D. Yancey, © 2006 Zondervan. Published by permission of Zondervan.

August 5, "Spiritual Therapy," is excerpted and adapted from *The Bible Jesus Read*, by Philip D. Yancey. © 1999 Zondervan. Published by permission of Zondervan.

August 27, "An Audience of One," is excerpted and adapted from *Rumors of Another World: What on Earth Are We Missing?* by Philip D. Yancey. © 2003 Zondervan. Published by permission of Zondervan.

September 7, "The Dangers of Success," is excerpted and adapted from *Meet the Bible: A Panorama of God's Word in 366 Daily Readings and Reflections*, by Philip D. Yancey and Brenda Quinn. © 2000 Zondervan. Published by permission of Zondervan.

September 28, "Showing Up," is excerpted and adapted from *Prayer: Does It Make Any Difference?* by Philip D. Yancey. © 2006 Zondervan. Published by permission of Zondervan.

October 9, "The Chain of Ungrace," is excerpted and adapted from *What's So Amazing About Grace?* by Philip D. Yancey. © 1997 Zondervan. Published by permission of Zondervan.

October 21, "God's Love Story," is excerpted and adapted from *Meet the Bible: A Panorama of God's Word in 366 Daily Readings and Reflections,* by Philip D. Yancey and Brenda Quinn. © 2000 Zondervan. Published by permission of Zondervan.

November 6, "Serve or Die," is excerpted and adapted from *Reaching for the Invisible God,* by Philip D. Yancey. © 2000 Zondervan. Published by permission of Zondervan.

December 14, "The Glory of Humility," is excerpted and adapted from *The Jesus I Never Knew,* by Philip D. Yancey. © 1995 Zondervan. Published by permission of Zondervan.

JOURNAL

JOURNAL

JOURNAL

JOURNAL